The Far Left
in British Politics

To Anne Marie and Rowan

The Far Left
in British Politics

JOHN CALLAGHAN

Basil Blackwell

Copyright © John Callaghan 1987

First published 1987

Basil Blackwell Ltd
108 Cowley Road, Oxford, OX4 1JF, UK

Basil Blackwell Inc.
432 Park Avenue South, Suite 1503
New York, NY 10016, USA

British Library Cataloguing in Publication Data

Callaghan, John
   The far left in British politics.
   1. Communism — Great Britain — History — 20th century
   I. Title
   355.43'3'0941   HX244

   ISBN 0-631-15488-4
   ISBN 0-631-15489-2 Pbk

Library of Congress Cataloging in Publication Data

Callaghan, John (John T.)
   The far left in British politics.

   Includes index.
   1. Communism—Great Britain.   2. Great Britain Politics
and government—1945—   I. Title.
   HX249.C35 1987 320.5'32'0941 87—5148
   ISBN 0-631-15488-4
   ISBN 0-631-15489-2 (pbk.)

Typeset in Baskerville 10.5/12
by Alan Sutton Publishing Ltd, Gloucester
Printed in Great Britain by
Billing & Sons Ltd, Worcester

Contents

Acknowledgements

The research for this book began at Manchester University where I was fortunate to receive the excellent assistance of Norman Geras and Lewis Minkin. I want to thank them both here together with David Coates who also read and criticized the original manuscript. I should also mention Danny Cunningham, Mike Gapes and Louis Sinclair who were good enough to provide many of the documents on which this book is based. Thanks are due also to my colleague Martin Durham whose erudition on the British political fringe is second to none. I alone am responsible for the final text.

Preface

Since 1983 there has been considerable talk of a realignment of the Left in Britain. Certainly there has been a great deal of change on the far left where new organizations appear as frequently as the mutations of insects. The pace of change was quickened in 1979 when the most reactionary government since the war was elected. Not the least significant feature of this result was the high percentage of Tory voters among the working class. The Left interpreted Labour's defeat as a punishment for the lugubrious performance of the right-wing Callaghan government. Since the latter had failed to implement the radical policy commitments with which it had won the 1974 election, left opinion was generally persuaded that this betrayal accounted for the 1979 defeat. Conveniently, then, the defeat of the Thatcher government and the calling to account of the Labour parliamentary leadership were seen as one and the same thing. A campaign for constitutional reforms designed to democratize and radicalize the Labour Party was led by Tony Benn and enthusiastically supported by most left activists with both these objectives in mind.

When Labour entered the 1983 election under the leadership of Michael Foot most leftists believed that it was a better organization with a better programme than ever before. Moreover, the Thatcher government had created mass unemployment, mass poverty, a housing shortage, a war, urban riots, a large reduction in manufacturing industry and much else besides: the misery factor could not have been higher. But the Tories remained in power and Labour registered its worst result

in 50 years. It was now that a new coalition emerged within the
Left comprising all of those who believed that the 1983 disaster
would not have happened had an uncompromising socialist
leadership clearly expounded the socialist alternative: this was
the position of the Bennite 'hard' left of the Labour Party
together with a variety of Trotskyist groups, 'Stalinists' from the
Communist Party and trade union militants. On the other side
were those socialists who questioned the very existence of a
coherent socialist alternative and recognized the errors of omis-
sion and commission by which the Left had contributed to its
own decline.

This book is chiefly concerned with the Leninist left whose
Trotskyist and Stalinist exponents found themselves on the
same side for once in the 1980s. It is not a detailed account of
either Trotskyist or Communist history though I have adopted
an historical approach and made use of a great deal of historical
information. Like its predecessor *British Trotskyism*,[1] this book is
concerned to analyse the Leninist ideology and the politics it
characteristically gives rise to. To that end I have included two
chapters on the Communist Party and an opening section on the
Communist International and the theory and practice of the
Bolshevik state in Lenin's day. In the earlier book a good deal of
detailed material can be found concerning the history of
Trotskyism and the divisions within it which is not included
here. I have also dropped a discussion of the Militant's analysis
of the present economic crisis. All the material which I have
used here has been rewritten and updated. Though the first two
chapters examine communism before 1945, the bulk of this
book is concerned with British Marxism in the post-war period.

During this period British communism was in almost unin-
terrupted decline but Trotskyism experienced a revival in the
1960s and Trotskyists subsequently became prominent in
single-issue campaigns, in the Labour Party and trade unions,
the new social movements and even local and national government. Until recently four Trotskyist groups were particularly
prominent and these are the ones which the book focuses on.
But it should be recorded here that a succession of splits and
regroupments since 1983–4 may well change the picture in the
next few years. The Workers' Revolutionary Party is now four

separate organizations: the International Marxist Group became the Socialist League which later split in two and produced the International Group. Likewise another entrist organization, *Socialist Organiser*, hatched the Socialist Group and even the Communist Party – hitherto the most faction-free of all these Marxist groups – purged a sizeable opposition which is now known as the Communist Campaign Group. The number of organizations on the far left can be gauged from the guest list produced by the Revolutionary Democratic Group for all those factions which like itself issued at one time or another from the Socialist Workers' Party and retain an interest in the latter's shibboleth of 'state capitalism'. A 'state capitalist forum' held in October 1986 included delegates from the IS Opposition, the Faction for Revolutionary Democracy, the Republican Faction, the Pro-*Women's Voice* Group, the Building Workers Faction and Red Action. The Revolutionary Democratic Group itself informed readers of *Republican Worker* (no. 4, October/November 1986) that unity was sought with the Socialist Federation, Workers Power, *The Leninist*, the Socialist Group and Red Action.

No doubt these organizations are small. But small groups can make their presence felt: like the Spartacist League which manages to disrupt an enormous number of political meetings in spite of the fact that its international membership is currently no more than 400; like the Revolutionary Communist Group which is prominent in the Westminster anti-apartheid group; like the readership of *Class War* which mobilized the 'Stop the City' demonstrations of March and September 1985. Some of the organizations of the Far Left are quite sizeable of course. The Communist Party in particular has always made its presence felt inside the trade unions, though the purge of its *Morning Star* faction in 1985–6 was at the cost of losing a considerable number of prominent trade union officials and communist industrial organizers. The changes inside British communism which brought about this schism are dealt with in chapter 6. In chapter 7 I analyse the politics of the Militant tendency – the organization which has been most successful in the application of the entrist tactic. Militant has also been able to boast a degree of industrial strength – especially in the CPSA where one of its members, Kevin Roddy, was elected president in 1982 and where another member, John Macreadie, currently holds this position. But Militant members also hold prominent positions inside the POEU, the Fire Brigades Union, the Bakers Union and ISTC. It is the Socialist Workers' Party, however, which more than any other Marxist organization in recent times has attempted to build a revolutionary party by means of a rank and file strategy within the unions. My analysis of this attempt to emulate the CP's Minority Movement of the 1920s occupies most of chapter 4.

Radical politics have changed during the last thirty years. Since the emergence of CND there has been an enormous number of campaigns and movements of protest which by no stretch of the imagination relied on the manual working class. Indeed in some quarters this has been invoked as evidence of the decline in the political significance of the working class. I do not share that view but it is worth observing that most far left groups habitually refer to the working class in sociological terms – that is, as if only the industrial manual workers counted. Yet it is precisely on this narrow definition of working class that most of the forecasts are based which look forward to the end of proletarian politics. In practice the Marxist organizations have succeeded much more by their activities among students, feminists, peace campaigners and the like. But with the exception of the Eurocommunist CP most of the would-be vanguard parties are shamefaced that they have recruited more teachers and social workers than miners and steelworkers. In several chapters I take up this question of the 'new social movements' but give this issue particular attention in chapter 5.

Isaac Deutscher once predicted that Stalinism and Trotskyism would be transcended in quite different ways. There is no doubt that the CPGB is in the process of finally coming to terms with its Stalinist past: it does not have a Stalinist future. It may not be too long before the very term 'communist' is dropped – certainly if Lenin was justified in his rejection of the name 'social democracy' in 1914 there is a powerful case for dispensing with 'communist' and 'communism' now. The change in name is only significant, of course, if it denotes a change in ideology and political practice but these are well on the way. As for Trotskyism there are so many groups claiming this title that no one trajectory is possible. If one can make any generalization it is that these groups already combine militancy and sentimentality in equal proportions. My guess is that with respect to these groups Marx would once again declare himself not a Marxist.

1

Communist Ideology

In all countries after 1918 the radical and activist
elements who were dissatisfied with existing conditions
began to disregard democracy.

Arthur Rosenberg, Democracy and Socialism

We journeyed through bombarded towns, in countryside
dotted with wooden crosses on the railway
embankments, until we came into the territory of the
'Tommies'. One night in a port whose houses were
shattered by bombs, the sick man in our party, some
police officers and I went into a tavern filled with
British soldiers. They noticed our unusual appearance.
'Who are you lot? Where are you going?'
'Revolutionaries – we are going to Russia.' Thirty
tanned faces surrounded us eagerly, there were hearty
exclamations all round us and we had to shake
everybody's hand. Since the Armistice popular feeling
had changed again; the Russian Revolution was once
more a distant beacon to men.

Victor Serge, Memories of a Revolutionary

Bolshevism became a world movement in the immediate after-
math of the Imperialist war of 1914–18 and the Russian
revolution of October 1917 which the war had helped to bring
about. In the estimation of radical opinion the European conflict
had exposed the moral bankruptcy of social democracy, the
renegacy of its national leaders, most of whom threw their
weight behind the war efforts of their own governments, and the

impotence of the Second International which was unable to prevent these betrayals. Lenin himself first mentioned the idea of a Third International as early as November 1914.[1] The October Revolution supplied him with the prestige which enabled the Bolsheviks to launch and dominate the new International when it was set up in 1919 and it was the war which convulsed Europe and paved the way for new insurrectionary movements embracing the Leninist ideology.

On the eve of the war democracy, understood as a system based on universal suffrage, was confined to only three peripheral capitalist states – Norway, Australia and New Zealand. But among the principal protagonists both France and Britain could claim democratic credentials. It was the involvement of these countries in the European slaughter which lent credibility to the contention – by no means confined to the Bolsheviks – that parliamentary forms of the bourgeois state were mere masks concealing the dictatorship of a militaristic finance capital. The fact that systems of universal suffrage increased immediately after the cessation of hostilities (from three to ten) did not greatly impress their radical critics. No one expected the Scandinavian countries – which were prominent in the new democracies – to shape the destiny of Europe so these could be safely ignored. In Central Europe radical mass movements had certainly created democratic republics in Germany and Austria but here expectations had been higher and for many years after 1918 the radical left awaited socialist revolutions in these countries. The Weimar Republic, moreover, was only the shallowest of democratic arrangements and given the centrality of Germany in Bolshevik perspectives it functioned *par excellence* as proof of the sham character of the bourgeois commitment to democratic forms. Here too social democracy appeared in its most pusillanimous and treacherous guise. In 1918–19 and 1920 it wasted good opportunities to democratize thoroughly the state and left the army, the bureaucracy and the judiciary in the hands of the republic's right-wing enemies. Social democratic politicians, indeed, actually used these coercive institutions to crush the Spartacist revolt and – in one of the republic's first acts – murder the revolutionaries Rosa Luxemburg, Karl Liebknecht and Leo

Jogiches. Then too, this wing of social democracy only equalled its deference to German capitalism by its vociferous hostility to Bolshevism. All these factors no doubt contributed to the dim view of bourgeois democracy which increasingly characterized Lenin's thinking after August 1914.

But this also had a great deal to do with the widespread conviction – common even in liberal and social-democratic circles – that the World War marked the end of an epoch of bourgeois progress and signalled the beginning of an era of capitalist crisis and socialist revolution. Even when it became apparent that the revolutionary wave of 1917–21 had receded, the salient features of the European experience in the inter-war period could, without violence to the facts, sustain this mood. For these were, of course, years of successive economic and political crises during which the democracies prepared for another world war and sections of the ruling classes threw in their lot with fascist and militarist movements. The temper and achievements of the communist movement cannot be understood outside this context any more than can its perversions. Nevertheless Leninism was not a mere creature of these forces but also an active shaper of events within the European socialist movement. This is what I will focus on in the present chapter.

Although the Bolshevik experience and doctrine completely dominated the Comintern from the beginning and served as guide and model for all the other parties, Leninism was formed in the unusual conditions, for Europe, of Tsarist Russia. The state overthrown by the February Revolution was not even in any meaningful sense a capitalist state.[2] The Provisional Government which succeeded the Tsar and which survived only until October 1917 was never based on any sort of national suffrage or popular participation. Participation was of course channelled into the soviets which I shall discuss later. But the first point to note is the absence of any viable liberal regime in Russia and the corresponding lack of experience of the Bolsheviks of political arrangements common in Western Europe. The liberal tradition had always been weak in Russia and civil society was, as Gramsci noted, primitive by Western standards. Indeed, such as it was, civil society in Russia was in large measure engendered by the proto-bureaucratic autocracy forced by military competition from its economically advanced neighbours to stimulate industry. The Russian bourgeoisie was in part the creature of this dirigiste experience and never strong or independent enough to represent a political challenge to it. Moreover on the eve of the First World War foreigners owned some 40 per cent of all the stock capital in Russia and even more in the leading branches of industry.[3] None of this prevented the Bolsheviks from deriving lessons of universal applicability from their own revolutionary experience and instructing foreign communists on how to create mass movements in wholly different political systems.

Bolshevik authority rested on their success as revolutionaries and it was this which enabled them to 'Bolshevize' their Western admirers. In practice this meant exporting ideas and practices born of Russian experience to alien soil. The Marxism propounded by Lenin, to take an important example, was inevitably cast in a Russian mould. the Russian revolutionary tradition necessarily bore characteristics derived from the peculiarities of Russian backwardness. Not the least significant of these was the idolatrous attitude to science among the Russian intelligentsia and the absence of any sceptical element in the materialism of revolutionaries persuaded of scientific certainty and even scientific morality. Lenin inherited this cast of mind in full measure declaring that 'the Marxist doctrine is omnipotent because it is true. It is comprehensive and harmonious and provides men with an integral world outlook.'[4] Throughout his career Lenin's thought was characterized by a non-negotiable belief in the monopoly of truth possessed by him and his faction and a corresponding disposition to castigate any and all opposition as bourgeois or petty bourgeois. In Lenin's perspectives no issue was beyond social class determinations or impenetrable to Marxist analysis or even irrelevant to the politics of the moment.[5] Victor Serge saw in this 'absolute sense of possession of the truth, grafted upon doctrinal rigidity' the 'seeds of such serious evils as intolerance and the drive towards the persecution of dissent.'[6]

Complementing this intolerance for which political pluralism is completely alien was the theme of renunciation and ascet-

icism in Russian revolutionary thought which eschewed everything which distracts from 'the Revolution'. Taken together
these habits of the Russian tradition go a long way to explain
what Arthur Rosenberg described as the 'stony one-sidedness'
which marked the Comintern from its inception. But while it
was possible for the self-constituted Bolshevik leadership to
imagine the vanguard party as the embodiment of
consciousness in Russia, in a highly industrialized urban
civilization such as Britain with over a century of proletarian
self-organization behind it the singular exclusivist claims of the
Communist Party were inevitably held in suspicion. Yet in
Left-Wing Communism – where it was asserted that 'all the
primary features' of the Russian revolution 'and many of its
secondary features are of international significance' – Lenin
argued that of the lessons of the Bolshevik experience the first is
'the most rigorous and truly iron discipline in our Party'.[7]
Comintern propaganda was particularly concerned to create
and protect the doctrinal purity of the communist parties and
wage a war against ideologically dubious elements, especially
those calling themselves Marxist. From the first the purity of
revolutionary theory was determined by the degree to which the
cadre understood the Bolshevik model.

This ignored the fact that the model had arisen in definite
conditions which either did not exist in the West or could not be
easily reproduced there. Since 1905, revolutionary politics in
Russia was informed by what Lukacs called the 'actuality of the
revolution'. But this could not be sustained in countries where
there was no prospect of revolution without isolating the parties
concerned. Lenin, in truth, was aware of the circumstances
which had made the Bolshevik revolution possible. He referred
to the 'unusual political backwardness of the tsarist monarchy'
which ensured, among other things, that even bread-and-butter
issues assumed a revolutionary character since even the routine
activities of trade unions and parties were proscribed. Russian
backwardness also facilitated the 'peculiar' merger of the
proletarian revolution 'against the bourgeoisie' with the
peasant revolt against the landowners.[8] Lenin realized that the
Bolshevik success owed much to the fact that the October
insurrection could be linked to Russia's withdrawal from the

war. Russian geography and poor communications helped the
new regime survive a lengthy civil war. The continuing
imperialist war prevented an early united capitalist front
against Bolshevism. And so on.[9] But none of this touched on
what Lenin regarded as the essentials of the Bolshevik
experience – the emergence of soviets, dual power, polarization
of society, civil war, dictatorship of the proletariat, the need for
a rigidly disciplined vanguard party etc. – all of these possessed
universal significance. At its most abstract Lenin's summing-
up of the preconditions for socialist advance was that
'revolution is impossible without a nation-wide crisis (affecting
both the exploited and the exploiters)'.[10]

Perspectives of the Comintern

Lenin was in fact convinced from 1914 that these crisis
conditions were generalized in the capitalist world. In 1916 he
found a rationale for this conviction in his *Imperialism: The
Highest Stage of Capitalism*. Here Lenin contended that capitalism
had entered a new crisis-ridden stage in its development. The
competitive, expansionary historically progressive capitalism
of the nineteenth century had been transformed by the growth
of monopolies (which promoted trade combines, cartels and
other forms of collusion) into a system of domestic economic
stagnation and political reaction. Monopoly capitalism tended
to destroy the competitive dynamic within national economies
and transferred capitalist rivalries to the international stage
where national monopolies competed for overseas markets and
cheap sources of labour and raw materials – thereby generating
a struggle for territorial acquisitions. Thus the conflict between
monopolies was always likely to become an open, violent
struggle between capitalist states. This was because Lenin (in
common with Bukharin) reasoned that just as the old bourgeois
parliamentarism had rested on the progressive competitive
capitalism of the nineteenth century the new twentieth-century
capitalist states were the expression of monopoly capitalism.
Where once it had been appropriate and necessary to represent
diverse capitalist interests in an elected, politically-pluralist

bourgeois parliament it was now appropriate and necessary to dispense altogether with democracy – save where this continued to dupe the masses – and replace it with increasingly militaristic authoritarian states able and willing to enforce the interests of national monopolies abroad. The old divisions within the capitalist ruling class were now obliterated by the growth of monopolies controlled by finance capital. This new monolithicity of the ruling class made the relatively open political systems of the recent past superfluous. Since the real material conflicts between capitalists were now conducted and resolved on a world scale, vigorously imperialist states were the order of the day.

Thus the imperialist epoch was characterized by inevitable imperialist wars. Why then was the system able to generate support within the working class as 1914 had shown? For Lenin the super-profits derived from imperialism enabled the monopolists to buy off a layer of the working class at home in the form of higher wages. According to Lenin, it was this 'aristocracy of labour' which, having a stake in the system, was prepared to support imperialism. These corrupted elements were the backbone of the reformist trade unions and social-democratic parties which had betrayed the revolutionary cause in August 1914. In the early stages of the imperialist epoch then (according to Lenin it had 'begun no earlier than 1898–1900') there was an objective basis for reformism in the more or less perilous factor of extraneous super-profits rather than in the capacity of capitalism to discover new techniques of production for the development of the productive forces.

Lenin never specified the size of the labour aristocracy nor was he able to describe the mechanisms which redistributed the colonial plunder in the form of higher wages. The point of the analysis was rather to explain how 'The mightiest organisations of the working masses were dominated by parties which had become transformed into auxiliary organs of the bourgeois state.'[11] Lenin was also able to show that although 'a bourgeois labour party is *inevitable* and typical in *all* imperialist countries . . . in view of the desperate struggle they are waging for the division of spoils, it is improbable that such a party can prevail for long in a number of countries.'[12] He was equally adamant, however, that these parties would not conveniently disappear by virtue of some automatic economic mechanism: 'There is not the slightest reason for thinking that these parties will disappear *before* the socialist revolution. On the contrary the nearer the revolution approaches . . . the greater will be the part the struggle of the revolutionary mass stream against the opportunist petty-bourgeois stream will play in the Labour movement.'[13] This is why Comintern documents referred repeatedly to the need to 'brand not only the bourgeoisie but also its helpers, the reformists of every shade, systematically and pitilessly'.[14] The nature of this struggle was such that 'at any moment it may and actually does substitute criticism with weapons for the weapon of criticism.'[15]

The Leninists contended then that the objective basis for a Third International consisted in the alleged 'decomposition and collapse of the entire world capitalist system'.[16] Even 'the most democratic bourgeois republic', they reasoned, 'is no more than a machine for the suppression of the working class by the bourgeoisie, for the suppression of the working people by a handful of capitalists.'[17] The economic crisis was no mere conjunctural affair but rather the symptom of a profound malaise, a general crisis expressed in the predominance of the state in economic life, 'the complete subjection of the state power to the power of finance capital and the complete militarisation of both.' The first congress of the Comintern insisted that these were 'accomplished facts' from which there is *'no turning back'* just as the transformation of the mightiest organizations of the working class into 'auxiliary organs of the bourgeois state' had become a permanent feature of all advanced capitalist countries.

By this means Lenin and Trotsky reduced the differences between the capitalist democracies and the capitalist and quasi-capitalist dictatorships to negligible (and forgettable) proportions. The whole thrust of Lenin's analysis was to deny that the democratic form of some bourgeois states mattered. In his polemics against Kautsky, Lenin contended that the prospect of a peaceful transition to socialism in countries like England – countenanced by Marx – was only valid in the days when 'there was no militarist clique . . . *as there is now* – serving as the chief apparatus of the bourgeois state machine.'[18] It is clear moreover that Lenin did not confine this analysis to states in war conditions but believed that liberal democracy was 'always narrow, hypocritical and false; it always remains democracy for the rich and a swindle for the poor.'[19] Indeed he was persuaded that as bourgeois democracy became better-established so it was more shallow, more of a confidence-trick: 'The more highly developed a democracy is the more imminent are pogroms or civil war in connection with any profound political divergence which is dangerous to the bourgeoisie. . . .the *more highly* democracy is developed the *more* the bourgeois parliaments are subjected to the stock exchange and the bankers.' Losing patience with Kautsky's defence of democracy Lenin concludes that bourgeois democracy is in any case 'moribund'.[20]

In fact just as Lenin concluded that bourgeois democracy had no future a major extension of the franchise occurred in Britain. If the system persisted anyway communists were required to denounce it as a mere veil for finance capital. Lenin could not conceive that any but the corrupt workers would see any intrinsic value in the institutions and practices of liberal democracy. Those that did constituted 'a whole trend of socialism (that) has gone over to the imperialist bourgeoisie' and the conclusion which this 'bitter truth' revealed was that the mass reformist organizations were simply 'agents of international imperialism operating *within* the labour movement, permeating *that movement* with bourgeois influence, bourgeois ideas, bourgeois lies and bourgeois corruption.'[21]

Lenin and Trotsky seem to have regarded the whole question of legitimacy in capitalist states as a problem composed only of corruption and the betrayal of reformist leaders. In his 'Theses on the Fundamental Tasks of the Second Congress of Comintern' Lenin maintained that the labour aristocracy was among the 'chief causes hampering the revolutionary working class movement in the developed capitalist countries'. This 'small minority of the working class', he argues, 'might even be called the social mainstay of the bourgeoisie'.[22] War has to be declared against them and communists must direct their efforts to recruitment among 'those who are least organised and educated, who are most oppressed and least amenable to organisation'.[23] The strong implication in Lenin's argument and one made explicit by Comintern leaders such as Radek, as Arthur Rosenberg observed, was that 'a few marks sufficed to turn the workers into counter-revolutionaries and middle class citizens' an argument which 'would have deprived socialism of all meaning'.[24] The ultra-lefts inside the Comintern interpreted Lenin just in this way when theorists of the 'offensive' dismissed the organized workers and pinned their putschist hopes in Germany on the unemployed.[25] This was all the more bizarre because Germany was one of several countries – France, Sweden and Italy were others – where the better-paid workers joined the communist party in disproportionate numbers.

The same crude reduction of political prospects to economic misery – the principle of 'fewer, better' – emerges as the chief Comintern explanation for revolutionary optimism:

> The revolutionary character of the present epoch consists precisely in this, that the modest conditions of life for the working masses are incompatible with the existence of capitalist society and that therefore the fight for even the most modest demands grows into the fight for communism.[26]

In fact the inter-war slump may have slowed down but certainly did not stop the growth in influence of the Labour Party while the communists remained a tiny though often influential force. When mass communist parties emerged in the post-Second-World-War period in France and Italy their growth had little to do with economic decline and much to do with specifically political factors brought about by the war. Nevertheless the idea that economic crisis is the real objective basis of revolutionary politics lingers on with the Leninists and Trotskyists of today content to repeat the old formulae concerning the bankruptcy of parliament as an arena where real reforms can be made and even theorizing that the increases of living standards since 1945 are simply illusory. Writing in the mid-1920s when it was obvious that the course of events had not taken the expected turn Trotsky 'explained' the survival of British capitalism as follows:

It can be said without exaggeration (sic) that the Fabian
Society . . . is nowadays the most reactionary grouping in
Great Britain . . . [for] . . . the proletariat itself is restrained
by precisely its own top leading layer, ie the Fabian
politicians and their yes-men. These pompous authorities,
pedants and haughty, high-falutin' cowards are systematically poisoning the labour movement, clouding the
consciousness of the proletariat and paralysing its will. *It is
only thanks to them that Toryism, Liberalism, the Church, the
monarchy, the aristocracy and the bourgeoisie continue to survive and
even suppose themselves to be fairly in the saddle.* (my emphasis)[27]

Even allowing for the usual polemical excess the real pity of this
ludicrous passage is that it is consistent with the burden of
'explanation' constantly repeated by Comintern. Trotsky's
ignorance of Britain is wholly understandable: it is harder to
explain why such arguments were ever taken seriously by
communists *in* Britain. The myth – sedulously cultivated by
most of the Russians on the executive of the Comintern – of
Bolshevik infallibility aided this acritical reception of Lenin and
(for a while) Trotsky in British communism and for many years
'theory' was thought of as a Russian preserve.

The failure of the Western revolutions reinforced this
religiosity and all shortcomings of the Western communists
were understood as a failure to grasp Leninism. Thus,
encouraged by the Russians, Western communists tried to
improve themselves by taking extra lessons in 'building the
Bolshevik vanguard party' in their own countries for this was
the instrument which would bring success.

The party fetish

Rosa Luxemburg warned Lenin that opportunism could not be
regarded as a mere symptom of some purely organizational
malaise and so could not be stopped by means of a formula
written down in a constitution. Since the socialist movement
has to be a mass movement its problems she argued, arise out of

'unavoidable social conditions' not the insidious machinations of individuals and groups.[28]

> A manual of regulations may master the life of a small sect or a private circle. An historic current, however, will pass through the mesh of the most subtly worded statutory paragraph. It is furthermore untrue that to repel the elements pushed toward the socialist movement by the decomposition of bourgeois society means to defend the interests of the working class.

Lenin's theory of the labour aristocracy was no concession to these strictures because it functioned simply to reinforce the idea that reformism was the product of corruption and leadership betrayal. The 'great betrayal' of 1914 was diagnosed by Lenin as stemming in some measure from the organizational defects of social democracy. Parties of a new type had to be established combining doctrinal purity with democratic centralism and a wholly committed, active membership. In theory the ideological sophistication of the cadre together with the vigilant activism of these militants would guard against bureaucratic degeneration though the price paid for this cohesion included 'a substantial, sometimes enormous turnover of members'[29] which taken alone would seriously impair the capacity of the rank and file to reach that familiarity with organizational procedures and ideological lore required to exercise real democratic control. In fact the problem of democracy within the communist parties and Comintern was *always* much deeper than this.

Since the Comintern was conceived as the 'one world party' of international communism the national 'sections' of this 'army in the field' (as Comintern documents spoke of it) were subordinate to the centre.

> Its permanent leading organ, the Executive Committee, was endowed with extraordinary powers. Its directives had immediate 'force of law' for all the national sections. It could expel members or groups of members belonging

to any country or entire national sections, it could change
the leadership of a national section, even against the
majority of its members and so on. Under these
conditions, the national leaderships held in practice
merely the power that was delegated to them by the
Executive Committee of the Comintern.[30]

The militaristic conception of the Comintern required that the
national sections had to be built 'according to the principle of
the strictest centralisation and, in the epoch of civil war must
establish military discipline within its ranks'.[31] From the
beginning Moscow was necessarily 'combat headquarters of the
world proletariat' and since no other revolutionary current
could match the authority of Bolshevism – especially after the
Spartacists were decapitated – this meant that Lenin and his
co-thinkers were the real directing force.

The project of fashioning a single world communist party
required among other things a high degree of ideological
homogeneity. But despite the stringent '21 conditions' of
membership and ruthless splitting tactics designed to dislodge
only the 'true' revolutionaries from the European socialist and
centrist parties the supporters of the Third International were a
politically diverse lot and included syndicalists, freemasons,
Luxemburgists and radicals of various types. Years of mass
political experience and democratic self-criticism were
required if a genuinely unified world party was to emerge from
these elements but such a protracted developmental
perspective was ruled out by the belief of the imminence and
urgency of the European revolution. Instead the desired
political cohesion was to be achieved by virtue of organizational
norms, purges and splits. In the first place the main thrust of
these was to exclude Marxists who refused to follow the
Leninist canon. These 'centrists' were perceived as the main
threat which would 'water down' (as Trotsky posed it)
communist purity though no such problem was perceived in the
variety of ultra-leftists who, representing no mass movements,
could be moulded or ejected as circumstances dictated.
Accordingly the Comintern engineered splits in mass organizations such as the German USPD and the Italian socialists

which weakened the labour movements in those countries.[32] Likewise insistence on submission to its 21 conditions of membership led to a collapse of support for affiliation to Comintern in the Independent Labour Party.[33]

The Comintern claimed exclusive title to the role of revolutionary vanguard and depicted all other currents in the labour movement as wilful obstructors of the revolutionary process. Only the Communist Party, argued Lenin, 'is capable of leading the proletariat in a final, most ruthless and decisive struggle against the forces of capitalism.'

> Owing to the extreme intensification of the struggle, all groups, parties and leaders in the working class movement who have fully or partly adopted the stand of reformism, of the 'Centre' etc, inevitably side with the bourgeoisie or join the waverers or else (what is most dangerous of all) land in the ranks of the unreliable friends of the victorious proletariat.[34]

Zinoviev, president of the Third International, made the same point arguing that the communists, being the 'most advanced, politically conscious and revolutionary part of the working class' are able to 'survey the whole historical path of the working class in its totality'. Although at first a minority, after the seizure of power 'all, or nearly all, workers begin to join the Party'.[35] There was simply no room for any other organization. As Lenin emphasized, the Communist Party had to enter 'every nook and cranny of toiling workers' so that its 'all-embracing efforts' could systematically educate 'the party, their class, the mass'. And at the second congress of the Comintern he stressed that this involved 'old leaders being replaced by Communists in proletarian organisations of absolutely every type – not only political, but also trade union, co-operative, educational etc.'[36]

This emphasis on the communists as the only true precognitive proletarian party was reinforced, ironically, by the early defeats inflicted on the Spartacist insurrection in Germany and the Bavarian and Hungarian soviets. While these experiences might have led to a re-examination of Leninist assumptions covering the preparedness of the European workers' movement for socialist revolution they in fact provided arguments on the need for Bolshevik-type parties. By 1920 the combination of Comintern rhetoric on the impending 'final struggle' and an arrogant vanguardism encouraged the development of an ultra-leftist 'theory of the offensive' according to which mass revolutionary movements could be catalysed by the independent insurrectionary activities of the communist party. This putschist orientation culminated in the notorious March Action of the German communists (KPD) in 1921. Here an abortive insurrection was directed by the Comintern leadership against the wishes of the KPD leadership around Paul Levi. Levi, who had oriented the KPD towards joint action with the other German workers' parties, publicly denounced the adventure and was duly expelled from the Comintern. The latter, which had full responsibility for the German debacle, blamed the ineptitude of the KPD. To complete this bizarre episode Lenin who had sanctioned Levi's expulsion effectively adopted his policy for it was immediately after the failure of the German putsch that the Comintern, against the wishes of several sections, adopted the policy of the united front – the orientation taken by Levi in Germany. By refusing to acknowledge the real causes of the March putsch the Comintern perpetuated the myth of Bolshevik infallibility. Levi himself saw through the Comintern account:

> It's the same old nonsense that Moscow always wants to believe, namely that a Soviet-style revolution would have occurred by now if there weren't a Serratti in Italy or a Levi in Germany standing in the way. The Muscovites completely overlook the fact that conditions in Western Europe are utterly different from those in Russia.[37]

In particular Levi drew attention to the fact that in the Western lands the bourgeoisie practises its domination in the form of democracy. But the united front turn of 1921 represented no new realization of this by the Comintern since it called forth a tactical change devoid of new theoretical insights. The policy of splits was seen to have failed in creating mass communist parties – the masses were still with the reformist organizations.

But there was no new reflection on the nature of Western reformism. The communist united front was based on the assumption that joint work with reformists and centrists would serve to expose the timidity and duplicity of their leaderships. In this way the masses would be won to communism. The united front was a way of 'taking the reformist leaders by the hand so as to be able to get them more easily by the throat'. If anything the singular claims of the communists were intensified and the objective of destroying the opposition within the working class was trumpeted even louder than before. The rhetoric of imminent revolution did not abate and far from making changes that would allow the national sections more discretion in the framing of policies and tactics suited to local conditions, the Comintern took further measures to reinforce the rigidities of organization, centralism and discipline extant.[38]

Basic perspectives were unchanged. Capitalism was still held to be defunct and the objective basis of reformism was likewise in terminal decay. Mass consciousness, though evidently out of step with this process, would soon catch up and achieve a revolutionary content as Bolshevik-type parties conducted a ruthless war against the reformist and centrist misleaders of the proletariat. Bourgeois democracy, for ever denounced as a mere sham, was destined to give way to more open forms of capitalist dictatorship. Italy was one of the first European countries to see these predictions realized and it is instructive to note that there the Italian communist leadership saw no real difference between fascism and bourgeois democracy, standing back and refusing to join with the hated reformists in armed fights against the fascist thugs. Even when the fascists came to outnumber the leading parties of Italy, the second congress of the Italian communists, in March 1922, continued to denounce democracy as 'a snare and a confidence trick' and referred to the socialists and libertarians simply as 'two different forms of weakening the proletariat'.[39]

Lenin and Trotsky opposed the disastrous sectarianism of the Italian communists but neither of them acknowledged the consistency of Bordiga's posture with their own rhetoric concerning the purely sham character of bourgeois democracy and their own depiction of rival workers' parties as the chief obstacles to socialist revolution. The fact that in 1928 the whole of the Comintern swung round to Stalin's codified version of this ultra-leftism – the so-called theory of social fascism which maintained that fascism and social democracy were 'twins' – owes something to the theses of the Comintern's first four congresses which nurtured a mentality receptive to such thinking. The truth is that the communists took an all-or-nothing attitude to democracy: bourgeois democracy was nothing, soviet or council democracy everything.

Soviet democracy

It was Lenin who insisted that council democracy and parliamentary democracy were mutually exclusive. Indeed until the Russian revolution of 1905 council democracy had played virtually no part in Marxist thought. Lenin transformed this Russian experience into a question of principle especially after the Bolsheviks liquidated their own constituent assembly in January 1918.

In fact the Bolsheviks had repeatedly called for the convocation of a constituent assembly between February and October 1917. It was only after the Bolshevik insurrection, however, that elections to the assembly began to take place. This was a protracted and uneven affair because of the vastness of the country and in some districts elections never took place. Some 40 million votes were cast but less than 10 million were for the Bolsheviks and the Socialist Revolutionaries emerged with the biggest share, around 16 million. The Bolshevik central committee delayed the assembly's first meeting until January 1918. The previous December Lenin argued that soviet democracy superseded the constituent assembly which was merely the highest form of democracy known to the bourgeoisie. Soviets, he proclaimed, were the only type of institution 'capable of securing the most painless transition to socialism'. And in any case the assembly, Lenin argued, is convoked on the basis of electoral lists submitted in mid-October 1917: since then the 'people's will' had changed and the Socialist

Revolutionaries had split, with their Left going over to alliance
with the Bolsheviks. Clearly, he argued, if the people had voted
in knowledge of the full scope and significance of the October
Revolution the electoral results would have been different.[40]

On this basis the constituent assembly was dispersed by force
at its first meeting with Lenin explaining that the workers
would not submit to a peasant majority. Lenin always claimed
to find more virtue than necessity in this development by
insisting on the superior nature of soviet democracy. Here, he
argued, personnel were subject to immediate recall without
bureaucratic formalities obstructing the people's will. The
elected representatives had both legislative and executive
functions which, reasoned Lenin, prevented them from degen-
erating into mere talking shops such as bourgeois parliaments.
The Bolsheviks could see no value in a separation of functions
between legislators and executive members of the state. Indeed
such divisions were regarded as bourgeois devices to emasc-
ulate working class electorates. In *State and Revolution* Lenin
outlined the future socialist state – one that would from the first
day begin to wither away – without suggesting any distinctions
between the functions of government and opposition, party and
state, elected representatives and paid functionaries, state and
society. His guiding assumption was that the revolution created
an identity of interests between the revolutionary party and the
people. Coupled with the idea that advances in technique had
rendered all these tasks so simple that anyone could and would
perform them, this assumption conjured away all the usual
problems of politics which derive of course from the clash of
opposed interests in a context of many scarcities (of time,
resources, abilities etc.).[41]

Lenin presented an image of the Bolshevik state – and this is
what attracted foreign communists – as a pyramid of soviets
controlled from below. But no sooner were the Bolsheviks in
power than the process began whereby the soviets were
dominated by executive committees based on the party and
responsible to the party centre for implementing its decisions.
Such a process was required both by the situation of anarchy
and chaos which the Bolsheviks inherited as well as the
requirements of their conception of socialism which was statist

and centralist. Coercion and manipulation first reduced then
removed the influence of the other soviet parties.[42] Of the
revolution's sympathizers abroad only the anarchists and Rosa
Luxemburg saw through the legend of direct democracy.
Luxemburg brilliantly exposed the nub of the problem as
follows: 'The tacit assumption underlying the Lenin-Trotsky
theory of the dictatorship is this: that the socialist transformation is something for which a ready-made formula lies
completed in the pocket of the revolutionary party which needs
only to be carried out energetically in practice.'[43] Some features
of the direct democracy pursued by syndicalist and irrespons-
ible elements in the factories actually added to the all-pervasive
disorder but the Bolsheviks never deviated in any case before or
after October from a commitment to statist and centralized
solutions to the economic disintegration. The slogan of
workers' control was used by them to attract the radical workers
but the Bolshevik conception of workers' control was that of the
collective class control of the proletariat exercised through its
party – the Bolsheviks. From the beginning of 1918 the spontaneously created factory committees were absorbed by the
trade unions which were themselves redefined as organs, essentially, of the state.[44] By March 1918 Lenin demanded the
restoration of one-man management to solve the economic
crisis which had reached such proportions that the cities were
deserted by workers fleeing hunger. Many too left to join the
Red Army and fight in the civil war.

There was very little scope for any kind of democracy under
these circumstances. But once again it was Luxemburg who saw
the danger which 'begins only when they make a virtue of
necessity and want to freeze into a complete theoretical system
all the tactics forced upon them by these fatal circumstances
and want to recommend them to the international proletariat as
a model of socialist tactics.'[45] This is what happened but to a
large extent the Bolshevik authoritarian approach was consistent with conceptions which pre-date the insurrection and
which, therefore, had nothing to do with the exigencies of the
situation they confronted after coming to power. Before the
revolution Lenin emphasized the virtues of organization of the
population into compulsory consumer societies and compulsory

unionization and talked as if measures such as these, by implementing 'the fullest, strictest and most detailed account-ancy', were more than half the battle to achieve socialism. The model of organization for society was the factory since *unquestioning subordination* to a single will is absolutely necessary for the success of processes organised on the pattern of large-scale machine industry.'[46] Bolshevik thought was always devoid of any clear conception of institutional accountability as Lenin's *State and Revolution* attests. But matters were made worse by their conviction that the political and cultural prerequisites of socialism would emerge as automatic effects of advances in the productive forces. This, in turn, could best be achieved by imitation of the most advanced capitalist technique no matter how barbarous the methods employed.[47] Thus economic authoritarianism was regarded as a necessary devel-opment while political pluralism was a non-starter. As Sirianni argues,

> Virtually every exhortation on the need for mass participation during the transition, in *State and Revolution* and in Lenin's other works, speaks primarily in terms of participation in the technical tasks of administration. . . No statement whatever except those relating to the questions of revolutionary strategy and the seizure of power in 1917 before the Bolsheviks had established pol-itical hegemony . . . speaks of mass participation in the formation and revision of policy . . . Indeed Lenin later argues that the existence of division and differences pre-cisely disqualifies mass organisations embracing the entire proletariat from deciding policy and ruling directly and necessitates the imposition of a unifying line by the party . . . differences are never recognised as even possibly legitimate but are automatically branded an insidious threat to revolutionary unity, an expression of demoralisa-tion and degradation revealing the persistence of capitalist ideology and culture. The revolutionary interest is one and so must be the revolutionary will. Only one party can guarantee this.[48]

The fate of the soviets as agencies of working-class democracy was settled therefore by a combination of factors which includes the authoritarian nature of Bolshevism. No doubt circumstances of economic chaos and civil war would have destroyed them anyway. But the ideological factor is important because Lenin's authority could be invoked to justify further steps down the road of dictatorship taken by Stalin and because Leninism was the orthodoxy, after 1917, of a world movement. As early as 1920 it was Lenin who argued that 'the mere presentation of the question – dictatorship of the party *or* dictatorship of the class . . . testifies to the most incredibly and hopelessly muddled thinking.'[49] It was Trotsky at the tenth party congress who denounced the Workers' Opposition for 'placing the workers' right to elect representatives above the party . . . as if the party were not entitled to assert its dictatorship even if that dictatorship temporarily clashed with the passing moods of the workers' democracy'. These people, he said, had made 'a fetish of democratic principles'. But the Bolsheviks made a fetish of the party, as Trotsky illustrated in a polemic with Kautsky:

> We have more than once been accused of having substituted for the dictatorship of the Soviets the dictatorship of our party. Yet it can be said with complete justice that the dictatorship of the Soviets became possible only by means of the dictatorship of the party. It is thanks to the clarity of its theoretical vision and its strong revolutionary organisation that the party has afforded to the Soviets the possibility of becoming transformed from shapeless parliaments of labour into the apparatus of the supremacy of labour. In this 'substitution' of the power of the party for the power of the working class there is nothing accidental, and in reality there is no substitution at all. The Communists express the fundamental interests of the working class.[50]

The Trotsky legend

After Lenin's death in 1924, by which time all opposition parties had been outlawed and factions banned within the

Communist Party of the Soviet Union, the repression of dissent intensified and Trotsky's followers became its victims as members of the Left Opposition. Victor Serge, himself a member of the Opposition, later had this to say about it:

> I came to the conclusion that our Opposition had simultaneously contained two opposing lines of significance. For the great majority of its members it had meant resistance to totalitarianism in the name of the democratic ideals expressed at the beginning of the Revolution; for a number of our Old Bolshevik leaders it meant, on the contrary, the defence of doctrinal orthodoxy, which while not excluding a certain tendency towards democracy, was authoritarian through and through. These two mingled strains had, between 1923 and 1928, surrounded Trotsky's vigorous personality with a tremendous aura. If in his exile from the USSR he had made himself the ideologist of a renewed Socialism, critical in outlook and fearing diversity less than dogmatism, perhaps he would have attained a new greatness. But he was a prisoner of his own orthodoxy, the more so since his lapses into unorthodoxy were being denounced as treason.[51]

Until his death in 1940 Trotsky was both the greatest opponent of Stalin and the staunchest defender of the Bolshevik orthodoxies which helped to pave the way to Stalinism. That is to say he was incapable of finding in the first four congresses of Comintern or in the basic practices of the Bolshevik state in its early years the authoritarian roots of the Stalinist tyranny. Instead he was forced by his own convictions, his own role in these events, and his struggle against Stalin, to promote Bolshevism – the authentic Bolshevism of Lenin – as a thing wholly apart from developments in the Soviet Union and Comintern after 1924. Yet even among the doomed Trotskyist inmates of the isolator at Verkhne-Uralsk, among these victims of the dictatorship, the same intolerance was reproduced, with members insisting on the dissolution of factions and the suspension of their publications in the interests of a 'monolithic section'.[52]

In reality Lenin's own thought was dogmatic and intolerant.
The Bolshevik Party under Lenin did much to destroy soviet
democracy which was finished well before the personal
ascendancy of Stalin. The Communist International from its
beginning concentrated power at the top, was dominated by the
Russian party and incapable of admitting the mistakes and
fallibility of the Bolsheviks let alone that they had anything to
learn from other currents of Marxism. To this day the
Trotskyists persist in the belief that Stalinism and Leninism
have nothing in common and this is not the least reason why
organizations descended from Trotsky reproduce the practices
associated with Stalinism.

For ten years between 1923 and 1933 Trotsky sought to
organize his supporters as a faction of the Comintern striving to
reform an organization which had outlawed them and tolerated
no dissent. Though the International functioned largely as an
instrument of Soviet foreign policy Trotsky refused to believe
that the Stalinist dominance was permanent. His slogan was 'all
eyes to the Communist Party. We must explain to it. We must
convince it'.[53] All this was changed when the KPD, the
Comintern's most powerful section, succumbed to the Nazis
without a fight in 1933.

Since 1928 Trotsky had argued against the ultra-leftist lurch
taken by the Comintern when the so-called Third Period was
inaugurated. Between 1928 and 1934 the Third International
denounced the social democrats as 'social fascists' and refused
to countenance collaboration with them against the real
fascists. Trotsky saw through this nonsense and produced the
best analysis of fascism then available though it was completely
ignored by the communist audience for which it was intended.
Hitler's accession to power was made possible by the disastrous
policy which Moscow imposed on the communist parties but
even after this catastrophic event the International ruled that
the KPD's tactics had been 'completely correct'. Trotsky's
decision to found alternative communist parties was taken in
the months that followed: 'Only when it became clear that no
open indignation was aroused in the ranks of the Communist
International after the latter had surrendered without a fight
the most important of its positions did it become clear that no

hopes remained for the regeneration of this organisation.'[54]

Because reform of the Comintern had become a hopeless prospect the political necessity, by Trotsky's reasoning, was to create a new, Fourth International. Trotsky also revised his analysis of the Soviet Union concluding that a 'political revolution' was now required to shift the parasitic bureaucracy and restore a genuine workers' state. To those such as Isaac Deutscher and Victor Serge who recognized the bankruptcy of the Comintern but who believed that the European situation prevailed against the creation of a new International, Trotsky argued that the objection was devoid of all content although he delayed the founding conference of the Fourth International until 1938 in the hope that the intervening years would enable the miniscule Trotskyist forces to establish a real base within the working class. They did not and the Fourth International was launched regardless.

In the seven years after 1933 Trotsky laboured indefatigably to nurture the new organizations and was called on by his supporters to advise and intervene on every conceivable issue including a large amount of what he once, in exasperation, called 'disgusting trivia'. Despite obstacles of every kind Trotsky foresaw events which would undermine both capitalism and the rival mass parties which stood in the way of the Fourth International. In essence his hopes were pinned on the coming catastrophes which the growth of fascism, the world capitalist crisis and impending war represented. After 1933 he came to see fascism as the inevitable destiny of the capitalist democracies which only socialist revolution could avert. His reasoning was entirely reductionist and an echo of Lenin's analysis of the inevitable drift of the bourgeois parliamentary regimes to authoritarianism. For now he described fascism as 'the political regime that crowns the regime of economic decay'.[55] The Comintern, which in 1934 inaugurated the popular front tactic by means of which the communists sought unity with all anti-fascists, was now denounced by Trotsky for pursuing an orientation very similar to the one he advocated himself prior to 1933. Trotsky proposed instead that 'when the whole train is plunging into the abyss the distinction between decaying democracy and murderous fascism disappears in the face of the collapse of the entire system.'[56] The tables were now turned; popular feeling clamoured for unity as did the communists while Trotsky offered salvation exclusively through the socialist revolution led by his own negligible faction.

The isolation of the Trotskyists could not have been greater. But their situation was made tolerable by the conviction that the objective conditions were 'rotten ripe' for socialism and only the traitorous communist and social democratic leaders had prevented its realization. This sentimental reasoning brought Trotsky to the conclusion that 'the world political situation as a whole is chiefly characterised by a historical crisis of the leadership of the proletariat' which only Trotskyists could solve by 'freeing the proletariat from the old leadership whose conservatism is in complete contradiction to the catastrophic eruptions of disintegrating capitalism and represents the chief obstacle to historical progress'.[57] It was the refusal of anyone else to see the situation in this way which compelled the Trotskyists to embark on the entrist tactic. Since no one would join them in building mass revolutionary parties the Trotskyists infiltrated the organizations of their centrist and reformist rivals in the belief that by this means their message would gain access to the masses.

Trotsky even failed to persuade other small revolutionary groups to throw in their lot with the Fourth International. Trotskyists attended the conference convoked by the Independent Labour Party in 1933 where they urged delegates representing 14 such groups to take this course of action. But Trotsky failed to win over even those organizations which accepted many of his analyses and policies. Some of these policies failed to take account of the new European reality. The coming world war was depicted as a re-run of the first in which 'the victory of any one of the imperialist camps would spell slavery, wretchedness, misery, the decline of human culture.'[58] Though he insisted that the duty of his followers was to defend the USSR once it entered the fray he was convinced of its inevitable defeat. Among his own followers there were many persuaded that the USSR had become a form of state capitalism but Trotsky was adamant that the nationalized economic foundations of the Soviet Union represented a genuine socialist gain. For this reason only a political action was required to restore the state for the workers. But this 'degenerated workers' state' thesis was too much to swallow for many of those aware of the slave labour conditions which characterized 'normal' factory conditions inside Russia as well as its gulags. Like the question of entrism, Trotsky's characterization of the USSR soon became one of those shibboleths which Trotskyists have argued and split up about ever since.

But the bulk of the ideological legacy bequeathed by Trotsky was not of his own invention. Trotsky pledged himself to the defence of Leninism as manifested in the history of the Bolshevik Party until Lenin's death and in the policies of the Bolshevik state before 1924 and in the first four congresses of the Comintern. This is how it stands with contemporary Trotskyism.[59] To shed any more light on this Leninist theory it is necessary to turn now to its impact here in Britain in the early history of the Communist Party.

2

British Communism Between the Wars

Until the formation of the Communist Party in 1920 there were three main Marxist organizations in Britain. Hyndman's Social Democratic Federation became the British Socialist Party (BSP) in 1911 with John MacLean as its most prominent member after the departure of Hyndman himself in 1916. There was also the de Leonite Socialist Labour Party (SLP) and Sylvia Pankhurst's Workers' Socialist Federation. When the Communist Party was formed it consisted of a fusion of the British Socialist Party, the Socialist Labour Party and a number of intellectuals associated with the National Council of Labour Colleges. It did not result, therefore, as in so many other countries, from a split in the mass reformist organizations. From the beginning the key question for the 2,000-strong party was its relationship to the Labour Party: but this would be determined by its relationship with the Communist International.

Leninism drew the party's British converts away from the economistic and mechanical variants of Marxism associated with the SLP and BSP. Its initial impact was to discredit the fatalism which expected socialism to come from a final catastrophic breakdown of the system and urge instead the development of an immediate revolutionary strategy. Marxism in this its Leninist guise was understood primarily as a guide to action. This was its strength of course but it also became a source of weakness.

In the first place it was a foreign import which presented difficulties not simply of assimilation – the aspect of the problem emphasized by Lenin and the Comintern – but also of application in British conditions. The CP leaders were very soon 'dependent upon the guidance of Soviet interpreters' of Marxism.[1] This meant that Marxism was handed down as a body of definitive truths which required no further elaboration. Apart from Lenin's contemporaneous writings the key texts were taken from the later writings of Marx and Engels. Marx's early writings and his specifically political works were less well known, or unheard of, as were the books of Luxemburg, Lukacs, Korsch and Gramsci. On the authority of Lenin, British Marxism by the mid-1920s had become a new teleological doctrine in which the final victory of socialism was assured by virtue of the party guided by science and able to exploit the contradictions of an imperialist system in permanent crisis.

It has been argued that the complete conversion of the CP leaders to Bolshevism was so rapid and thoroughgoing that the individuals concerned were henceforth incapable of maintaining a critical distance between themselves and the Russian party leaders for the rest of their lives.[2] But it was not so much the speed of the conversion as the nature of the original relationship which produced this result. Harry Pollitt expressed it this way:

> The thing that mattered to me was that lads like me had whacked the bosses and landlords . . . These were the lads and lasses I must support through thick and thin . . . for me these same people could never do nor ever can do any wrong against the working class . . . you cannot be a real Socialist and enemy of reaction and at the same time assist in any way to carry on a struggle against the Soviet Union . . . however cunningly you try to pretend that it is 'only the tactics of certain Soviet leaders' that you are protesting against.[3]

Pollitt, Campbell, Gallacher and the rest were tough-minded militants, not the stuff that lackeys and sycophants are made of. Their allegiance to Lenin and the Soviet Union was based on the fact, as they saw it, that by creating the first workers' state the Bolsheviks had struck the most important blow for progress and could instruct them in the ways of achieving the same in Britain. They were no theorists and within international communism there was no alternative source of authority to that of the Bolsheviks. They did not *want* to believe that the Soviet system was defective. Well before the purge of Trotsky and his supporters, reports of Bolshevik repression against other socialists were either denied by the British communists or accepted as the just punishments of criminals and counter-revolutionaries.[4] (Of course the Trotskyists see no connection between the waves of repression and the fact that acquiescence in the first may have prepared the ground for acceptance of the second.)

Since there had been very little theoretical attention or critical debate in the socialist movement on what the future society would look like or on how it would cope with the many serious problems actually faced by the Bolsheviks even abstract criteria against which the Russian experience could be judged were thin on the ground. In the 32-year history of the German Social Democratic Party's theoretical journal *Neue Zeit*, for example, only one article considered post-revolutionary society. Yet until 1914 this was universally acclaimed as the world's biggest and best Marxist party. It is little wonder then that the tiny British Communist Party was inclined to take on trust what the Bolshevik pioneers presented as the components of an authentic socialist experience. In 1920, the year the British party was formed, soviet democracy was already dead and the dictatorship of the Bolsheviks, rather than the proletariat, was the cardinal feature of Russian society in the grip of a civil war.

At this time the British Marxists were in any case considerably confused as to what the soviets actually were.[5] Opinion ranged from the idea that they promoted exclusively workshop-based political representation to the notion that they were a way of running industry. But if the British were ignorant of Russian arrangements the Bolsheviks were equally confused about the situation in Britain.

Sylvia Pankhurst was believed to be lying in a dungeon undergoing the tortures of a Rosa Luxemburg. John MacLean was thought to be the particular personality around which rallied the Communist movement in Great Britain . . . The Guild Socialists had virtually captured the trade unions and the unofficial Workers' Committees were endeavouring to smash the unions and had rejected political ideas like the International Workers of the World.[6]

Comintern paid no heed to advice which failed to correspond with its own perspectives. The strength of the British party was overestimated but, more damagingly, the International would not acknowledge that its perspectives of mass industrial struggle had no purchase on the British situation.[7] This was characterized by the collapse of the militant shop stewards' movement and, indeed, of trade union strength generally. Unemployment in engineering, the main base for industrial radicalism before the CP was formed, was 27 per cent by 1921. Generally 17.8 per cent of insured workers were out of work and trade union membership was falling – from 8.3 million in 1920 to 5.6 million in 1922 to 4.4 million in 1933. The number of strikes also fell and those that did occur were overwhelmingly defensive in character.[8]

While the slump did little to promote the political radicalism anticipated by the Comintern, the defining feature of working class politics in the same period was also the opposite of what the International predicted in Britain. I am referring, of course, to the rise of the Labour Party. Until 1931 the Labour Party's share of the vote rose inexorably without however doing much to strengthen the position of the minority of socialists within its ranks. Labour's electoral growth was chiefly an expression of defensive solidarity akin to trade union membership and even in these terms it was as Hyman says 'an uphill struggle to win workers' support . . . as an expression of common social interests.'[9] Not surprisingly the International did not really know what to make of the Labour Party but this did not prevent it from dictating the attitude of the British CP on this vital issue.

The Labour Party and trade unions

According to Lenin 'the only correct point of view' on the question of the Labour Party was that it is 'a thoroughly bourgeois party . . . led by reactionaries and the worst kind of reactionaries at that'.[10] However, the Comintern also described it as 'the political organisation of the trade unions' and emphasised its unique structural link with them. Since the Bolsheviks attached crucial significance to organization at 'the point of production' and within the unions, the fact that many of these were affiliated to the Labour Party and that the latter was organized federally recommended communist affiliation as well. Comintern accordingly insisted on a campaign for communist affiliation to the Labour Party, this 'thoroughly bourgeois party', against the wishes of a reluctant CP leadership in Britain and at a time when Comintern propaganda was denouncing reformism as a spent force. Thus the British CP was in effect directed to the united front tactic shortly before the rest of Comintern was reoriented in the same way. But on top of the problem encountered by the united front tactic everywhere – the difficulty of bringing about joint work with organizations that the communists were loudly denouncing as traitors, misleaders, cowards, etc. – the British communists were expected to secure affiliation. The Labour Party's response can be summarized as follows:[11]

Summary of labour movement actions against the Communist Party

1920   Rejection of the first application for affiliation
1924   CP members banned from individual membership of the Labour Party and from adoption as Labour candidates
1925   Trade unions prevented from electing CP members as delegates to Labour Party meetings
1929   General council of the TUC attempts to ban communists from election to office
1933   Labour Party proscribes organizations which include communist members

1934   TUC general council issues 'black circulars' urging
         trade unions to amend their rules to exclude com-
         munists from office and from trade councils
1946   Labour's annual conference votes against affiliation
         and changes the party's rules to bar any further
         applications for affiliation from national organiz-
         ations
1947   Labour's NEC calls on trade unions to remove com-
         munist officials
1948   Attlee government purges civil service of communists
         (or tries to!)
1949   TGWU prevents election of communists to official
         union positions

If the objective of the united front was to destroy the
political influence of the reformist organizations within the
working class the Labour leadership understood this rather
better than the British communists. The response to the
affiliation campaign was predictable from men whom the communists openly compared to the Mensheviks – an organization
outlawed and terrorized by the Bolsheviks. There was no
chance of gaining their assent and the communists must have
known it. Where they miscalculated was in supposing that a
major rift would develop between the Labour leadership and
the rank and file when in fact even in the 1930s dissident
constituencies were easily disciplined precisely because no
such cleavage of opinion was ever generalized in the organization. A major avoidable blunder in these early years which
compounded the problem was the Comintern's identification
of the Independent Labour Party (ILP) as *the* powerhouse of
Fabian (therefore bourgeois) influence within the Labour
Party.[12] In fact the ILP had for a time considered affiliation to
the Comintern and consistently contained most of the
individual Marxists active in the Labour Party. Here was an
organization with which some sort of united front *was* possible
but the communists often reserved their most vituperative
language for it.

'Fractional' entrism within other organizations was obliga-
tory in situations where at least two communists were active.

Thus in the unions and the Labour Party – which individual CP members could join until 1924 – communists organized themselves into caucuses. In 1923 the CPGB was pressurized by the Comintern's belief that the unions could be transformed into 'mass organizations of revolutionary struggle' to create a Minority Movement organizing the rank and file for confrontation with the trade union bureaucracy. Since 1921 this had been on the agenda of the British Bureau of the Red International of Labour unions (Profintern). In reality the CP's Minority Movement answered no felt need among trade union members except, perhaps, among the miners. But around the end of 1923 the attention of the Comintern switched from Germany – where another KPD putsch was aborted in October – to England where Zinoviev saw 'conditions . . . now being created for the establishment of a mass communist party.'[13] The fifth congress of the Comintern saw the CPGB's tasks as comprising a struggle against parliamentary illusions and preparation 'to snatch the workers' movement out of the hands of its reactionary leaders'.[14]

The Minority Movement sought to bring militant trade unionists under the direction of the CP in a campaign which included the demand for reorganization of the unions on an industrial basis and the assumption of responsibility for the whole trade movement by the TUC General Council – the better by means of such centralization for the ultimate revolutionary transformation of the movement. 'Merciless criticism' of the trade union bureaucracy was deemed an essential feature of this process. But it is arguable that the greatly increased majority for exclusion of CP members from individual membership of the Labour Party recorded in 1925 owed something to the antagonism which the communists' industrial entrism created in the preceding year or so. Following this decision which Pollitt disingenuously attributed to mere organizational manipulations by the reformist leaders, the CP in December 1925 created the National Left Wing Movement as a means of organizing its members and sympathizers within the Labour Party.

By 1926 the CPGB had 150 'groups and fractions' operating within the Labour Party – 87 in London alone.[15] Some 48

constituency labour parties endorsed the CP's campaign for
affiliation and by 1927 the party was reckoning that 1,455 of its
members were active within the Labour Party. By 1926 the
Sunday Worker (launched in March 1925), the CP's mouthpiece
for the united front, claimed a circulation of 85,000 and was
able to depend on the active collaboration of prominent Labour
left-wingers. Nevertheless Labour's NEC responded to these
developments by disaffiliating 27 local labour parties between
1926 and 1929 and threatening disciplinary action against
dozens more.[16] Most of these were in London – Bethnal Green,
Stratford, Hackney, Lewisham, Southwark, Poplar, etc – where
over one-third of the membership of the CP was engaged in
entrism. Here Herbert Morrison led the campaign against CP
infiltrators. But apart from failing in its ultimate objective of
affiliation the CP was unable to arouse the degree of sympathy
required to mobilize the constituencies against official Labour.

The reasons for this failure are not hard to find. Until 1945
the Labour leadership could claim that it had never received a
parliamentary majority and the fact that it was untried and
untested in government was a powerful reason for its supporters to reject the communist alternative. Entrism in an organization which enjoyed the support of its members was always
likely to antagonize more individuals than it won into the CP
and may even have been, as McIntyre argues, one of the biggest
causes of estrangement from the CP in these years.[17] Then we
have to consider the effect of the CP's propaganda. This set
communists the impossible task of persuading trade union and
Labour Party members that the Marxists were the best defenders of their interests even though they did everything to
oppose the elected leaders and policies of these organizations.

Matters were not helped by the CP's own confusion. In 1920
the leadership evidently believed that it could go it alone and
made no secret of the fact by proclaiming the reformists a spent
force. Once, however, the prospect of the trade unions being
transformed into 'instruments of revolutionary progress' was
held out to them by the Comintern, the CP was emboldened to
relax these polemics in the interests of co-operation and R.
Palme Dutt even spoke of the need for patience while Mac-
Donald and company paved the way for a workers' society

when the first minority Labour government was formed.[18] It was the Comintern which blew the whistle on this conciliatory line and Radek complained of a 'reformist epidemic' in the British section. Over a year later, in 1925, when the united front line seemed to be bearing fruit and the party was reaching a mass audience through the *Sunday Worker*, doubts remained over its ultimate objective. By now Palme Dutt was fearful that the party had conceded too much and had lost sight of its purpose which was to replace the reformist influence by a mass communist party while others, such as J. T. Murphy, looked forward to fusion with a radicalized Labour left as the means of bringing about such a mass revolutionary party. If Murphy was right did this not entail nurturing the non-communist left? If Dutt was correct the reformists, however 'left' their pretensions, had to be openly damned.[19]

The mood in the Comintern favoured Murphy's approach while Dutt toyed with Trotsky's line only to abandon it on the eve of the General Strike when in a review of Trotsky's *Where Is Britain Going?* he concluded that 'the English working class is not yet ready for a mass revolutionary party.'[20] These vacillations reflect the problems of building a revolutionary party in a non-revolutionary situation. The best proof that this was how things stood lies in the failure of the Minority Movement to become the revolutionary rank-and-file power which the CP tried to construct in industry. By the spring of 1926 the party was still a tiny force of only 6,000 which despite an urgent drive in the period 1924–6 could only count 17 per cent of its members in factory cells. The party clearly foresaw major industrial conflicts ahead – indeed in October 1925 its leaders were arrested and imprisoned as the government anticipated a similar scenario. There is no doubt that as the General Strike approached, the CP possessed no clear agitational line. Sometimes it argued that the miners' struggle could only be defended by civil war (though the party did not prepare for such an outcome). But much of its propaganda suggested that the leadership of militant trade unionists was enough and since the formation of the Minority Movement the party had demanded that the General Council of the TUC should take full responsibility for conducting the strike – which of course it did with disastrous results. But whatever these confusions Trotsky's argument that the CP wasted a revolutionary situation because it was compromised by the International's opportunism is wrong. In fact the British party stood to the right of the Comintern in its application of the united front line. At the end of the General Strike, with its membership temporarily swollen to 10,730 and *Workers' Weekly* with sales of 80,000, the CP swung to the 'left' declaring that there were now 'millions of workers more Left' than left trade union leaders such as A. J. Cook of the miners.

Class against class

It is ironic that it was the *defeat* of the General Strike that persuaded the CP that things had changed for the better. It now argued that the Labour lefts had been exposed as betrayers and the masses had been radicalized. The party was more than ever persuaded that decaying imperialism was destroying the basis for the labour aristocracy and the reformist politics it sponsored. This was the message which Dutt dwelt on in *Socialism and the Living Wage* and at the eighth party congress in October 1926 the delegates were told that 'in the period of capitalist decline there is no basis for a reformist leadership and party like the Labour Party'.[21]

Yet during 1927 CP membership fell rapidly as did its newspaper sales. The worsening economic situation provided every indication that the militancy of the trade unions had been completely undermined. It was precisely now, however, in this low ebb that the Comintern under Stalin's direction imposed its new 'Class against class' line on a reluctant CPGB leadership. In May 1927 the Comintern was emphasizing the alleged shift to the left of the British working class. At the same time the Russian party was preparing for the onslaughts of forced collectivization. But the CPGB's ninth congress took place in October in sublime ignorance of what was about to descend on it in the form of the ultra-leftism of the Third Period and passed the usual resolutions concerning work in the Labour Party and trade unions. After the congress the party received a telegram from Bukharin informing it of a reconsideration of relations with reformist organizations. Both Pollitt and Dutt acquiesced although they were initially in a minority within the British leadership. However by March 1928 the central committee and politbureau of the CPGB accepted the new sectarianism with virtually no discussion.[22]

The new line argued that social democracy was no different from fascism save in the respect that it was more insidious and corrupting of the workers. Though the Labour Party was *not yet* social democratic, according to the Comintern, its degener- ation was such that communists had to stand against it in elections. The tiny CPGB, in other words, had to pose as an alternative to the Labour Party at every turn and denounce its left wing in particular. *Communist Review* referred to the 'fascis- ation' of the 'sham Lefts' such as Maxton, Cook and Kirkwood. Dutt asserted that Labour had become 'an integral part of the capitalist state'.[23] A Labour government was duly elected and the CP was more marginalized than ever. All the party's efforts to woo the workers through united fronts were eventually dissolved – the Minority Movement and National Left Wing Movement no longer had a function and CP membership collapsed to 3,500 by January 1929.

This disastrous experience was imposed on the CPGB by the Stalinist Third International and the collapse of membership of the British section and the initial opposition of its leaders testifies to a local awareness of its self-destructive conse- quences. Nevertheless the fact that the British party persisted for six years with this line is not entirely explained by its blind loyalty to International directives. The Trotskyists in par- ticular ignore the continuities with Comintern ideology before the ascendancy of Stalin. These include the vilification of left reformists as one of the chief obstacles to socialism within the working class; the conviction that reformism has no future except as a form of false consciousness; and the belief that *only* the communists represent the interests of the working class. At the Unity Convention in 1920 delegates emphasized the use- lessness of parliament.[24] The *Manual of Party Training* (1924) repeated that organs of local and central government were 'really useless for serving the real interests of the mass of the

workers'.[25] By fostering illusions in parliament it followed that
the leaders of the Labour Party were 'willing tools of the
bourgeoisie'. So what then of those leading Labour Party figures
of the Left? Were they moving away from such illusions and
towards communism or were they merely a most effective
means of securing legitimacy for the Labour Party's reformist
fantasy? Marxists are still divided over this question. But since
the communist ideology insisted on the unique and exclusive
role of the Leninist party in advancing the workers' cause there
was always an in-built hostility to anyone who refused to put
themselves under the direction of the communist party. Thus
other leftists were regarded with favour only if they joined the
party or worked under the leadership of one of its front organizations. In this sense the tenth congress of the CPGB was correct
in describing 'the new line of complete opposition to the Labour
Party' as 'the highest stage yet reached in the transition to
direct Party leadership of the masses'.[26] It brought to the fore
the party's singular objective: 'Let there be no misunderstan-
ding about this. No man or group can represent the workers or
endeavour to carry forward the workers' struggle without
following the leadership of the Communist Party. *For the Communist Party is the political party of the workers.*'[27]

Under communist leadership

The need for a socialist party informed by Marxism and
independent of the Labour Party is not in doubt. Despite the
zig-zags of its policies, its slavish relationship to the Russians,
the narrowness of its vision and the arrogance of its self-
perception the Communist Party was able to meet this need in
many respects. The party was alone in formulating a clear and
consistent anti-imperialist policy. For a time it was able to gain
the collaboration of some Labour and ILP leaders in the
League Against Imperialism which it set up in 1927. But this
was outlawed in 1930. Nevertheless the party's anti-imperialist
campaigns made a real impact even though official Labour and
the trade unions were deeply imbued with the imperialist

ideology. Thus at the 1925 congress of the TUC, for example, it was the communists who proposed a motion denouncing 'the domination of non-British peoples by the British Government' as 'a form of capitalist exploitation'. The motion was supported by a majority of 3 million votes.[28] Nor was this anti-imperialism confined to resolutions and the many solidarity campaigns which the party initiated. British communists were actively involved in helping to establish militant trade unions in India. Indeed two party members were jailed and sentenced to twelve years transportation and ten years respectively for this activity at the beginning of 1933. When initially arrested in March 1929, it was of course a Labour government at Westminster which permitted the communists – Philip Spratt and Ben Bradley – to be charged with conspiracy to 'deprive the King-Emperor of Sovereignty over British India'.[29]

Just as communist theory was occasionally able to penetrate even in areas where the labour movement was arguably at its most backward and reactionary the selflessness and organizational talents of the communists enabled them to transform the unemployed from a condition of atomized impotence into one of the most militant sections of the labour movement. The communists led the National Unemployed Workers' Committee from 1921. In the autumn of 1927 communist dominance of the unemployed movement was the excuse for TUC withdrawal and the active sabotage by some trade union leaders of campaigns such as that of unemployed miners marching from South Wales to London in November 1927. By the end of 1930 around one-third of the CP's membership was unemployed but the sectarian politics of the previous two years had reduced *total* membership to 2,555 – its lowest official level. When, in 1931, the second MacDonald government collapsed ignominiously CP membership rose again to 6,000 with the majority of the new recruits coming from the growing numbers of unemployed. The complete impotence and paralysis of the Labour government on this issue (and, in truth on almost all the issues which confronted it) no doubt contributed to the CP's apparent recovery. For it is significant that while most communist activities suffered dramatically during the Third Period this was not true of its work among the unemployed. The dues-paying membership of the National Unemployed Workers' Movement (NUWM) increased from 20,000 in 1930 to 50,000 in 1932. Despite its inevitably shifting membership, Labour and trade union bans and the prohibition on meetings outside labour exchanges, the NUWM organized the unemployed around the slogan 'work or full maintenance' and inspired five national hunger marches between 1929 and 1936.

The extreme timidity of both the Labour and trade union national leaderships in relation to mass campaigns is not the least important reason for the recovery of the Communist Party's influence in the 1930s. The worsening economic slump after 1929 and the manifest failure of the Labour government to do anything about it finally destroyed the cosy Fabian belief in the 'inevitability of gradualism' and stimulated the Labour left to discover a programme for the introduction of 'socialism in our time.' The inauguration and apparent success of planning in the Soviet Union after 1928 attracted many British socialists so that by the mid-1930s the 'cult of planning' was embraced by most Labour leaders. To some extent the CP probably benefited from the belief that the Soviet Union had found a rational, scientific solution to the problems of unemployment, poverty and instability which bedevilled Britain. Certainly technocrats such as the Webbs thought that this was the case. Many others were drawn to the party after the accession to power of Hitler in 1933 when the communists seemed the only force determined to stop fascism. When the Comintern's seventh congress turned the communist parties away from Third Period sectarianism towards the popular front the communists took the initiative in demanding unity of all forces opposed to fascism. In Britain where the National Government pursued a foreign policy of appeasement and the Labour leaders rejected any collaboration with the CP, the communists were seen by many leftists as vitally important allies in the practical struggle against fascism at home and abroad.

It was the CPGB which mobilized a huge counterforce (perhaps as many as 250,000) to prevent Mosley's blackshirts marching through the Jewish East End of London in October 1936 when Labour Party leaders were urging people to stay at home. The CP also created the British Battalion of the

International Brigade to fight in Spain and of the 2,200 or so volunteers who went from Britain between a third and a half were members of the party.[30] Membership of the party began to grow; from 6,500 in February 1935 to 12,250 in May 1937 to 17,539 in March 1939. In the same period weekend sales of the *Daily Worker* were sometimes as high as 200,000 while pamphlet sales exceeded one million in the two years 1935–7.[31] The CPGB also reached an important audience through Gollancz's Left Book Club. Established in May 1936 this recorded a peak membership of 57,000 and about one-third of its titles were written by party members.

The limits of left unity

In July 1932 the bulk of the ILP membership was taken out of the Labour Party by leaders disgusted with its performance in office between 1929 and 1931. James Maxton spoke now of the need for 'unity of revolutionary socialist forces'. As Pimlott points out Maxton had 'misread the auguries' in believing with most of the other ILP leaders that 'there was a real possibility of crushing the Labour Party in open competition for working class support'.[32] But a substantial minority of the ILP refused to disaffiliate. It was these who formed the Socialist League inside the Labour Party in 1932. Although it was set up originally as a centre of socialist research the 'loyal grousers' of the League were eventually disaffiliated by the Labour Party in 1937. Like the ILP the Socialist League was impelled by the international crisis to engage in united activity with the communists, and this could not be countenanced by the Labour leadership.

The summer of 1932 also marks the beginning of Trotskyism in Britain when a group calling itself the British Section of the Left Opposition was expelled from the Communist Party.[33] Over a year later this group, styling itself the Communist League, only numbered around 50 members. In view of the small size of the organization Trotsky advocated its entry into the ILP, the better to reach active militants. The ILP had signed an appeal for unity of the Second and Third Internationals in a common front against Nazism in February 1933.

It seemed to Trotsky that the ILP was bound to disintegrate unless his own followers were able to inject the necessary political clarity which as a 'centrist' organization wavering between reform and revolution it sorely lacked. There was also the danger of the ILP being hijacked by the Communist Party. In March 1933 the ILP accepted united front activity with the CP. The latter made no secret of the fact that the object of the exercise was to bring about a single mass communist party. Harry Pollitt made this clear in a letter to Fenner Brockway. 'You are asking the question: Can there be two revolutionary parties? Common sense tells you that two parties both professing to lead the militant struggle of the workers is an absurdity.'[34] The ILP leaders understood communist intentions well enough and this may partly explain the use they made of Trotsky's analyses of the Soviet Union and Comintern. They certainly needed something to counteract communist influence. Within the ILP the pro-Comintern lobby was organized by the Revolutionary Policy Committee led by Jack Gaster. But invoking Trotsky to prevent a communist takeover of the ILP was rather like dousing flames with petrol since it encouraged the Trotskyists to set up their own faction within the already faction-ridden ILP. But when Trotsky pressed the matter with his British followers by advocating their complete commitment to entrism the tiny Communist League was unable to comply and duly split. In the upshot only eleven Trotskyists made the recommended tactical turn and organized themselves as the Marxist Group within the ILP.[35]

The drift of the ILP membership towards the Comintern was halted at its Easter conference in 1934 when the delegates voted 98 to 51 against 'sympathetic affiliation'. The CP seems to have reacted by instructing its factions within the ILP and the Guild of Youth to step up their pro-communist propaganda and prepare for splits which would maximize the numbers dislodged. In October 1935 the Revolutionary Policy Committee resigned en bloc from the ILP taking 50–100 members into the CPGB. Earlier a similar operation had been conducted in the ILP's Guild of Youth. No doubt knowledge of these CP machinations influenced the Socialist League's Derby Conference in October 1934 to vote against joint action with the CP and ILP. Certainly Cripps explained the decision to Strachey in terms of the fear of disruption which would follow such collaboration.

The policy pursued by the CPGB up to 1935 was conditioned by the prejudices of the New Line adopted in 1928. Since reformists and especially left reformists were then regarded as 'social fascists' there could be no talk of unity with such people. However this did not preclude a 'united front from below' whereby communists would seek to influence rank and file leftists of other organizations with a view to bringing them into the CP or at least into organizations directed by the CP. This was the meaning of CP entrist activity in the Labour Party and the ILP and the purpose of front organizations such as the British Anti-War Movement and the Relief Committee for Victims of German Fascism. However the communist line had already begun to soften when Hitler came to power in 1933. Thereafter the CP tried to pursue a united front from above in the sense that it was now prepared to approach the leaders of the ILP and Labour Party as well. In 1935 the seventh congress of the Comintern turned all the communist parties towards the popular front tactic.

The central slogan for the communist parties had henceforth to be 'the fight for peace and for the defence of the USSR'. The Third Period had seen the practical destruction of 43 of the 67 communist parties between 1928 and 1935. Fascism now threatened to destroy the rest and the Soviet Union as well. Dimitrov, Stalin, Thorez and company now believed that Soviet foreign policy and communist party tactics required co-ordination around the goal of securing the widest possible set of alliances against the fascist menace. So just as the USSR would seek an alliance with capitalist France and Britain, the communist parties would join hands not only with the reformists but with any organization genuinely intent on combatting fascism. Though Trotsky had advocated such anti-fascist alliances during the previous six or seven years of communist sectarianism he now pronounced the new popular front strategy anathema. Indeed he had predicted that the earlier ultra-leftism would be succeeded by 'right opportunism'. Popular frontism as far as Trotsky was concerned only set out to fight fascism by sowing illusions on the nature of capitalist democracy and the bourgeois parties and thus obstructed the socialist project. He insisted that only the socialist revolution could prevent the forward march of fascism.

In emphasizing the need for a broad alliance to preserve peace the communists undoubtedly struck a chord with left activists in Britain. However the CPGB was unable to adopt the policy of alliance of *all* anti-fascists until 1938. The Socialist League and the ILP – the only left organizations interested in alliance with the communists – insisted on a united front of *workers'* parties excluding Liberals, Tories and the like. The national executive committee of the Labour Party never wavered in its rejection of such co-operation. Harry Pollitt, backed by the ILP, was rebuffed in March 1933 when the CP first proposed joint action with the Labour Party. The NEC drew a distinction between democracy and dictatorship and told all the constituency parties to regard the communists as firmly aligned with the latter. A Labour pamphlet drew attention to the '*Communist Solar System*' warning party members against joining the numerous front organizations of the CP. Nevertheless scores of constituency parties did work hand in hand with the communists, despite threats of expulsions and disaffiliation.[36] In 1935, for example, the National Unemployed Workers' Movement led the opposition to new uniform rates of unemployment relief which were designed to reduce payments. Those eligible for relief were required to accept training, sometimes in camps, and this too was vigorously opposed by joint CP and local Labour demonstrations. In Wales ad hoc united front committees were formed by lodges of the South Wales Miners' Federation and associations of the unemployed. Even the executive of the South Wales Labour Party declared for collaboraton with the CP.

United fronts also emerged in the form of anti-war councils in response to government circulars on air-raid drills. By November 1935 60 local authorities refused to implement the air-raid precautions circular on the grounds that this was fostering a war psychology. Communists and Labour members worked together on this. Similar united fronts developed against British fascism and in 1935 electoral co-operation between the CP and many CLPs was possible. In London the CP claimed that offers of electoral assistance had been accepted in 57 of the 62 constituencies of the County Council. In July 1936 1,121 Labour and trade union organizations declared in favour of communist affiliation to the Labour Party including the Fabians, the Socialist League and the Miners' Federation.[37]

Though the issue of communist affiliation was once more massively defeated at Labour's Edinburgh conference in 1936 there is no doubt that the CP was able to recruit many Labour members by virtue of its tough stance on issues such as the Spanish Civil War where the contrast with official Labour was sharpest and feelings for positive action ran deep. But the party's tactic was to keep these new recruits in the Labour Party in order to bolster the affiliation campaign. The London Labour Party organizer argued that 'Large numbers of trade union branches are completely under the domination of Communists and other Left-Wing organisations so far as their political activities are concerned.'[38] It has been estimated that when the Unity Campaign – launched by CP, ILP and Socialist League in January 1937 – was at its height around one-fifth of Labour's 90,000 individual members in London were involved.[39] The combined forces of the CP and ILP in London were about 10,000 in 1937 and given their greater devotion to political activity this represented a high ratio of zealots for unity against loyal Labour members. London was exceptional but the CP itself rated Lancashire as the bastion for unity so far as rank-and-file Labour sentiment was concerned.

The communists were undoubtedly handicapped in their appeals for unity by memories of the Third Period and by the Moscow Trials of 1936. The CP's disruption of the ILP in 1934–5 could not have helped either. The party also orchestrated a strong faction within the Labour Party's League of Youth – between 1933 and 1935 around the issue of the united front and thereafter for a popular front. The communist line was propounded by *Advance* while a smaller Trotskyist group published *Youth Militant*. With the exception of one Trotskyist all the members of the League of Youth's national committee supported the positions of *Advance*. In 1936 the NEC proposed to disband the leadership of the League of Youth while the League asserted its intention to merge with the Young Communist League. Ted Willis led the pro-communist faction within the League and championed the CP's positions in Spain, the hunger marches, the Moscow Trials and anti-Trotskyism. Until 1939, however, everything was done by the CP to keep this faction within the League of Youth but in June of that year Willis, the editors of *Advance*, leading officers and federation secretaries resigned en bloc to join the Young Communist League taking many of the League's branches wholesale with them. The high visibility of communist penetration in the youth section was another reason for keeping a large distance between the CLPs and the communists: here the NEC could point to a communist takeover and the eventual destruction of this 24,000-strong organization as proof of communist intentions.

The CP's focus on entrism was quite simply intended to boost its chances of affiliation (and, of course, party membership) but provided all the evidence – in the form of duplicity and disruption – that the NEC needed to make this impossible. In this connection it is noteworthy that when the NEC disaffiliated the Socialist League – three days after it helped to launch the unity campaign – it was Pollitt and Dutt who proposed that the League should voluntarily dissolve itself so that its members could avoid expulsion and thereby remain in the Labour Party as proponents of communist affiliation. This also had the merit of removing a rival organization from the scene. As for the ILP Trotsky was correct to predict its rapid fall in membership and influence and we may suppose that what he could foresee thousands of miles from the scene was well within the range of Pollitt and Dutt. Since the Trotskyists were too few in numbers to seriously count – though this did not stop the CP regularly denouncing their insidious 'fascist' influence – the CP was left with the field to itself and easily succeeded in taking over defunct wards and constituencies of the Labour Party. By 1938, 120 CLPs declared for the popular front though there is no reason to believe that CP–ers were present in all of them. But to put this in some sort of context it is important to remember that the individual membership of the Labour Party rose from 300,000 in 1931 to 447,150 in 1937 and this was in spite of the lugubrious record of the MacDonald government. Communist Party membership in 1937 was a mere 12,250. Further growth was possible via popular frontism but always subject to the unpredictable interventions of Moscow.

Some more zig-zags

In August 1939 the Hitler–Stalin non-aggression pact was signed and from then until 21 June 1941 the CPGB, which had been campaigning for the defence of democracy against fascism, insisted that there was nothing to choose between Hitler and the governments of France and Britain. Once again the CP's subservience to the dictates of Stalin's foreign policy made a mockery of its political work in Britain. All the unity and popular front campaigning was now wasted and the CP's entrists departed from the Labour Party. According to one account 'in some districts the effect was crippling for small Labour Parties. Overnight groups of active members resigned from the Labour Party ... and a good many were later expelled.'[40] Even so Labour's annual conference of 1940 was still confronted with 10 resolutions expressing the CP's characterization of the war and in the same year the NEC disaffiliated 4 local Labour Parties and trades councils in London reorganized the Sheffield Trades and Labour Council, the Cardiff Labour Party and the Central Southwark and Bermondsey Borough Labour Parties.[41]

With the signing of the Hitler–Stalin pact it became convenient for communist theorists to invoke, once again, Lenin's analysis of imperialism.[42] Campbell explained that 'the main danger of Fascism ... lies in the attempt of British Imperialism to regiment the people for war.'[43] For in order to protect the Empire for its own exploitative purposes the British ruling class must introduce a range of compulsory methods in industry which produce 'the same results as the Nazi economy'.[44] The worker, argues Campbell, is merely 'the pawn of monopoly capitalism and the monopoly capitalist State'.

This monopoly capitalism, he contends, is in an advanced state of decay and forever likely to produce imperialist wars.

Harry Pollitt resigned the leadership of the CPGB in October 1939 and like Campbell was obliged to sign a grovelling 'self-criticism' for their failure to respond quickly enough to Moscow's rapprochement with Hitler. As late as September Pollitt had argued that 'the Communist Party supports the war, believing it to be a just war which will be supported by the whole working class and all friends of democracy.'[45] It seems that only Dutt read the auguries while the rest of the politbureau had to wait for the intervention of a Comintern emissary before they could see the light.[46] No such outside aid was needed when the Nazis invaded the USSR: it was again immediately obvious that the war was after all a struggle between the democratic and progressive camp and the forces of fascism. The danger now was that Britain would not fight because its leaders had no wish to help the USSR and Transport House was full of defeatists.[47] Within a month of the invasion beginning the CPGB was demanding a Second Front. It was now necessary to 'mobilise the people', increase war production and persuade the workers that they needed to work 'maximum hours compatible with health'. Yet well before operation Barbarossa the CP had envisaged just such a Nazi assault and had argued as follows:

> But supposing Fascist Germany attacks the USSR: are you now in favour of the workers supporting the British or French governments in an attack on Germany?. . . *Under no circumstances.* Such action would help the German capitalists to represent the war as one of self-defence: it would immensely strengthen the British capitalists and weaken the British workers . . . it would mean suppressing the inevitable revolt in India and the Empire.[48]

CP membership collapsed from 18,000 in 1939 to 12,000 in June 1941 in response to the party's volte face. But once the USSR entered the war, membership rose rapidly again and reached a peak of around 64,000 in September 1942. Between 1943 and 1945 membership stood at 55,000 and was sustained at such a high level by the popularity of the Red Army and official encouragement of pro-Soviet sentiment. The party was also able to take advantage of the torpor of the Labour Party confined as it was by the electoral truce and its participation in the war coalition government. Labour membership fell from 400,000 in 1939 to 219,000 in 1942 and the constituency parties were generally inactive. The CP, on the other hand, had plenty to campaign about: the Second Front, bureaucratic obstacles to adequate air-raid precautions, managerial incompetence, the insidious influence of the 'men of Munich' and so on. It is true that CP propaganda was patriotic and bent on increasing industrial production but this alone could not explain the rapid increase in the party's factory branches after 1942. In Coventry alone there were 30 factory cells of the CPGB. This also had something to do with the party's continued role as watchdog of the shop floors' interests.[49]

Nevertheless the party's enthusiasm for the alliance knew no bounds. In 1943 Stalin quietly dissolved Comintern no doubt to show the USSR's enthusiasm for the alliance. No word of protest, indeed no discussion, was recorded to mark this event inside the CPGB. Pollitt argued that the opening of the Second Front and the Teheran Conference represented blows against those 'who have poured scorn on the possibility of capitalist and socialist nations uniting together, pooling their common resources and carrying through a common strategy'. These developments give us 'a right to suggest that [they] offer exactly the same splendid prospects for co-operation in solving the gigantic economic and social problems in the days of peace that are now coming so much nearer'.[50] As a general election drew closer the CP distinguished between old-fashioned Tories and Labour men on one side and their progressive counterparts on the other who saw the need for continuation of the wartime coalition.[51] Clearly collaboration between capitalists and socialists was the CP perspective at home and abroad.

In the event the election produced a landslide majority for Labour (though few expected it) and the best results the CPGB has ever had. Two communists were elected to parliament – Gallacher in East Fife and Phil Paratin for Stepney. By the end of the round of local elections concluded in November 1946 the CP had 256 councillors but most of these local gains were lost

immediately thereafter and both MPs were defeated in 1950.
An unusual combination of circumstances had helped the
party.[52] The swing of opinion to the left, the party's new
patriotic image and the temporary popularity of the Soviet
Union played their part. But in the local contests – and there
was an unprecedented number of these because of the backlog
accumulated since 1939 – communist gains also had something
to do with the absence of Labour candidates in some of the
contests, especially in the parishes, and widespread plural
voting which allowed electors to vote for both Labour and
Communist candidates. The ballot papers did not then show
the candidate's party and this may also have aided the CP. By
1947 most of these conditions had gone. Membership had
already fallen to 45,000 in 1945 and this slide continued when
the Cold War was resumed two years later and the CP,
following Stalin's creation of Cominform, lurched to the left
again. Much of the CP's energies were now devoted to
exposing the pernicious influence of American economic and
political interests in the foreign and domestic policies of the
Attlee government. Paradoxically 1947 is also the year when
CP leaders began to talk of a peaceful parliamentary road to
socialism. But this will be taken up in another chapter.

Conclusions

The failure of the CPGB to achieve a stable and viable
alternative to labourism has been explained – most notably by
the Trotskyists – as the result of its degeneration to a pure and
simple instrument of Soviet foreign policy under Stalin. This
sort of argument sometimes supposes that genuine revolutionary opportunities were missed, as in 1926, because of an
opportunist policy or because, as in 1945, the CP was so
discredited by its subservience to Moscow that it no longer
figured as an authentic expression of the revolutionary tradition. But whatever we make of the 'missed opportunities'
argument this approach ignores the continuities of CP theory
and practice and focuses on the Moscow-inspired zig-zags.
However gross the latter it seems to me that the communist

project was deeply flawed from the outset. The failure of the Trotskyists to realize this is the main reason why they – the great critics of Stalinism – reproduce the features of Stalinism in their organization's politics and theory.

Lenin's theory of the state is characterized by a one-sided emphasis on its coercive role. This is one of the reasons why he regarded bourgeois democracy as a mere sham destined to disappear entirely and give way before open dictatorship. Capitalism was defunct, so the argument ran, and would not survive in any shape or form were it not for the traitors of social democracy and trade union reformism. Not only is this a virtually useless explanation of reformism and a complete underestimation of the popular significance of bourgeois democracy but also a rationale whether intended or not for the belief that the coming economic crisis was the basis for revolutionary advance and the corresponding collapse of the reformist influence. Nothing of the sort happened in the interwar years in Britain (or for that matter during the present economic crisis). But it does incline those who subscribe to this scenario to imagine that the job of socialists is to fashion the correct agitational line or list of 'transitional' demands so that no matter how few their number the revolutionaries will be catapulted to mass leadership once the working class is 'triggered' by 'objective' events. The political arena, in a sham democracy, is to be used to expose the system and serve as a platform for socialist propaganda. There is no confidence among Leninists that intrinsically useful and progressive reforms can be extracted from politics within the system. The CP *did not* emerge before or after Lenin's death as the best champion of democratic and structural reforms. There was no recognition of the immense scope for such reforms which, though well short of the socialist revolution, would bring a socialist democracy that much nearer. On the contrary nothing was to be expected short of the socialist revolution. When this arrived it would solve everything or nearly everything though nobody bothered to spend much time describing how it would work or what it would look like.

One really big task which consumed a vast amount of time and ink was the job of exposing the pernicious influence of the reformists. It is impossible to read early Comintern accounts on the nature of reformism and the struggle against it without identifying the roots of the social fascist argument. The mass reformist parties were described as agencies of the bourgeois state: the latter was increasingly authoritarian. It followed that the reformists and especially the left reformists and centrists were the main impediment to mass socialist consciousness. A ruthless and systematic war had to be waged against them. When real fascists emerged openly pledged to destroy bourgeois democracy consistent communists could say 'so what?' – it is only a sham democracy anyway and those who defend it sow illusions; indeed it might be better that this is demonstrated once and for all by a fascist government.

There was no recognition by the communists that they *shared* responsibilities and insights with the reformist parties. The communists believed that they possessed a monopoly of truth and as the sole fount of political wisdom would solve everything themselves. The united front made not a shred of difference to this logic since it occasioned no re-thinking of the original Comintern perspectives. It was designed to deal with a temporary delay. In December 1934 Dutt explained that the united front required 'the exposure of reformism' and 'advance to the necessary revolutionary policy, to Communism.'[53] This was all about the crushing of reformism and the complete dominance of the CP, a perspective which 'since 1928 has been increasingly justified by the whole subsequent development and evolution of the Labour Party into a full social democratic party leaving no freedom for revolutionary Marxist leadership within its ranks'. So 'whatever militant struggle develops in Britain today develops increasingly under the direct leadership and influence of the Communist Party.'[54] Pollitt made a similar point in connection with the unity issue: 'The importance of the leading role of the Communist Party increases extraordinarily. Only the Communist Party is at bottom the initiator, the organiser and the driving force of the united front of the working class.'[55] No wonder he thought that the CP had 'to conduct a considerable explanation of this.'

One explanation was already available though it is doubtful

that this is what Pollitt had in mind. In 1935 Ralph Fox, a party intellectual, explained that 'unlike other classes the working class can have (only) one party.' This is why, he reasoned, other classes seek to influence the CP and 'endeavour to disrupt the Party by various policies sometimes of an openly opportunist character, sometimes by covering them with all kinds of extraordinary "revolutionary" sentiments'. Hence, 'The party does not allow the growth of such fractions and groups inside its ranks considering that they represent alien influences whose aim is to split the party.'[56] It was this mentality which helped make the CP a dubious and suspicious ally of the working class. Though it was able to make at times an important contribution to working-class politics it could never build beyond single-issue campaigns. The party was hamstrung by Leninist perspectives on reformism and reformists. Reformism was supposed to have no future: the reformists were enemies. How was joint work with the Labour Party then possible? Who would ally with an organization claiming a monopoly of truth and openly swearing its determination to crush its rivals?

The Labour leaders might well have refused collaboration with the CP under any circumstances. But the ILP was a different matter. This was wrongly identified by Lenin's Comintern as a 'tool of the ruling class'. The CP poured its harshest invective upon it. But it also chopped and changed according to the tactical imperatives of the moment. In 1924 the ILP was 'an organisation openly working for the defence of capitalism': in 1925 the CP proposed joint work with it. In 1928 it had become 'an inseparable part of social fascism' meriting only 'irreconcilable' opposition while the early 1930s saw a concerted CP campaign to take it over. These zig-zags undoubtedly made the CP synonymous with duplicity and mendacity in circles much wider than those of the rival working-class leaderships. They were justified in the eyes of party members in terms of that 'ruthless' war which Lenin recommended against reformism and centrism and by the conviction that only the CP could be right. And when all else failed, when the polemics became hysterical and the party lost all credibility as in

1928 it could always fall back on the reassuring delusion that 'while the Communist Party exists there can be no security for capitalism for at any time a direct working class issue similar to the miners in 1926 may arise, and the whole working class may swing round behind the militant policy of the Communist Party in a determined attack against the very foundations of capitalist power'.[57]

3

Apocalypse Now: The Politics of 'Orthodox Trotskyism'

During the war the Trotskyists attempted to implement the so-called 'proletarian military policy' bequeathed to them by Trotsky.[1] He argued in 1940 that to combine the revolutionary defeatist policy which Lenin advocated during the First World War with 'defence of the Soviet Union' once the latter became involved was the duty of revolutionaries. Practically this meant demanding that the workers' organizations take control of military training since the bourgeoisie could not be entrusted with either the anti-fascist struggle or the defence of the USSR and the workers' objective was in any case the ultimate defeat of their own bourgeoisie by means of revolution. This policy illustrates only too well the apocalyptic vision which imagined small propaganda groups actually directing mass movements. Among the Trotskyists considerable confusion and disagreement was engendered by the discrepancy between policy and reality; with lines of communication broken and over a hundred leading cadres killed in the conflict, national groups pursued quite different agitational lines.

In Britain two rival Trotskyist groups – the Revolutionary Socialist League (RSL) and the Workers' International League (WIL) – were divided on a number of basic issues. The RSL was regarded as the official section of the Fourth International (FI) but the WIL regarded it as the artificial result of an unprincipled fusion. The International dismissed the WIL as an instance of those 'national groupings' which it called 'reactionary in essence'. While the RSL remained submerged in the Labour Party, the WIL maintained an independent organization and actually grew. To some extent the CPGB's enthusiasm for the war effort after the invasion of the USSR enabled the Trotskyists – where their small numbers permitted – to champion shop floor militancy.

The Revolutionary Communist Party

Trotsky's confidence in the actuality of the revolution was unshaken by the major reversals experienced by the European workers' organizations in the 1930s. Indeed after 1933 he emphasized more than ever the decay and coming collapse of the capitalist system. The Fourth International (FI) was established in 1938 on the basis of just such a catastrophist rationale. Although his party was tiny and marginal Trotsky supposed that the war and the economic collapse that would follow would create the conditions for mass radicalization which would propel his followers to the fore. The Stalinists and social democrats would be swept aside by the same process.

These prognoses soon proved to be wildly inaccurate. The Stalin leadership survived and presided over a major expansion of Soviet power into Eastern Europe. Mass communist parties emerged in several West European countries and even in Britain communism was able to survive in an outwardly stronger condition than before the war. The end of the war also witnessed the restoration of bourgeois democracy in a number of countries and its strengthening in others. Certainly Trotsky's prediction that it was doomed proved baseless. Worse still, from a Trotskyist perspective, some of the parties of the old Comintern actually led successful revolutions. It was obviously necessary for the Trotskyists to think again.

Felix Morrow began this process during the war as a member of the American Socialist Workers' Party (SWP). He pointed out that the strengthening of Stalinism did not support the FI's perspective of imminent revolution under Trotskyist leadership: instead 'decades of struggle' lay ahead before a genuine socialist party could be created.[2] The Trotskyists would

necessarily remain merely one among many tendencies within
the mass reformist parties during this protracted period. But
this was denied by the defenders of Trotsky's pre-war prognoses who persisted, despite all evidence to the contrary, with
the either–or of triumphant socialist revolution and a picture of
Europe governed by police states supported by American
military might. There was no prospect in this the official view
for the survival of any form of bourgeois democracy. The
political task was to construct mass revolutionary parties
straight away. In 1946 Morrow's disagreements with the
guardians of orthodoxy led to his expulsion from the
movement.

In Britain similar developments aided and abetted by the
leadership of the FI ensured the ascendancy of the most
dogmatic wing of the Revolutionary Communist Party (RCP).
The RCP had been created in 1944 from the fusion of the RSL
and the WIL. Until 1947 the RCP was the sole representative
of Trotskyism in Britain but it was dogged from the beginning
by intense factionalism which soon destroyed the organization.
The fragments which emerged from its break-up eventually
became the three principal tendencies of British Trotskyism.
Each of these groups, passing through a succession of names,
were henceforward dominated by the views and personalities
of the individuals who originally led them as factions of the
RCP. In this chapter I will examine the politics of the group led
by Gerry Healy.

To an outsider not versed in Trotskyist esoterica nothing
could seem more orthodox than the RCP leadership's belief
that it stood 'on the threshold of the greatest crisis yet
witnessed in the history of British capitalism . . . indeed the
period of the world crisis from 1929 onwards . . . will appear a
rosy picture in comparison with what the working class faces in
the next period.' The organization's 1945 conference envisaged
a bloody collapse of British imperialism in India and imagined
that the consequent loss of 'economic tribute' would entail a
greater rate of exploitation at home. Mass redundancies, the
repression of the trade unions and the elimination of the
labour aristocracy would be the principal features of the ruling
class offensive. But this would create conditions which would

be 'the most revolutionary in the whole of British history'.[3] However the leadership around Jock Haston also entertained 'the possibility of a temporary post-war boom lasting for one or two years'. By 1946 RCP delegates to the world congress of the FI were prepared to go further. They now argued that Europe's economic recovery 'will be on the basis of US loans' and saw that American hegemony was compatible, even dependent upon, the revival of capitalism in countries such as Britain. The International leadership insisted the contrary and emphasised the old argument that the productive forces 'remained on a level approaching stagnation and collapse'.[4]

Haston and his co-thinkers believed that the RCP could prosper as an independent organization though this did not stop them from maintaining entrist fractions in the Labour Party. Given the connection in the Trotskyist mind between party-building and economic and political convulsions, this commitment to an independent RCP indicates that Haston was as convinced as anyone could be about the coming catastrophe. Nevertheless the International which was so persuaded of the heretical economic perspectives of the RCP that it struck up a campaign to stamp them out was also equally adamant on the need for a total immersion of the RCP in the Labour Party. In January 1947 the International Secretariat of the Fourth International (ISFI) wrote directly to the RCP central committee informing it that there was no prospect of any economic recovery no matter how shortlived: the same message also insisted that the situation involved 'the setting into motion of *the entire awakened British working class* along the path of revolutionary action this time within the framework of the Labour Party itself'. On the issue of economic recovery the RCP was able to observe that it had already surpassed the limits envisaged in 1946 but doubted that the boom could be sustained for more than a few years. In any case it assured its inquisitors that 'the orientation and strategy of the RCP is firmly based on the long-term perspective of crisis and decline'. Where entrism was concerned it pointed out that fractional activity in the Labour Party produced only disappointing results and there was no reason to suppose that complete entry would improve the situation. But the Inter-

national's idea that the whole working class could be 'set in
motion' by a group of 300 to 500 Trotskyists was simply fantastic.

This nonsense was authentic Trotskyist doctrine for the
international leadership and its prodigy within the RCP – the
faction led by Gerry Healy. Healy bombasted that the perspective of economic revival 'calls for complete revision of our
programmatic estimation of capitalism . . . they must revise
the Marxist analysis of imperialist decline.'[5] In September
1947 Ernest Mandel entered the fray to make a similar point:
an economic boom, he said, was 'impossible' because 'in the
period of capitalist decadence British imperialism can no
longer overgrow the stage of revival and attain one of real
boom.'[6] The ISFI produced another lengthy and scholarly
document in November, *The World Situation and the Tasks of the
Fourth International*, which not only foresaw 'a period of
economic and political difficulties, convulsions and crises in
one country after another' but also singled out Britain (with
France and Italy) as an instance of where this trend threatened
'to become catastrophic'.

Healy linked this argument with a parallel debate concerning
the pros and cons of entrism although, needless to say, there is
no logical connection between advocacy of entrism and a
religious faith in the terminal state of capitalism. However it
seems that all the participants supposed the contrary. The
entrist row began before the general election of 1945 and was
resumed immediately after, with Healy seeking to demonstrate
that the Labour landslide signified mass determination to
'break with monopoly capitalism.[7] Many people on the left –
Pollitt and Laski among them – argued that the Tories would
never form a government again so complete was the Labour
victory. Healy followed this lead adding that this meant the
beginning of extra-parliamentary measures by the Conservative Party. No evidence was needed to back this assertion: when
Haston, on another occasion, demanded empirical evidence
from Healy the latter was arraigned at great length for 'renunciation of the methodology of Marxism'.[8]

In this spirit Healy backed by the ISFI pursued a faction war
against the RCP leadership well before this was officially

acknowledged just prior to the 1947 conference. Though
Healy's group never amounted to a majority of the organization the rules of democratic centralism allowed him to get his
way since these rules permit the higher international bodies to
intervene in the affairs of the national sections. Thus it was
that the Healy group, in defiance of the RCP leadership, came
to pursue total entry in the Labour Party from 1947. The
International had effectively split the organization in two. By
December 1948 Haston's Majority reluctantly realized that the
prospects for independent party building were non-existent
but rightly refused to accept that entrism could be justified by
reference to an illusory upsurge in working class radicalism as
indicated by the International Secretariat. Haston, hounded
for an alleged conspiracy with renegades and heretics such as
Morrow and Goldman (one is tempted to say Goldstein) of the
American SWP, resigned from the Fourth International in June
1950. He had come to the conclusion that it had no future as an
organization. He cited considerable evidence to support this
judgement in the form of the doctrinal gibberish which passed
as Marxism within the International:

> the incredible thesis of the 'ceiling above which produc-
> tion could not possibly be pushed' and the whole discuss-
> ion of boom or slump

> the fact that India had achieved political freedom and the
> right to determine its own form of government under the
> leadership of the Indian bourgeoisie . . denounced as a
> denial of the theory of the permanent revolution

> five years after the event . . the beginning of a grudging
> admission . . plain to every petty bourgeois politician that
> capitalism had been overthrown in Eastern Europe.

> In China, the FI . . failed to recognise a revolution when it
> was in the process of taking place.

In short the International was too concerned to protect the
Lenin and Trotsky scriptures to take much note of reality. By
its action in Britain it encouraged those of the same religious
faith and repelled more critical spirits.

Inside the Labour Party

Most of those who remained active Trotskyists were by 1949 members of the Labour Party. But as already indicated there was no unanimity over the purposes and prospects of entrism and the experience of the RCP had soured relations between the individuals concerned. Effectively there were now three main groups: Healy's supporters whose expectations of mass radicalism were sanctioned by the International; a small group who subscribed to the state capitalist heresy propounded by Tony Cliff; and another tiny group who believed that entrism was justified by the wholly unfavourable political environment which precluded party-building. This last group eventually surfaced in the mid-1950s under the leadership of Ted Grant. For a short while these contradictory elements tried to work together under the low profile name of 'the Club' which published *Socialist Outlook* from December 1948. This proved incompatible with Healy's ambitions.

On the grounds that his faction had been proved correct on the entrist issue (and in the knowledge that the International supported him) Healy demanded and gained a majority on all the group's executive bodies. Before a congress could be arranged to finalize these 'temporary' accommodations democratically, Healy's group began a series of expulsions to eliminate prominent opponents. As an example of the procedure adopted let us look at the removal of Haston and Jimmy Deane. The latter asked that Haston be given the chance to produce a written statement in his defence before the vote of expulsion was taken and was told instead that 'it is necessary that you indicate in writing political support for the Executive Committee resolution condemning Haston without any reservations *immediately*.[9] Refusing to do so Deane was expelled for 'cryptic sympathy' with Haston. Clearly it was impossible to work in an organization run along these lines. Most of the strong personalities left – including Grant and Cliff.

In some respects the Labour Party looked a useful environment in these years for the growth of Trotskyist influence.

Labour's individual membership rose in almost every year between 1945 and 1953 as did membership of its sections for women, students and youth. But the returns from entrist activity recorded by the RCP's Labour fraction were worse than the meagre results of independent work as measured by newspaper sales and recruitment. Indeed the Haston majority alleged that the constituencies were characterized by low levels of political activity and absorption in the humdrum of purely routine administrative work.[10] The Healy minority seem to have conceded some of this by insisting that only total entry could properly test the validity of their high expectations. The chances of exerting influence were severely circumscribed, however, by the tremendous solidarity of Labour MPs behind the Attlee government. Labour's rising vote between 1945 and 1951 indicates that the public's sympathies were also in support of the government's performance.

Yet there was plenty of scope for a socialist opposition and alternative to the government's policies. Labour could plead that the economic situation set severe limits on its domestic reforms. Much more dubious though was the use of troops against strikes, the early introduction of charges in the health service and the exhaustion of Labour's reforming zeal well before the end of its term of office. The Labour government was forced to preside over tighter rationing and general austerity. It is all the more objectionable then that it pursued a foreign policy indistinguishable from that of the Tories. This meant defending Britain's 'national interest', as if it was self evident and taking for granted its continued great power status. Not only did this involve national service to prosecute colonial wars and the preservation of British influence in South-Eastern Europe, the Eastern Mediterranean, the Middle East, Indo-China and the rest: it also meant that the Labour government was prepared to support reactionary regimes actively whenever the 'national interest' demanded it. Thus it endorsed the Shah of Iran, helped to install a neo-fascist government in Greece and worked with former Nazis in West Germany. Labour's development of nuclear weapons was only the 'logical outcome of (its) assertive and highly self-conscious foreign policy'.[11] It was a thoroughly orthodox foreign policy devoid of socialist principles.

The rhetoric of a socialist foreign policy had been heard, however, during the 1945 election. But even the Labour left soon dropped any serious concern with it and the government was never really threatened on this issue.[12] The choice seemed to be between the USA and the Soviet Union and, as Orwell observed at the time, the communists were the only ones who would choose an alliance with the USSR. Once Marshall Aid was made available the *Tribune* left became unequivocally pro-American. The behaviour of the communists contributed to this uncritical stance. With the establishment of Cominform the CPGB adopted the sectarian and denunciatory tones of former times. Soviet policy seemed determined to prove that social democracy could not work. Stalin's aggressive and treacherous dictatorship was vividly displayed by the blockade of West Berlin. Crossman and Foot were not alone in rallying to Bevin's foreign policy when its belligerent anti-communism seemed vindicated by such communist policy.

Nevertheless the *Tribune* left's inability to formulate an alternative to Bevin was deep-rooted. In the 1930s it had been vigorously pro-Soviet and very close to the CPGB until the betrayal of 1939 when the latter 'changed its mind' on how to deal with Hitler. In the 1940s its anti-communism was just as sentimental and blind. It gave unequivocal support to NATO. which Bevin had helped to initiate, describing it as a defensive alliance. It enthusiastically supported Truman and the doctrine of containment whereby the Americans reserved the right to intervene against peoples so foolish as to choose communist governments. *Tribune* denounced opposition to the A-bomb as 'the new pacifism'. It feared the loss of Malaya to 'communist bandits', defended the repression of ELAS (the communist-socialist movement) in Greece and believed that Britain's continued presence in Africa was necessary to save that continent from 'catastrophe'. Not until 1950 did it realize that these sentiments aligned it with the enemies of socialism and thereafter its anti-communism became more measured.[13] But the collection of individuals who supported *Tribune* never developed an analysis of the Soviet Union any more than they understood the character of American imperialism in the new conditions of American hegemony.

The Trotskyists were for a short while able to work alongside a small group of Labour MPs in the Socialist Fellowship which Fenner Brockway and Ellis Smith founded in 1949. Within a year they had created a following within the constituencies and the unions for a more vigorous socialist policy: the Merseyside district alone claimed 120 members drawn from eighteen local Labour parties.[14] At its second conference in 1951 the group adopted the familiar concoction of catastrophist perspectives and maximalist demands which is the hallmark of Trotskyism in the 1940s. It argued that only a 'vigorous socialist policy can save the country from economic collapse, subservience to international capitalism and destruction in a third world war' and advocated state ownership of all large-scale industry under workers' control as the means of achieving it. The Socialist Fellowship was proscribed in April 1951 and dissolved itself, though *Socialist Outlook* was allowed to continue publication until 1954. The newspaper was in any case deprived of any influence it may have had among a small group of left MPs when Bevan resigned from the government in 1951 and began a close association with *Tribune* which became the organizer of Labour's left opposition.

Socialist Outlook claimed a circulation of 9–10,000 when the Bevanite revolt began. It campaigned in defence of North Korea in accordance with the Trotskyist view that workers' states, no matter how deformed, must be championed against their capitalist adversaries. The conflict in Korea was the occasion for the departure from the Club of those who refused to accept this thesis. Tony Cliff had fashioned a theory of the state capitalist nature of the so-called workers' states. For his supporters it was impossible to side with either North or South Korea and their journal *Socialist Review* proclaimed 'neither Washington nor Moscow' from its first issue in 1950. Thereafter adherence to the state-capitalist theory was a sufficient reason for exclusion from the Club though this did not stop the defenders of orthodoxy hailing Tito as an authentic revolutionary socialist though his position on the Korean war – neutrality – was similiar to that of the heretics.

The International splits

The Healy group's passion for doctrinal orthodoxy dates from its first appearance as a faction of the RCP in the restricted sense that it couched all disagreements with fellow Trotskyists in these terms. By 1953 it led the Club out of the FI over an issue which was suitably esoteric and for reasons which remain opaque. The argument within the Fourth International began with the publication in February 1951 of an article by Michel Pablo entitled 'Where are we going?' This was an elaboration of certain arguments which first appeared in the document *Theses on International Perspectives* which was adopted at the second world congress of the International in 1946. Pablo's basic contention was that the antagonistic blocs into which the world was now divided made global war inevitable in the near future. The capitalist bloc exhibited 'basic, chronic disequilibrium' and was allegedly enfeebled by the division of Europe and the colonial revolt. For these reasons the capitalist bloc was supposed to be inclined to precipitate a war.[15]

Pablo believed, however, that the world war would be rapidly transformed into revolution. The political and economic power of the Soviet Union, he argued, had increased and combined with the growing colonial revolt would prove sufficient to overturn capitalism in Europe and Africa. China and Yugoslavia proved that the Communist Parties could still find a 'revolutionary orientation' and given the greater size of these parties the leadership of the masses would fall under their control with the Trotskyists reduced to the part of a 'left opposition'. Clearly if Pablo was right about this, Stalinism would find, had already found, a new lease of life and he did not fail to point out that 'an entire historical period of several centuries' would elapse before genuine socialist societies could emerge from the transitional regimes that the communist parties would dominate.

The prospect of centuries of deformed workers' states did not please the American section of the International although only the French Trotskyists perceived 'liquidationism' in Pablo's ideas.[16] This was because Pablo advocated entrism *sui*

generis – submergence of the Trotskyists within the mass communist parties – in anticipation of the appoaching war-
revolution. The French were instructed to enter the PCF and
refused to do so. Neither the American nor the British Trotskyists complained when the International replied by suspending
the majority of the French leadership. Pablo's position was
deemed 'completely Trotskyist'.[17] It received further elaboration by Pablo and Ernest Mandel in the course of 1951.[18] The
third congress of the International agreed on the 'Theses on
Orientation and Perspectives' which contained Pablo's arguments,[19] and the tenth plenum of the International executive
committee instructed all the national sections to adopt entrism
in either the reformist or the communist parties – whichever was
dominant in the countries concerned. Here, incidentally, are the
origins of the entrist *strategy* (pursued most successfully in
Britain by Militant) since Pablo is at pains to stress the very
long-term nature of the new entrist orientation which is predicated on the *transformation* of the reformist party (or mass Communist Party) placed under new conditions which generate
centrist currents capable of leading radical mass movements.
Even the slogan associated with Militant 'Labour to Power on a
Socialist Platform' was coined to fit the new orientation.

In Britain the Healy group was already installed within the
Labour Party when the row over entrism *sui generis* began.
Having failed to locate the revolutionary upsurge anticipated
since 1945, the Club was now assiduously cultivating links with
the Bevanites whom they took to be the first indication of a new
and powerful centrist trend winnable to revolutionary positions.
The tone of *Socialist Outlook* was tempered in order to build the
necessary bridges though the movement was all in one direction:

'Bevan gives the lead that workers want' 3 October 1952
'Bevan and Morrison: it is a difference of principle' 14 May
1954
'The Tories must resign: Let's have a petition to get 'em
out!' 27 November 1953

There is nothing here to suggest a 'left opposition' pressing
reformists to adopt radical policies. After 1954 the Trotskyists,

divested of *Socialist Outlook*, sold and wrote for *Tribune* and the story is told that the cognoscenti were directed to pukka articles by pencil marks in the margins. Healy even talked of enacting socialism from parliament as the Militant entrists do today.[20] The Club evidently needed no lessons from Pablo in the disciplines of deep entrism yet it was soon to denounce him for revisionism.

The lead in the campaign against Pablo was taken by the American SWP whose leader, James P. Cannon, had earlier found Pablo's arguments 'completely Trotskyist'. The change came when Cannon's own leadership was challenged by a faction claiming allegiance to the Pablo theses. Henceforth Cannon was persuaded that Pablo was the centre of an international conspiracy and Pablo's ideas were reappraised in this light. Why Healy should follow Cannon down the path to schism is unclear. What can be said for certain is that no one in the British section made contributions to the 'theoretical' debate which consumed the International up to the split of 1953. Perhaps Healy, who knew all about Pablo's high-handed interferences in wrecking national sections from the time of their alliance in 1947, feared that he might be on the receiving end of a similar 'reorganization'. In any event the Club and the SWP left the International in 1953 to establish their own International Committee for the Fourth International. Twenty years later the Healy organisation was devoting considerable time and money in the ideological war against Pabloism even though Pablo had long since left the International and Healy had paid scant attention to the 'deviation' at the time of its appearance.

Apart from shedding light on the character of British Trotskyism under Healy's leadership the Pablo affair is interesting as an instance of what periodically happens within the FI when one of its leading members actually tries to think for himself. In 1953 the East Berlin riots, the death of Stalin and the subsequent Malenkov reforms posed problems for those who would grasp the changes operating within the Eastern bloc. Articles by Pablo, the Americans Cochran and Clarke and, in Britain by John Lawrence, the editor of *Socialist Outlook*, seemed to stress the relative mildness of the Soviet repression

of the East German uprising, in 1953. This group was optimistic about the extent of the disintegration of Stalinism then
taking place. Like Isaac Deutscher whose *Russia After Stalin* was
influential in these circles, the optimists believed that the
decay of Stalinist othodoxy was in process and sure to be
followed by an intense ferment of ideas which could transform
the outlook of the communist parties everywhere. Within the
USSR they stressed the undermining of Stalinism by developments which it had itself initiated such as industrialization and
the modernization which that process demanded. In *The Rise
and Decline of Stalinism* Pablo cited the Malenkov reforms as
evidence of an internal thaw with the external consequence of
relaxing somewhat the Kremlin grip on the foreign communist
parties – making them potentially more responsive to local
conditons. Pablo specifically argued that the European parties
were being penetrated by 'ideas opposed to the interests of the
Soviet bureaucracy'.[21]

1956

If the leadership of the FI had been unduly optimistic about
the extent of the reforms embarked upon in Russia after Stalin
it was more guarded when, in 1956, Kruschev's 20th Congress
speech was made known in the the West. Though the secret
speech was taken as confirmation of the bureaucracy's retreat
in the face of 'pressure from the masses' the International
argued that the bureaucracy's self-reform could not be fully
concluded in the absence of the 'political revolution' specified
by Trotsky.[22] While it discounted the possibility of a return to
the politics and methods of the Stalin era, the International
also precluded the transformation of the CPSU into a genuine
revolutionary party by a series of reforms from the top. It saw
the Kruschev reforms rather as a bureaucratic self-defence: a
return to Leninism would require a 'qualitative break' involving whole sections of the CPSU rank and file. Mandel's report,
from which this analysis is drawn, also observes of Hungary
(where it is acknowledged that 'the masses . . . seem more
passive than in other countries') that 'the whole situation

seems ripe for [it] to be one of the first countries where a more
or less open struggle between tendencies will take place inside
a Stalinist party which holds power.'[23] When the Hungarian
revolution finally erupted the FI drew the lesson, again, that a
revolutionary party was needed if the bureaucratic regimes
were to be deposed. This and the fact that it did its best to
intervene practically in the uprising was the best possible proof
that Healy and Cannon were wrong to charge the Pablo
leadership with revisionism. The analyses of the Hungarian
revolution proffered by the FI were substantially the same as
those of the recent splitters.[24] The American SWP thus began
the process which led to re-unification in 1963: the Healy
organization stayed apart and redoubled its anti-Pabloite
polemics.

So peripheral were they to the struggles which preoccupied
both wings of the Labour Party that, on the eve of the split
which tore the Communist Party apart in 1956, the Trotskyist
entrists had declined in numbers to the point where
membership of the Club amounted to no more than one
hundred. Ironically Healy had recently lost John Lawrence to
the Communist Party and the former editor of *Socialist Outlook*
supported the CP line on Hungary and its rejection of
unilateral disarmament – hardly evidence of entrism *sui generis*
as alleged. The uprising in Hungary now provoked such a crisis
in the Communist Party that it lost around a third of its
members in the two or three years which followed. Of these
10,000 Healy managed to recruit perhaps 200 but among them
were individuals of some talent who quickly became members
of the leadership around Healy or who clashed with him and
soon left the organization. Among the former were Tom Kemp
and Cliff Slaughter, among the latter Brian Behan, Peter Fryer
and Brian Pearce.

Fryer was the *Daily Worker* correspondent who was sent by the
CPGB to cover the Hungarian events within six days of the
start of the revolution. He had previously covered the show
trials of Slansky and Rajk and was a trusted member of the
party. Yet within days of his arrival in Hungary he was sending
reports which disquieted King Street and which were eventually suppressed by the CP leadership. On his return to Britain,

Fryer resorted to the mainstream press and then in 1957 started *The Newsletter* as a non-sectarian journal of the Left. This was able to serve for a time the needs of a broad radical left associated with the socialist forums, begun after the Wortley Hall conference in April 1957. These emerged to cater for the many Marxists disoriented by the events of 1956.

The communist monolith was already cracked and less sure of itself when news of Kruschev's secret speech began to filter through. By March 1956 the flood of letters to the *Daily Worker* debating the Stalin experience was stopped by J. R. Campbell who pre-emptively closed the discussion. A few days later the actual contents of Kruschev's speech became known and the debate continued unofficially. The CP leadership was itself disoriented in the absence of a clear line from Moscow which it had become accustomed to await before taking action. A section of the membership was already clamouring for more freedom of discussion and in July took unilateral action by publishing *The Reasoner* for the benefit of CP members. The leadership conceded to dissident opinion to the extent of creating a commission on inner-party democracy in the summer of 1956 but before this could report the Hungarian uprising began and the hoped-for return to normality was quashed. When the Soviet tanks rolled into Budapest the CP was given the firm line which its leadership was dependent on. Party members were now reminded that Hungary had pioneered fascism, that it was staunchly anti-semitic and anti-Russian and that the regime lacked 'revolutionary maturity'. Crimes and errors had been committed by the Hungarian party leadership but the uprising threatened 'a real menace of a Fascist Hungary'. The Soviet invasion was thus a regrettable necessity.[25]

The Club seized on these events as an opportunity to intervene actively in the internal affairs of the CPGB and win over as many of its members as possible knowing that as Trotskyists they had the advantage of a ready-made analysis of the Soviet Union which could make sense of the Hungarian tragedy. Dissident CP members did not. Healy exhorted that 'all members of the Communist Party and Young Communist League should immediately demand a special Congress to repudiate the leadership line on Hungary. Stay in the Communist Party and fight it out.'[26] This is, in fact, what happened. By 1957 opposition in the CPGB had cohered around the minority report of the commission on inner-party democracy which essentially argued for greater independence from Russia. But the dissidents were heavily defeated at the party's 25th (Special) conference of that year which accepted the majority report and effectively left everything as before: that is the democratic centralist arrangements which involve the domination by higher party bodies over lower levels remained untouched. The leadership followed up its victory with 'a political letter to members' warning that 'it is harmful to give assistance to Trotskyist and anti-Party people who will try to cover up their aims by the participation of one or two Communists as sympathetic contributors to journals or conferences whose main political content is anti-Communist and anti-Party.'[27]

Although the Club was greatly strengthened by these events and was soon to pose as an independent party, the intellectual leadership of the dissident communists was not Trotskyist and seems, indeed, never to have even considered the Trotskyist option. E. P. Thompson and those like him who set up the *New Reasoner* in 1957 embarked on an altogether different project. Although they were concerned to develop a Marxist understanding of communism it borrowed nothing from Trotsky and perhaps for this reason made little headway in understanding Stalinism and the Soviet Union. Its emphasis was on the need for socialism to be desirable as well as practicable and this made a moral critique of Stalinism imperative. It rejected the economistic and mechanistic variants of Marxism which necessarily included the Leninist–Trotskyist heritage. It emphasized the cultural, experiential and ideological facets of life which the Leninist tradition virtually ignored altogether. In promoting the analysis of these aspects of reality the *New Reasoner* moved closer to a Gramscian Marxism and saw insurrectionary Leninism as unable to meet the needs of socialists in advanced capitalist societies.[28] Together with the *Universities and Left Review* which began publication in spring 1957, the *New Reasoner* helped to bring a new left into existence which was critical of both Leninism–Trotskyism and social democracy.

The Socialist Labour League

The Campaign for Nuclear Disarmament, which began in February 1958, was seen as a potential mass base for socialist politics of this type. It seemed to represent a 'march out of apathy' and owed nothing to the policies and leaderships of the Labour or Communist Parties. The Trotskyist entrists contributed to the emergence of CND, albeit indirectly, at Labour's 1957 conference. One of their number, Vivienne Mendelsohn, seconded the resolution calling for unilateral disarmament. It was defeated with the assistance of the communist-led unions and this defeat dented somewhat the cosy assumption that unilateralism could be achieved through activity in the Labour party.[29]

The Healy group's slogan for CND was 'ban the bomb and black the bases' in order to stress the need for trade union action if the campaign was to progress. But the Trotskyists were disdainful of CND's 'pacifism' and considered that the movement was 'an indirect reflection of the growth of the class struggle in the ranks of the professional and middle classes'[30] – a characterization intended to explain why it could not be regarded as a top priority. Nigel Young points out that in practice the Healy group 'mainly kept aloof' from CND for fear of losing their class perspective in a bigger pacifist movement.[31] Within the organization there were those persuaded that class was slightly irrelevant in relation to an issue – atomic warfare – which threatened complete annihilation: these people – Ken Coates and Peter Cadogan among them – were summarily expelled for advocating 'a vast united front for peace – a front which cuts across class boundaries'.

It is amusing to note in connection with this incident that Healy had pledged himself and advised the first socialist forum to 'examine every point of view'.[32] Of course such uncharacteristic tolerance was expedient when the objective was to make a favourable impression on the heterogeneous audience briefly created by the crisis in the CP. The Club won over Fryer's journal *The Newsletter* in this way. But by December 1958 Healy had joined its editorial team and soon afterwards Fryer left the organization, taking the commitment to non-sectarian politics with him. A similar metamorphosis affected *Labour Review*. Begun in 1952 this functioned between 1957 and 1959 as a forum for Marxists concerned with 'principled discussion of every aspect of revolutionary theory'. In this period the journal discussed Gramsci and Lukacs as well as Trotsky and took articles from independents such as Deutscher as well as group members. But from 1959 onwards all this changed and from having described itself as *'not* a sectional Trotskyist journal' *Labour Review* degenerated into a house journal reflecting the esoteric and sectarian obsessions of Healy and his co-thinkers.

While some of those associated with the socialist forums advocated the creation of a new Marxist party – Peter Worsley, Eric Heffer and Ken Coates were of this opinion – *The Newsletter* advised in favour of the Labour Party despite the fact that the Bevanite movement was past its peak. Within the Club however the argument for an independent party was taken up by Brian Behan. Ten years of entrism had profited the Trotskyists very little and there were those persuaded that an independent alternative to the CP would have gained more from the crisis in that organization than the Club achieved in the obscurity of entrism. Healy believed, however, that entrism was still justified and looked forward to rank-and-file campaigns in the trade unions as the future source of leftism within the Labour Party. It had long been canvassed in Trotskyist and communist circles that a campaign for democracy in the bureaucratic unions would result in increased left-wing representation at national level, and thus shift the balance of power in the Labour Party.

The growth of shop steward power was one reason for this optimism. Another was the new-found ability of the entrists to intervene in industrial disputes. Brian Behan was prominent in the Shell-Mex strike on the London South Bank site in 1957 and *The Newsletter* was used to promote the cause of the sacked and locked-out building workers involved. This strike was also used as a springboard for the Club's highly successful national industrial rank-and-file conference of November 1958. The 500 trade union activists who attended were urged by Behan to build rank-and-file committees capable of challenging bureaucratic power in the labour movement. Again there was division over the question 'in or out of the Labour Party?' Behan faithfully stuck to the Club's line; others dissented – notably Lawrence Daly – and called for 'a genuinely revolutionary socialist party'.[33] The Club's diagnosis of the Labour Party was reproduced for the benefit of the assembled militants and makes interesting reading as a specimen of the petrified schema which it passed off as revolutionary common sense:

> the basic aim of the Labour Party, as laid down in its 1918 constitution, is to work for the social ownership of the means of production. . . The right-wing leaders have abandoned this aim. Only the rank and file can bring the party back to its original purpose and restore the socialist vision and energy of the pioneers of our movement.[34]

The Trotskyists did not trouble themselves with the poverty of this 'socialist vision': to the extent that there was any recognition of waning support for nationalization they imagined that this could be put right by the panacea of 'workers' control' though this did not figure prominently in the 'Charter of Workers' Demands'. As entrists they were compelled to believe (or agitate as if they believed) that the leadership of the Labour Party and trade unions were simply 'middle class' usurpers of an otherwise radical movement: either way they directed their energies so that the focus was on changes in political representation within these organizations.

Despite the fact that unemployment in 1958 stood at a mere 500,000, the Club demanded a one-day general strike in protest. Its 'Charter' drew the attention of Labour's NEC and Healy provocatively answered charges of 'infiltration' by acknowledging authorship and the intent of 'launching . . . a socialist organisation inside the trade unions'. In this reply Healy availed himself of the opportunity of warning that 'unless the Labour Party takes real socialist measures to solve the problems that capitalism places before the British people, then the middle class will be won over to fascism.'[35] Why Healy adopted these apocalyptic tones at this time (when certainly the middle class had 'never had it so good') is a mystery if we look for an answer outside his own tiny group. Such a prospect was simply fantastic.

However Healy had returned constantly to the theme 'socialism or fascism' since the 1940s.[36] The evidence presented here is surely enough to indicate that the prospect of imminent catastrophe has always played a significant part in the Leninist–Trotskyist tradition, if not so ludicrously as when invoked by Healy to justify a tactical turn not noticed by anyone else. Within six months of Healy's dire warning he had launched the Socialist Labour League. To justify this move, which was clearly the first step towards leaving the Labour Party, Healy asked: 'What is the situation in which the Socialist Labour League is born to inherit and carry forward the best traditions of four Internationals? If we were to choose one word to sum up the salient features of this period, that word would be "crisis".'[37] In this way Healy sought to use the old recipe of approaching seismic changes to justify a move – independent party-building – which he had spent a good portion of his time rubbishing during the previous decade. By launching the SLL with a fanfare Healy did everything to make it a public event and thus stir the wrath of Labour's NEC. The SLL was duly proscribed within one month of its foundation in Whitsun 1959.

Nevertheless the SLL constitution referred to the need for 'all members of the League' to 'be members of the their appropriate trade unions and, where possible, Labour parties and play an active part therein'.[38] The point was to delay the group's departure from the Labour Party for as long as possible so that it could maximize the publicity and recruitment thereby attendant on expulsion. The foundation conference referred to 'a movement to the left inside the trade unions [which] required the formation of an open organisation which could recruit trade unionists direct to the Marxist programme and organisation while at the same time training them for continuing struggle from their unions into the Labour Party'.[39]

Some members objected to this lingering attachment to entrism and Brian Behan proposed that the new organization should pass directly to independent status. Behan's faction were therefore expelled *before* the next conference in 1960 but not before he had time to reflect on Healy's authoritarianism and the latter's personal ownership, with Mike Banda, of the SLL's printshop. The energetic Healy was also general secretary of the SLL, editor of *The Newsletter*, secretary of the International Committee of the Fourth International, treasurer of the SLL and manager of the printshop. It is not surprising that a man of this importance should take exception to the Behan faction which was formally expelled for ignoring the correct procedure for launching a tendency. But Alasdair MacIntyre, one of those expelled, was nearer the truth when he complained that 'it has now been established that minorities cannot exist in your [i.e. Healy's] organisation. I say your organisation advisedly because of your private ownership of the assets and personal dominance.'[40]

Though the SLL was a proscribed organization almost from its foundation entrist activity continued, amid expulsions from the Labour Party, and alongside the open organization. One good reason to persist with entrism was Labour's new youth section – the Young Socialists – which was created in response to the party's electoral defeat in 1959. Corresponding to the 'law' that Labour's youth section will be taken over by whichever entrist group happens to be the biggest, the SLL was able to dominate the organization until, in 1964, it decided to take 4,000 Young Socialists to an SLL rally. The following year the Labour Party disbanded the organization after losing a war with Healy which had begun in 1961 with the proscription of *Keep Left*. Meanwhile another battle was being fought with Healy's erstwhile allies in the International Committee and co-splitters of 1953, the American SWP, which had become re-united with the Fourth International in 1963. The protracted unity talks discovered an 'acid test' to sort out revolutionaries from revisionists in the Cuban revolution. This was pronounced a genuine socialist revolution by those who favoured unity but the SLL demurred arguing that it merely represented 'the most radical of a whole series of petty

bourgeois national rebellions in the underdeveloped countries'.[41]

We should not suppose, at least on this occasion, that this
was simply a question of finding a shibboleth to guarantee the
dissent of the arch-doctrinaires of the SLL. There was so much
bad faith involved in the split of 1953 that it is impossible to
take any of the participants at face value on matters of doctrine
then or ten years later. All that can be said for certain is that
the SLL found reasons for staying apart and thereby guaranteed itself dominance of the rump of the International
Committee. It is perhaps something more than coincidence
that the SLL was steered towards independent party-building
at this very time. The 'struggle' against 'Pabloite liquidation'
was intensified in SLL polemics as Healy set out to build a
mass revolutionary party.[42] It was at this time that the SLL
adopted the procedure of recruiting en masse at the many
discotheques organized by its branches: the innocent young
boppers would not know that in paying for admission they had
'joined' the revolutionary party – though no doubt everything
became clear as the music stopped, the lights came on and
Gerry Healy appeared on the stage to commence a bracing
harangue.[43]

Demise and final derangement

The SLL was launched on the 'apocalypse now' perspective
and stuck to this theme throughout the 1960s. Membership
was undoubtedly a shortlived experience for most of those who
entered the organization but the leadership echelon was stable.
It follows then that the politics of the SLL is not reducible to
the influence of one man though we may be sure that Healy's
status as founder of the group, owner of its assets and most
energetic representative was real enough. The fact is that
Healy was supported by the likes of Michael Banda, Cliff
Slaughter and Tom Kemp and with the aid of these people
(and a high turnover of members) was able to eliminate
challenges from the ranks by expulsion. This has led some
critics of the SLL to reason that emphasis on Healy's personal

dominance is a species of demonology to be avoided in favour of an explanation of the doctrinal or political sources of the group's peculiarities.[44] They should not be so concerned. It is perfectly in order to attribute much of a group's style to one individual when the group is tiny and unstable and dependent on authoritative doctrine: what better authority than that of the founder? Obviously this leader needs the support of a clique of full-timers in order to dominate the organization's 'representative' bodies. But if this is forthcoming opponents can be removed from the group before they can build a following among the ranks.

The leadership around Healy was unanimous in promoting the idea that Trotskyist politics depend on the prospect of a major crisis triggered by an economic crash. In 1968 one member of the SLL privately confided

> I cannot emphasise too strongly the extent to which the SLL is committed to the view that a crisis will develop very quickly and that within months Britain will have six to seven million unemployed and general slump conditions. This is constantly reiterated at branch meetings and aggregates. It follows (of course!) that a crisis will, at one fell swoop, provide a mass readership for the daily, build the 'Young Socialists', provide forces to flood into the Labour Party, win the unions – and most importantly – provide masses of recruits for the League . . . this line, while guaranteeing a certain amount of enthusiasm in the short term, is bound to produce a backlash when in 6 months or a year the SLL is no further on.[45]

But the backlash never came – in part because 'six months to a year' was as long as many members could endure in the organization. And we know, on the authority of former leading members, that the group moved closer and closer to the style of a millenial religious cult as the 1960s progressed.[46] Hyperactive in selling papers and attending meetings, discouraged from the distractions of the outside world, the group members lived in a sealed atmosphere. Those who dared to question the sect's internal arrangements were often beaten, 'arrested' and tried by 'courts' in which Healy or his lieutenants presided. A religious faith in the purity of the organization's ultimate goals justified such terror in the eyes of the membership.

There is, moreover, plenty of textual support for authoritarianism in the Leninist–Trotskyist tradition. This could be turned to good effect in preserving the dominance of the leadership coterie. Their opponents could be drummed out of the organization as purveyors of the enemy's values. After all it is custom and practice for Leninists to find factional opponents guilty of representing alien class forces. It is also customary to stress the virtues of discipline and centralism and emphasise the singular value of the party. As Healy said in the 1940s:

> We are monopolists in the field of politics. To make a successful revolution in Britain, the working class will require to do it through one party and one programme. We are the nucleus of such a party and our programme is the Transitional Programme of the Fourth International. That is why we are out to destroy all competitive parties such as the ILP.[47]

Rival organizations and rival points of view are on this reasoning alike guilty of error and the wrong class viewpoint: they must be spurned or, if the occasion permits, stamped out. All this was made worse by Healy's readiness to regard himself as the personification of the revolutionary party: 'I am the party' or so he declaimed on more than one occasion.[48]

By the standards of rival Trotskyist groups the SLL was successful under Healy's leadership. Indeed Healy's success story begins in 1947 when the International made him de facto leader in Britain. By 1953 Healy was (with J. P. Cannon of the SWP) co-leader of an international faction by virtue of an opportunist split with the International Secretariat. In Britain Healy's group was the biggest Trotskyist organization until the early 1970s. In 1972 it organized a national Right to Work march which culminated in a rally 8,500 strong. *The Newsletter* was already published twice a week by February 1968: in September 1969 it was succeeded by *Workers' Press* – the first

Trotskyist daily newspaper by the early 1970s. A further expansion was recorded in 1972 when the paper was increased from four to twelve pages and *Keep Left* became a weekly. Moreover by the late 1960s the SLL had once more established a presence in the factories and could set up the All-Trade Union Alliance (1968) to mobilise militant trade unionists.

It would seem that the unity of the leadership was preserved by these developments and for as long as it chose to ignore the fragile basis for grandiose schemes like the daily paper all was well at the top. Only the frenetic activity of a declining membership could sustain the notion of turning the SLL into the Workers' Revolutionary Party (WRP) but this was done in November 1973. By then general predictions of the approaching catastrophe had become altogether more detailed. The WRP's prominent members – such as Vanessa Redgrave – warned of an imminent military coup headed by a section of the Heath Cabinet representing the 'squirearchy'.[49] In February 1974 *Workers' Press* declared 'Four Days to Military Dictatorship' and talked of concentration camps ready to deal with stubborn trade unionists. The apocalypse had at last arrived!

But, of course, the predicted events failed to materialize. Members of the WRP with one foot in the real world – significantly its members in the trade unions were prominent among them – were at last incapable of accepting any more of this rubbish – at least when the deadline for catastrophe was specified with such precision. The result of their rebellion was a further round of expulsions, intimidation and violence but this time the expelled numbered around 200 and were able to set up their own organization – the Workers' Socialist League (WSL) – and the WRP lost its supporters in the Cowley division of British Leyland.[50] Thus depleted the WRP continued to decline while, incredibly, persisting with its daily paper thanks to the wealth of the Redgraves and certain 'bourgeois national movements' in 'the Arab countries'.[51] The purists who could not co-exist with 'Pabloites' in the FI and who declared that it was now run by 'Soviet police agents'[52] were perfectly happy to receive money from Libya and Iraq. In return it seems the Healy group supported the Ba'athist regime's murder of 21 Iraqi communists and took the view that in destroying the Iranian section of the United Secretariat of the Fourth International, the Khomeini regime had only disposed of CIA and KGB agents.[53]

The derangement of the Healy organization had taken place in stages. The authoritarian internal regime had existed since the 1940s. The ludicrous 'apocalypse now' perspectives were present from the beginning and central to the group's rhetoric from 1959. This includes the spectre of fascism as an imminent threat in Britain. By the 1960s a range of idiosyncratic doctrinal positions were added to the group's repertoire which guaranteed its demise. It took no part in the Vietnamese Solidarity Campaign on the grounds that it was pro-Stalinist: it virtually ignored the campaigns in Northern Ireland and boycotted the Troops Out Movement; likewise it was completely by-passed by the student and women's movements which it considered petty bourgeois. In the 1970s it was only present as a daily newspaper obtainable in left bookshops, remarkable not so much for its bizarre politics as for the fact that it existed at all. Its last burst of publicity came in October 1985 when the organization's founder and cult leader Gerry Healy was expelled at the age of 74 for, among other things, using his power in the organization to obtain the sexual favours of female members who were enjoined to 'do it for the party'.

Healey's sexual proclivities nothwithstanding, it is much more likely that his expulsion can be explained by the WRP's descent into dementia and the inability of its septuagenarian founder to enforce acquiesence on the whole leadership. The 'gangster' tactics which formerly ensured his total dominance were now beyond him.[54] Banda, Slaughter and some other leading members rebelled and Healy was ejected from the organization only to be followed by the Redgraves and Alex Mitchell. There were now two WRPs but even the pro-Healy group soon dropped the cult figure from its central committee. By February 1986 the implosion of the WRP was complete when further splits were announced in both the Mark 1 and Mark 2 models. At least two of these sects were now preoccupied with establishing control of the publishing rights and assets of the original group, valued at over one million pounds.[55]

If an authoritarian personality is important in explaining the politics of an intolerant group it is not a sufficient explanation of the fact that Healy found support even for his most absurd policies and predictions from a loyal band of co-thinkers. These people made his control of the SLL and WRP possible. Within the International Committee, after the departure of the American SWP, the Healy group was supported by similar organizations in the USA, France, Australia, Germany, Sri Lanka and Peru. The organizations concerned came together for a variety of reasons ranging from personal interventions by Healy which resulted in the emergence of a leader of the same mentality to splits in other organizations over questions of doctrine. For as long as they consorted together all these groups supported the doctrinal positions of the International Committee. These must be regarded as a collective 'achievement' no matter how influential Healy may have been at one time. This applies to the absurd 'Security and the Fourth International' campaign according to which the leaders of the ISFI were agents of the KGB and CIA just as it applies to the intellectual thuggery which culminated in the deal permitting receipt of Arab money in exchange for lies and distortions in the 'revolutionary' press.[56]

If one is tempted to ascribe the later machinations to some form of madness it is as well to remember that almost every aspect of the WRP's politics in the 1970s and 1980s have precedents in the three earlier decades. The pure gobbledygook served up in book-length diatribes against dissidents who had allegedly deviated from 'dialectical materialism' is a case in point. Thornett's inability to accept the predictions of 1974 was interpreted as an 'attack against dialectical materialism' requiring 157 pages of 'philosophical' rebuttal.[57] Haston's mention of 'empirical adaption' in 1946 was likewise denounced at length as a renunciation of Marxist philosophy. The obscurantism of the International's arraignment of the RCP's leaders in the 1940s helped promote Healy in the first place: an equally fantastic doctrinal debate justified the split of 1953. Throughout this period, sometimes with, sometimes without the aid of the International, the Healy faction remained in the saddle by means of expulsions. Doctrinal justification for such authoritarianism was amply provided by the Leninist-Trotskyist perception of factions as the representatives of bourgeois and petty-bourgeois values. The group's theoreticians did not fail to make use of this authority: the membership did not fail to swallow it.[58] The politics of the Healy group was a fusion of the dogmatic, arrogant and authoritarian elements of the Leninist–Trotskyist tradition with the personal shortcomings of individual leaders and the sectarian condition of a marginal group. The only surprise is that its spontaneous combustion was so long in coming.

4

The Socialist Workers' Party and Leninist Industrial Politics

Until 1933 Trotsky linked the danger of the restoration of capitalism in the USSR with the idea of Thermidor. But after 1933 he revised his position, arguing that the Thermidorean reaction had already succeeded – the revolution's radical phase had given way before a reactionary process which allowed the state and party bureaucracy to triumph. This bureaucratic degeneration of the revolution had enabled the 'Bonapartist clique of Stalin' to come to the fore. Capitalism had not been restored but the isolation and material backwardness of the USSR precluded the victory of socialism. Bureaucracy grew instead in conditions of acute scarcity: it was able to take deep roots during the civil war and then with the inauguration of the New Economic Policy it received another boost with the growth of the petty bourgeoisie. Trotsky minimized the personal role of Stalin but argued that 'the degeneration of the party became both cause and consequence of the bureaucratisation of the state'.[1] Political factors such as the decision to ban factions within the Bolshevik Party in 1921 had thus contributed to the demise of Soviet power but the burden of Trotsky's explanation was elsewhere – on the backwardness of a country surrounded by hostile capitalist states.

But Trotsky refused to accept that the degeneration of the revolution had resulted in the appearance of state capitalism as some of his sympathizers urged. Trotsky insisted, against this view, that since the bureaucracy had no independent position in the process of production and therefore no independent property roots it was to be understood as a parasitic outgrowth privileged in consumption rather than property relations. In short, because the state had taken over private property and had kept control of it, this fundamental step towards socialism ensured that it remained a workers' state – albeit a *degenerated* workers' state given the demise of working-class political power. On this reasoning Trotsky supposed that the USSR could rediscover the socialist road if a 'political revolution' against the bureaucracy occurred. This amounted to saying that the problem inhered in the domination of the state by men of the wrong class and political policies. Yet Trotsky was fully aware of the virtual extinction of the working class of 1917 and the terrorized, atomized and super-exploited condition of its successor. How could it possibly be that the state which had created and continued to control the slave camps and the slavish conditions in the factories could in any meaningful sense represent the workers? Some of Trotsky's supporters reasoned that his emphasis on nationalized industry as the sound socialist foundation of the USSR gave disproportionate weight to the legal form of this property which was after all *controlled* by an unrepresentative and unaccountable party-state for purposes altogether remote from the interests of the workers. This suggested that the system was state capitalist or at best some form of bureaucratic collectivism.

Even those who loyally adhered to Trotsky's analysis of the Soviet Union were unable to make much sense of it after the war. Trotsky had insisted that Soviet foreign policy was 'counter-revolutionary through and through' yet the Fourth International witnessed the instruments of this foreign policy – the communist parties – seize power in Yugoslavia and China and become mass parties in France, Italy and Greece. By 1947 the Trotskyists were forced to envisage that these parties were articulating 'a real class policy'.[2] At the same time they argued that any trial of strength between imperialism and the USSR would be disastrous for the latter: indeed only the proletarian revolution could prevent an imminent fatal outcome from this collision.[3] Moreover such a collision 'is predetermined as soon as accounts are finally settled with the Nazis and the Japanese; perhaps even before' concluded the American SWP.[4] The considered position of the International was that an offensive against the USSR was inevitable and imminent and bound to result in its defeat unless the situation was radically altered by virtue of socialist revolutions in Europe. At the same time, the Stalinists were seen to be capable of promoting and leading successful revolutions. But if this was true how could the warmongers ignore working-class sentiment in Europe and go ahead with an anti-Bolshevik war?

The RCP drew attention to this contradiction and observed that the USSR had emerged from the war as the second world power – an event foreseen by nobody. But if the RCP saw more than the Fourth International its own debate on the nature of the USSR shows that its leaders were also struck by the profoundly negative features of that system. Haston argued that the Soviet state 'occupies the same position in relation to the economy as the capitalist to the single enterprise': he maintained that production was for profit as in the West – and yet his conclusion was that the system was *not* state capitalist. Similarly the International argued in 1947 that the USSR was 'a workers' state degenerated to the point where all progressive manifestations of the October conquest are more and more neutralised by the disastrous effects of the Stalinist dictatorship'. The RCP leaders essentially concurred with this description by portraying the Russian system as one in which 'wage slaves' were 'brutally exploited' by a bureaucracy which devoured a 'growing proportion of the social product'. The obvious conclusion was that the system was a new form of exploitative and particularly ruthless capitalism. But most Trotskyists were content to hold on formally to the degenerated workers' state thesis while actually denying that there was anything progressive about the USSR. A minority within the RCP, however, were prepared to go further and denounce the Soviet system as state capitalist.[5] The fullest version of this theory was expounded by Tony Cliff in *Russia: A Marxist Analysis* and distributed to all RCP members in 1949. The following year its supporters created the Socialist Review Group.

At the time of its first appearance 'the founders of the group saw themselves as mainstream Trotskyists differing only on important questions from the dominant group in the International, but belonging to the same basic tendency.'[6] Their objective was reform of the International which they would seek by entering its ranks: but in the event they were debarred from membership because of their belief in the state capitalist nature of the USSR. Though Trotsky once quipped that state capitalism 'has the advantage that nobody knows exactly what it means',[7] his commitment to the defence of the Soviet Union against internal or external reaction, which he placed among the first principles of revolutionary duty, could find no support among its adherents. On this crucial issue everyone knew exactly what state capitalism meant – neutrality or a 'plague on both your houses'. The Cold War presented the reality of a permanent campaign against the USSR which always threatened to become a real war and thus the argument with the state capitalists was much more than an abstract dispute between rival theorists. At issue was the correct stance to adopt over the war in Korea, for example, and even the original purpose of the FI. According to the state capitalists Trotsky specifically excluded the possibility of the Stalinists establishing worker's states – and yet the FI slowly came to accept that this was exactly what had happened in Eastern Europe after 1947. Cliff's followers believed that the historical justification for the FI was precisely the contrary and when the latter finally concluded that the People's Democracies were deformed *workers'* states they concluded that it had capitulated to Stalinism.[8]

The International itself had earlier referred to a 'fundamental tenet of Marxism – the conception of socialism as the self-emancipation of the working class'. This was the criterion subsequently employed by Cliff to establish the class character of the People's Democracies. He argued that 'in no way is it possible to demonstrate that the statifications [of property in Eastern Europe] were the culmination of the activities no matter how deformed of the working class.'[9] And yet 'the political supremacy of the working class is a prerequisite for its economic supremacy.' This being so, Cliff argued that 'where the state, which is a repository of the means of production, is

totally alienated from the working class, by this very fact of
political alienation the workers are separated from the means
of production, they are wage slaves.' As for the Soviet Union,
Cliff tells us:

> When I came to the theory of state capitalism I didn't
> come to it by a long analysis of the law of value in Russia
> ... Nothing of the sort. I came to it by the simple
> statement that if the emancipation of the working class is
> the act of the working class then you cannot have a
> workers' state without the workers having power to
> dictate what happens in society.[10]

This is an eminently sensible statement though it should be
pointed out that in Leninist discourse 'the act of the working
class' invariably means the act of the revolutionary party.
Trotsky never argued, of course, that the workers of the Soviet
Union exercised state power. The USSR was designated a
degenerated workers' state just because a privileged bureaucracy monopolized state power. But this analysis, according to
the state capitalists, had become 'hopelessly outdated' by the
early 1930s.[11]

The turning point in the history of the Bolshevik revolution
was the first five-year plan of 1928. According to Tony Cliff:

> It was now, for the first time, that the bureaucracy sought
> to create a proletariat and to accumulate capital rapidly. In
> other words, it was now that the bureaucracy sought to
> realise the historical mission of the bourgeoisie as quickly
> as possible. A quick accumulation on the basis of a low
> level of production, of a small national income per capita,
> must put a burdensome pressure on the consumption of
> the masses, on their standard of living. Under such condi-
> tions the bureaucracy, transformed into a personification
> of capital, for whom the accumulation of capital is the
> be-all and end-all here, must get rid of all remnants of
> workers' control, must substitute conviction in the labour
> process by coercion, must atomise the working class, must
> force all social-political life into a totalitarian mould.[12]

Trotsky viewed these events altogether differently arguing that the terror against the kulaks and NEP-men was a belated and bureaucratic response to real dangers of capitalist restoration. Hallas is right to observe that that 'Trotsky could initially see all this as a turn to the *left* (although he was not aware of the full facts until some years later) indicates that he had relapsed into substitutionism so far as looking at the USSR was concerned.'[13] The truth is that such substitutionism was endemic to Trotsky's position based as it was on the record of the Bolshevik state up to the death of Lenin. But like Trotsky the state capitalists subscribe to the fiction that 'workers' control' survived the Lenin era, which it did not. In fact the 'totalitarian' dictatorship which both Cliff and Trotsky refer to was installed well before Stalin became 'leader' of the party. In refusing to acknowledge the known facts the state capitalists, like Trotsky, subscribe to the legend that the Stalin dictatorship was a deviation from Bolshevism rather than its grotesque but legitimate offspring. They were never able, therefore, to discover the contributions of Bolshevik ideology and Leninist practice to authoritarianism in the party, the state, the factory and so on.[14]

Instead Cliff focuses on 1928 – the year when the Soviet state inaugurated forced collectivization, massive violence against the kulaks and the first economic plans. It was then, he argues, that the bureaucracy became the 'historical essence' of the capitalist class.[15] And yet his fidelity to Leninism prevents Cliff from regarding state capitalism as a new stage in historical development. Though it claims that state capitalism has spread to Eastern Europe and China and has been the inevitable outcome of communist revolutions everywhere else – Cuba, Vietnam, Angola, etc. – the Cliff group refuses to see it as a new type of exploitive society.[16] Were they to argue this it would clearly undermine the Leninist conception of the imperialist epoch as one in which the politics of revolutionary socialism (i.e. Leninism) are the singularly appropriate response to the decay of capitalism. In fact by their own logic socialism is only possible if a number of advanced capitalist countries simultaneously succumb to revolution – a socialist 1848. Otherwise it is argued that the isolated command economy is distorted by the capitalist world economy. Cliff's analysis of the Soviet economy is the model for this argument.

Cliff acknowledged that the Soviet plan replaces the price mechanism or law of value as the regulator of production. The entire economy functions like a single capitalist enterprise with the various parts producing use values for each other. But according to Cliff the Soviet economy behaves like a capitalist enterprise in competition with other enterprises within the world economy. In this context international competition ensures that the price mechanism does operate and the priorities of the Soviet economy are determined by forces beyond its control. Like Bukharin, Cliff reasons that 'because international competition takes mainly a military form the law of value expresses itself in its opposite viz, a striving after use values.'[17] Weapons production therefore has the chief determining role in 'the whole development of the Russian economy'[18] and therefore production is governed not in accordance with the requirements of socialist criteria but in accordance with the dictates of the capitalist world economy. In this way isolated revolutions made in the name of socialism inevitably result in state capitalism. Among the peculiar consequences of adherence to this theory is the Cliff group's support for the Vietcong as against American imperialism only to conclude that the former's success produced state capitalism.

But the most useful theoretical spin-off from Cliff's state capitalist heresy was the propositon concerning the centrality of armaments production. Since 1945 this has obviously loomed large in the world economy not simply in terms of the arms race between the super powers but also by way of massive exports of conventional weapons in part designed to offset the nuclear bill. Cliff and Michael Kidron elaborated the notion of permanent arms economies to explain the unexpected postwar boom which for so long disoriented their orthodox Trotskyist rivals. Their basic idea is very simple: 'Insofar as capital is taxed to sustain expenditure on arms it is deprived of resources that might otherwise go towards further investment'.[19] In this way surplus investment funds are siphoned out of the economy into expenditure on fast-obsolescent weapons systems. By thus leaking potentially productive capital it is argued that these economies avoid the over-heating and speculative booms which normally terminate periods of capitalist expansion and precipitate slumps. So just as the great boom in capital exports was once said to have stabilized capitalism before 1914, arms production was responsible for the equilibrium of the 1950s and 1960s. According to Kidron 'this was because seen from the angle of the system . . . arms production is the key and seemingly permanent offset to the tendency of the rate of profit to fall.'[20]

Kidron thus explained the post-war boom and addressed a number of other issues which the orthodox had ignored. Capitalism clearly no longer required colonial possessions and was now much more involved in the export of capitalism than capital. Lenin's *Imperialism: The Highest Stage of Capitalism* was no longer useful. The world economy was now more integrated than in Lenin's day and the Cold War, the 'unrestrained competition' between East and West, further undermined national solutions to economic and political problems. Trotsky's theory of permanent revolution also, on this view, requires revision because the obsolescence of colonies has rescued the national bourgeoisie of these countries from the oblivion it previously faced. Whereas it seemed to Trotsky that this small and compromised class would be forced to cede the leadership of national independence to the proletariat Kidron argues that the dissolution of empire had given it a new lease of life and even 'the levers of economic development and its own growth'.[21] However this development also serves to remove the national question from the Third World agenda since having already played this card it is impossible to present problems of development and real political independence as amenable to any solutions other than class solutions. But economic backwardness, according to Kidron, obviously handicaps such nations and greatly diminishes the ability of the proletariat in these countries to solve local problems by means of socialism. Thus while other Trotskyist groups were persuaded that the key to socialism in the West was to be found in the underdeveloped world, the Cliff group emphatically rejected this short cut.[22]

These two distinctive theories – state capitalism and the permanent arms economy – were useful practically in a variety of ways. The Cliff group were freed from those allegiances which compelled other Marxist groups to take sides in the Cold War. They were obliged to go beyond the crude catastrophism which sustained the faithful in the Socialist Labour League. They were, most important of all, able to say that they regarded the Soviet system as at least as bad as capitalism. During the Korean war they argued that 'the immediate result of the victory of Stalinism in Korea would be the liquidation of the independent socialist movement and the disorienting of the socialist vanguard ... We can therefore give no support to either camp since the war will not achieve the declared aims of either side.'[23] As Birchall later explained, the Koreans were rapidly reduced to the role of mere victims as two great world powers engaged in a trial of strength across their territory.[24] The struggles in China which led to the revolution in 1949 and the war in Vietnam after 1965 were of a different character. Because both were based on mass move-ments of the people, it is argued, it was appropriate to support them even though the outcome of these wars was the very state capitalism which the group found so repulsive about North Korea. Sometimes therefore Cliff's Socialist Review Group gave the impression that they regarded state capitalism as an advance – as in China – while on other occasions such as Korea they assumed neutrality. They have argued that state capitalism 'was founded on a more systematic exploitation of labour than was possible in the old capitalism of the West' and Cliff even asserted that the system 'needs the blood of the purge to make the wheels go round.'[25] On yet another occasion it was argued that a 'welfare state capitalism' was being developed.[26] To complicate matters further Cliff has also spoken of state capitalism as 'a transition to socialism' though the intricacies of dialectical thinking allow that it is also 'the extreme opposite of socialism – they are symme-trically opposed and they are dialectically united with one another.'[27] It seems that Trotsky was right – the theory has the advantage that nobody knows what it means or rather it means what the Cliff group want it to mean as the occasion demands.

The permanent arms economy thesis is similarly versatile,

for while purportedly explaining capitalist equilibrium it paradoxically advances the view that prospects for revolution are strongest in 'the heartland of the system' rather than its economically backward periphery. Kidron argued that the capital-intensive nature of the permanent arms economy creates technological unemployment especially among marginal groups such as immigrants, ethnic minorities and women. By accelerating the concentration of capital and draining resources away from the periphery of the advanced capitalist world it also revives previously-dormant nationalist movements. By virtue of its unparalleled irrationality the arms economy incites the dissent of students and calls forth mass movements for peace. Thus in these ways the short-term stability bought by the arms economies only recedes before bigger crises in the future. The principal bearers of the military burden eventually find that competitors absolved of this responsibility such as Germany and Japan encroach on their markets and achieve higher growth rates. Eventually, argues Cliff, the proportion of Western resources spent on arms is cut back to meet the needs of this competitive struggle and the stabilizing effect of arms expenditure is reduced or lost altogether.[28]

It is all rather neat. But even Kidron was moved to disclaim the multi-purpose uses to which it was being put by his comrades;[29] and other Marxists demolished the claim that the arms economy was the principal cause of the post-war boom and the subsequent recession.[30] The specific claim that armaments expenditure arrested the tendency for the rate of profit to fall – in Kidron's words 'there (has) been no long-term slide in profit rates' – does not even command consistent support from Cliff who in 1975 asserted that 'in the last 25 years pre-tax profits for large companies have almost halved.'[31] Nevertheless the elaboration of these distinctive positions showed that there was life in the Socialist Review Group and its successor from 1962 International Socialism, and it was the contrast with the dogmatic and sterile Socialist Labour League which drew young radicals to the state capitalists in the 1960s.

Growth of the organization

Entrism contributed little to the growth of the organization;
the 1950 membership of 33 had only increased to around 250
in 1962 when the main field of recruitment was in the Young
Socialists. Here the entrists sold *Young Guard* in competition
with the SLL's *Keep Left*. The official historian of the organization tells us that the Socialist Review Group saw itself even
in those days as 'the nucleus of a Marxist party [which] . . .
can be built firmly only on the acceptance of party discipline
in the tradition of Bolshevism under Lenin's leadership'.[32]
This may well have been how the leaders intended to steer the
organization but Cliff was publicly extolling the merits of
Luxemburg's rather than Lenin's ideas on the role of the
party. It was also timely for a small group buried in the
Labour Party to emphasize the politics of the mass movement
and it is in this context that Cliff applauds Luxemburg's
opposition to

> abstention from the main stream of the Labour move-
> ment, no matter what the level of its development. Her
> fight against sectarianism is extremely important for the
> Labour movement in the West, especially at the present,
> when welfare-statism is such an all-prevailing sentiment.
> The British Labour movement, in particular . . . can gain
> inspiration from Rosa Luxemburg for a principled fight
> against reformism which does not degenerate into flight
> from it.[33]

The group's practical opposition to sectarianism was
apparent in its use of the journal *International Socialism* (1960)
as a forum of socialist debate. There was no evidence of
Lenin's influence in the structure of the organization either,
since, until 1968, this was federal rather than centralist. Cliff,
the future hagiographer of Lenin, was even persuaded that
Lenin's *What Is To Be Done*? 'can much less serve as a guide
than Rosa Luxemburg's [position] notwithstanding her
overstatements on the question of spontaneity'.[34] It is clear

that Cliff was principally concerned to establish the democratic strengths of Luxemburg over Lenin:

> Rosa Luxemburg's conception of the structure of the revolutionary organisation – that they should be built from below up, on a consistently democratic basis – fits the needs of the workers' movement in the advanced countries much more closely than Lenin's conception of 1902–4 which was copied and given an added bureaucratic twist by Stalinists the world over.[35]

Quite – but this is a long way removed from Trotskyism. That only a 'bureaucratic twist' separates Lenin and Stalin is an unthinkable proposition in this quarter and Cliff's acolytes have been quick to describe these remarks as something of a temporary aberration. But Cliff's 'slip of the pen' also included the remark that Trotsky's 1904 prophesy concerning Lenin's substitutionism was a brilliant insight on the dangers 'inherent in Lenin's conception of the party'. Even Birchall is forced to admit that in the period up to 1968 International Socialism members 'inherited a somewhat libertarian attitude to organisation; a tendency to distrust discipline or any kind of formalised or centralised structure',[36] and though he evidently disapproves of such laxity he concedes that at this time they were relatively free of the sectarianism of self-appointed vanguards.

On this basis the group grew to around 1,000 members by the end of 1968. Along the way changes in its political orientation were signalled by changes in the name of its paper. Begun in 1961 with the hopeful name of *Industrial Worker* it was given the more accurate title of *Labour Worker* in 1964 though it continued to concentrate on industrial news, if that is what long lists of strike reports amounts to. The decision to withdraw from the Labour Party – after a year of the first Wilson government persuaded the group of impending conflict between Labour and the unions – was carried out in 1965–6. Although membership was less than 400 the leadership was persuaded that a viable independent existence was possible on the strength of militant trade unionism, tenants' struggle and anti-racism. Circulation of the paper was only 2,000 per month in 1964 but this was big enough to justify a fortnightly the following year and probably seemed colossal to those who could remember that *Socialist Review* sold no more than 350 copies in 1950. Within two years of independent activity the International Socialists were confident of sales of 10,000. The paper became *Socialist Worker* in 1968.

1968 was a peak year for the International Socialists. Membership doubled in this twelve months primarily because of student radicalism in the colleges and solidarity campaigns (notably on Vietnam) and abroad (Paris, Prague, Berkeley etc.) – where radicalism outstripped the British experience but briefly seemed to show what might happen soon in London. Tony Cliff was less than euphoric, however, because for some years – since 1965 in fact when entrism was dropped – the chief object of the organization had been to establish itself in the trade unions. The growth of shop-steward militancy promised to develop a base for a new revolutionary movement firmly anchored in the factories. But despite its growth the International Socialist group was more visible at the London School of Economics than in any part of British industry in 1968. Unhappy about this situation Cliff instigated an organizational upheaval to fashion Leninist norms and the next year a so-called 'turn to the class' was instituted in a bid to establish a working-class base. This amounted, at first, to encouraging the student members to find industrial work and focus political activity at the factory gates.

Not all the leading members of IS were as enthusiastic as Cliff and Harman about the turn to Leninism after 1968. Hallas dismissed as irrelevant Lenin's model of 1903 since 'the vanguard, in the real sense of a considerable layer of organised revolutionary workers and intellectuals [has] been destroyed. So too has the environment, the tradition, that gave it influence . . . the crux of the matter is how to develop the process, now begun, of recreating it.'[37] If the point was to move 'towards a revolutionary socialist party' it involved something more than sorting out the politics of a small group 'and then offer(ing) it as an alternative to the uniting workers'. This procedure, said Hallas, was only appropriate to 'some sect or other' whose self-appointed role was to safeguard the purity of the programme. Hallas seemed to be saying that the symbiotic relationship between party and class which alone made vanguard politics relevant was a very long way off and could only come about by the reciprocal growth of class politics and the organized revolutionaries. But only eight years after Cliff rediscovered the virtues of Leninism and on the strength of just four thousand members, the International Socialists proclaimed themselves the revolutionary party as if this process was so well developed that they could pose as a national alternative to the CP and the Labour Party.

The local cause for the turn to vanguardism seems to have been connected with the rapid growth of IS during 1968 and 'the failure of the May events to lead to revolution'.[38] The issues of discipline raised by these experiences could be solved by democratic centralism. In the same year, however, Cliff was sufficiently worried by the support for Enoch Powell's 'rivers of blood' racist campaign within the working class that he called for unity of the revolutionary left and raised the spectre of 'socialism or barbarism'. In the event only Workers' Fight answered the call and for the next three years this small group kept its own faction within IS. For a time there were no less than five factions within the organization. Democratic centralism was not adopted, therefore, simply to put the IS house in order since in some ways this deteriorated after 1968. It has to be seen as a stage in the drift to proclaiming IS as the revolutionary party. If this was supposedly justified by the claim that 'objective' circumstances dictated it we had better look at the rationale for this argument.

The Wilson governments were held to provide empirical support for the 'theory' that Labour had ceased to promote useful reforms and parliament was no longer a vehicle for the achievement of 'direct, felt reforms'. The redundancy of mass politics in this way suggested that strikes were more important in advancing the workers' interests. This position was common to all the IS leaders. Repeatedly Cliff, Kidron and the rest argued that elections only provided a choice between 'Tweedledum and Tweedledee'. Remember that the decision to establish IS as an independent group in 1965 was based on these beliefs and the alleged potential of the shop stewards to form the working-class base of a new revolutionary party. Wage militancy was certainly growing and the attempts to curb trade union power by Wilson and Heath did much to provoke a rise in the number of specifically political strikes. In turning IS towards Leninism and the industrial working class Cliff attempted to create a vanguard party which at the least would eclipse the CP. Centralism was thus a concomitant of this rank-and-file industrial strategy.

Accordingly, in place of an executive committee based on delegates from IS branches, an elected national committee determined by conference was created. *Socialist Worker* was expanded from four to six pages in 1969 (by 1972 it was 16 pages). The first IS rank and file group was established in the National Union of Teachers and two of its members were elected to the union executive. Its *Rank and File Teacher* reached a peak circulation of over 9,000 in 1974. But the real difficulty was how to establish such groups in heavy industrial occupations where IS had few if any members. Membership actually dropped to 880 by 1970 under the strain of this 'turn to the class'; the Bolshevization of the organization led to the elimination of Workers' Fight in 1971 and the so-called Right faction in 1973 (which then set up the Revolutionary Communist Group). Nevertheless IS recovered and actually succeeded in creating rank and file groups in the car industry, local government, mining, docks and building as well as in the civil servants union, and among social workers and hospital employees where it was easier to recruit members. All of these groups published their own rank and file newspapers which ranged in circulation from 1,000 to 10,000. In 1973 IS also began publication of *Chingari* to build support among Urdu-speaking communities as well. But the central thrust was concerned with the establishment of an industrial base for IS.

By 1972 the organization was 2,351 strong, of whom 26 per cent were classified as manual, 31 per cent as white collar workers. In 1973 IS set up 40 factory branches and reached 2,667 members: the following year the growth continued and membership stood at 3,900. The print order for *Socialist Worker* also increased by leaps and bounds from 8,000 in 1969 to

21,000 in 1972 to over 40,000 in 1974. Edited by Roger Protz
Socialist Worker was by now devoted to the view that the strike
wave and the economic crisis would be sufficient to produce an
even bigger audience for revolutionary politics. Protz with the
help of journalists such as Paul Foot and Eamonn McCann had
made *Socialist Worker* the best read on the revolutionary left but
Cliff believed the potential existed for a circulation of 80,000,
despite the fact that during the February 1974 election only
35,000 copies were sold from a print order of 50,000. Cliff also
insisted that the journal should take on a more proletarian
character by turning its readers into writers. Protz was
removed from the editorship in April 1974 for opposing these
perspectives which he believed would dilute the politics of the
journal by increasing the number of short descriptive articles
covering industrial disputes. Protz was not the only opponent
of Cliff's forced march to the mass party. Andreas Nagliatti
resigned as industrial organizer and an opposition led by
Hallas, Jim Higgins and John Palmer tried to put the recent
growth of IS into some sort of perspective.

It was pointed out that the 1974 registration disclosed an
enormous turnover of members – some 48 per cent had
belonged to IS for a year or less. This pointed to a high degree
of political innocence among a membership 'unusually unin-
formed' and insufficiently integrated. Yet Cliff fancied that a
further spurt in membership was in the offing as well as a mass
circulation for *Socialist Worker*. His proposal was that both the
journal and the organization now be 'proletarianized' to make
ready for this spectacular growth. If this all sounds too
whimsical to be true let Protz describe it:

> It was always Cliff who advanced these sudden ideas.
> Cliff would drag a new theory out of his left ear one
> morning and it became holy writ the next day . . . If Cliff
> wanted to change the line, the line would change. He was
> IS to start with and people paid him enormous respect,
> which was due to him. But he would be very friendly to
> you one week and the next week he would be cutting you
> dead because you weren't agreeing with some new line
> he'd devised.[39]

Exit Protz who resurfaced some years later in the Campaign for
Real Ale no doubt tired of a politics which was more froth than
body.

Cliff led the IS along the chosen path of attempting to
emulate the CP's Minority Movement of the 1920s in spite of
the fact that 70 per cent of the membership were still either
students, housewives, unemployed or white-collar workers.
Only 368 of the 1974 membership were organized in factory
branches. With the election of a Labour government it was even
recognized that the immediate prospect was a decline in the
number of industrial disputes – the fragile basis for the whole
enterprise. Yet

> it is now possible to talk and to talk credibly, of the need
> to build a socialist workers' party that will sweep away
> capitalism. Building such a party is now fully on the
> agenda. It is a challenge IS willingly accepts . . . such a
> party has its mainspring in workplace branches. That is
> where workers' power lies. And that is why last year IS
> built 38 factory branches and this year the IS Conference
> decided to aim at 80 factory branches plus a number of
> white collar branches by autumn 1975.[40]

This was Cliff's conviction and he set about reorganizing IS
accordingly. Almost the entire executive committee was
replaced by provincial organizers from the group's growth
areas. But the result of this was that the EC meetings became
irregular and poorly attended affairs. It also became clear that
transforming IS into a Leninist workers' party was incompatible with the sort of united front which IS members in the
Birmingham AUEW were committed to. These people resisted
the new edict to stand independent IS candidates in union
elections. But all the dissidents were silenced when Cliff
changed the rules of the game. The national committee of 40
was replaced by a central committee of nine with the larger
body relegated to a purely advisory role. According to Martin
Shaw the delegate system for conference was gerrymandered so
that districts replaced branches as the representational basis
of the organization, ensuring that an estimated oppositional

minority of one third to two fifths of the membership was reduced to fifteen per cent of the conference delegates in 1975.[41] This gave Cliff an unassailable position and enabled him to launch major initiatives – such as the Right to Work campaign of 1975 and the Socialist Workers' Party in January 1977 – without the need for a discussion within the ranks.

In reality the peak of IS membership and paper sales had passed before the SWP was launched. Not until 1983 did the print order for *Socialist Worker* climb above 30,000 and reach the position occupied in 1975. The attempt to build rank-and-file trade union organization under SWP control failed miserably and those that existed withered on a limb. It will be recalled that when in the 1920s the CP set out on this path at least 17 per cent of its 6,000 members were organized in factory branches: only 11 per cent of the much smaller IS membership were so organized when it embarked on a similar course. Ironically it was pointed out by two of Cliff's opponents within IS that one consequence of the Minority Movement was that the CP ended up with a 'militant defensive reformism' because it tried too hard to identify with a non-revolutionary move-ment.[42] By 1982 the SWP acknowledged that it had also suffered this way but the truth is that within a year of launching the national rank and file movement its objectives were defined in defensive terms: 'these rank and file organis-ations linked together in a national movement . . . will act primarily in defence of workers' interests.'[43] This was reflected in the pages of *Socialist Worker* which, in the 1970s became almost exclusively preoccupied with pay disputes and the celebration of trade union militancy.

The SWP became characterized by an uncritical 'workerism' which rejoiced in the belief that strikes measured the growth in workers' class consciousness: by a disdain for collaboration with other socialists since it was asserted that the SWP was the only party needed; and, as a corollary of the foregoing, a tendency to force every issue into the service of the class struggle in industry and the construction of the SWP. Para-doxically the organization was saved from decline by the anti-racist campaigns organized by the Anti-Nazi League which the SWP set up in November 1977 to combat the

influence of the fascist organizations on the streets. Thus an
issue not reducible to class and of much more varied sources
than factory politics was capable of mobilizing 80,000 people at
its carnival of April 1978 in spite of the attempt to use it as a
mere recruitment vehicle for the SWP. On the latter issue Cliff
was perfectly frank:

> where the question of the rank and file or the Anti-Nazi
> League being independent of the SWP was a problem for
> us a few years ago, at the present time it's not a problem
> at all. We simply always say quite clearly that the
> leadership of the Rank and File is the SWP. The lead-
> ership of the Anti-Nazi League is in reality the SWP and
> we don't give a damn.[44]

Fortunately the anti-racist struggle was far too important for
the SWP's self-interests to deter participants who disagreed
with its politics. But the determination to subordinate every
other interest to that of party building was exposed as petty
sectarianism elsewhere.

Thus in the interests of its own self-projection the SWP
stood candidates in the 1978 local elections in constituencies
where there was already a Socialist Unity candidate standing
on a 'class struggle left wing policy': the SWP rejected all
overtures for unity during this period and so succeeded in
gratuitously weakening the far left vote. Of course arithmetical
party building such as the SWP was now embarked upon has
never succeeded anywhere in creating mass socialist parties.
But the SWP had fallen into the trap which Hallas earlier
described as imagining 'that all that is necessary is to build a
new leadership around some sect or other and then offer it as
an alternative to the waiting workers.' They were also guilty of
'the assumption that the answers to all problems are known in
advance'. Nowhere was this clearer than in the attitude of the
SWP to the women's movement.

The SWP was perfectly incapable of acknowledging that sex
inequalities could not be reduced to those of class. There was
therefore no question of acknowledging the need for an

autonomous women's movement. When in 1979 the SWP set up
Women's Voice groups to enable its female members to meet
separately the object of the exercise was simply to speed up the
recruitment of feminists into the SWP. In fact it seems that the
SWP's socialist theory was no match for feminism and so the
Women's Voice group acted as the wrong sort of transmission – of
feminists ideas into the SWP.[45] The *Women's Voice* groups were
closed down by the SWP's 1981 conference because they
offended against Leninist organizational norms and failed to
recruit effectively. Once again the main lesson was that only the
working class, male and female, can advance the cause of
women and only through workplace battles could the working
class acquire the necessary consciousness.[46] There was
therefore nothing to learn from the 'autonomous women's
movement'; just as there had been nothing to learn from the gay
group which the organization suppressed in the early seventies.
The only politics which really mattered were those concerned
with building the SWP in the factories.

One reason why the organization ended up with all its eggs
in the same basket was its identification of the Labour Party as
an entirely superfluous organization from the standpoint of
working-class reforms. This was not an argument about the
insufficiency of reformism but a conviction, utterly ultra-leftist
in nature, that reforms simply could not now be extracted in
any meaningful sense. Perhaps the Labour Party could one day
be 'captured' for socialism but only in circumstances of mass
struggle which would render it irrelevant. In any other
circumstances it is, so the argument developed, 'a positive
danger' which threatens to switch the struggle from the
factories to the redundant polling booth.[47] Cliff added that the
Labour Party membership – largely inactive, middle-aged and
middle-class servants of an electoral machine – was not the
frustrated socialist force of entrist fable.[48] But the self-
indulgent rhetoric of 'Tweedledum and Tweedledee' which
was habitually employed to describe the Labour and Conservative parties was much more than an argument against entrism
or even a close association with the Labour constituency
parties: it represented the conviction that little or nothing
occupied the gap between factory politics and the socialist

revolution in terms of winnable positions and policies. When reforms came they were simply a spin-off of economic boom periods and Labour was an entirely secondary factor: during slumps it was incapable of resisting the roll-back of existing reforms. The deduction from this was that only the industrial struggle counted strategically.

There is no doubt that there was a pressing need to politicize trade union struggles and develop a socialist programme capable of resolving the crisis. The shop stewards looked realistic contenders for this task but only in association with a socialist party. Shop steward power was real enough – some 45 per cent of recorded strikes in the boom years were unofficial and by 1965 it was estimated that the number of shop stewards was around 175,000.[49] Cliff asserted that ten years later the number had grown to 300,000.[50] Since *In Place of Strife* (1969) – the Labour Government's industrial relations proposals – both Labour and Conservative governments were determined to reduce this power but only helped to provoke a massive strike wave. Though this was overwhelmingly economic in character it contained by British standards a large number of specifically political strikes against trade union legislation and in solidarity with those imprisoned for defying Heath's Industrial Relations Act. The flying pickets used during the successful miners' strike of 1972 and the wave of occupations following the work-in at Upper Clyde Shipbuilders also testified to the growing militancy in British industry.

But the mistake of the SWP was to believe that all this trade union militancy was inherently political. The organization was in any case too small to influence such spontaneous and widespread struggles as were actually taking place but its spokesmen and its press argued as if this was unnecessary anyway. Cliff perceived 'both the rise of shop stewards' organisations and the number of unofficial strikes [as] symptoms (among other things) of the common aspiration of the working class: towards workers' control'.[51] Hyman also argued that 'collective action represents a reaction against the economic exploitation and deprivation of control inherent in the institution of wage-labour and possesses a dimension of revolt which can never be wholly suppressed.'[52] In conditions of economic contraction, it was argued, wage militancy is necessarily political: 'pure-and-simply trade union activity *does* pose a substantial threat to the stability of the capitalist economy.'[53] This being so it was left to Cliff to argue that more means better: 'when workers ask for a few shillings a week in a single shop, the ideological veil covering the system as a whole is not pulled aside but when 100,000 workers demand a 20% rise to keep up with rising prices the class struggle moves to centre stage.'[54] Politics then was reduced to a nebulous demystification which emerges automatically from wage militancy. This is why *Socialist Worker* was content to cheer on the strikers as if the bigger the pay demand the greater the socialist commitment and consciousness involved. But even at the time it was plain that a widespread revulsion against the wages scramble was taking place within the working class and in this context it was possible to attribute responsibility for this free enterprise chaos to greedy and overweening trade union power. Here are the roots of Thatcherism not socialism.

The Cliff strategy was essentially syndicalist. The first national rank-and-file conference was called in March 1974 with 500 delegates representing 300 sponsoring bodies. The organizing committee which this established consisted entirely of IS members. But nobody seriously believed that an organization of less than four thousand members could lead a mass rank-and-file movement. The hope was that 'untrammelled by a reformist bureaucracy they (the union militants) will also be capable of challenging capitalism itself.'[55] This was the only way the initiative could be justified within IS. Internal dissenters argued that the rank-and-file movement 'is not the product of the realisation of leading sections of the class for unity in struggle, but rather the result of the behind-the-scenes activity of IS.'[56] Of course they were right. Proponents of the strategy had to believe that all would 'come out in the wash' as spontaneous wage militancy simultaneously converted the unions 'into organizations of real revolutionary struggle'[57] and transformed the Trotskyist group into a revolutionary party. The objective need for a national rank-and-file movement was supposed to stem from the alleged conflict of interests between shop floor workers and trade union leaders. The latter constituted a bureaucracy with a material stake in industrial peace; the former were always straining to break this leash.

The 'two souls' of the trade union official are explained by Cliff as follows: 'Even the most 'left' of the top officials is trapped by his social environment. Worse still, he has to work though an official machine whose personnel is very much a prisoner of this same environment. The official is, and feels that he is, a member not of the working class but of the middle class.'[58] Thus the emphasis is on an embourgeoisement of upwardly mobile trade unionists. But the tension between trade union leadership and the ranks also stems in large measure from the *function* of officialdom which precisely inclines the leaders to approach industrial conflict as a problem to be solved. The rules of the game are such that every trade union negotiator is structured to go for compromise. Trade unionism is based on such compromise and tends to reflect class differences rather than seek their abolition. By stressing the syndicalist theory of leadership betrayal the IS–SWP polemics against trade union bureaucracy implied that the distinction between left and right trade union leaders was of negligible consequence. Following Trotsky, Cliff argued that in conditions of economic crisis any trade union leader was faced with a simple choice of submitting to the rank and file – which is assumed to be militant – or becoming integrated into the state.[59]

Most of these arguments surfaced during the year-long miners' strike of 1984–5. According to the SWP's analysis 'Without the sabotage of the right-wing leaders and the failure of the left leaders, Thatcher could not have beaten the miners.'[60] Within the NUM bureaucracy, it is argued, only Arthur Scargill was prepared to mobilize the full strength of the union. Communist Party elements within the miners' leadership who were infected by the Eurocommunist strategy of building a broad democratic alliance were alleged to have undermined the executive's resolve for industrial confrontation.[61] Similarly Labour leftists such as Jack Taylor – leader of the Yorkshire miners – were guilty of restraining their own militants though in Taylor's case 'he was not in a strong enough position to campaign openly for surrender like Emlyn Williams' of the South Wales NUM. Here Callinicos and

Simons argue that 'lower-rank officials' were left to do the dirty work of lobbying for a return to work in Yorkshire.[62] Taylor is also found responsible for the fact that the Nottinghamshire coalfield was not closed down. If Scargill had campaigned in Nottinghamshire from the beginning and Taylor had not kept the Yorkshire militants at bay the Nottinghamshire miners would have stayed out. Even in Scotland the leadership 'blocked attempts to use the methods necessary to win'.[63] What was required, according to the SWP strategists, was more faith in the power of rank-and-file initiative and concerted mass picketing to close specific targets. Indeed the strike proved the need for independent rank-and-file organizations to provide an alternative to the perfidious national executive of the union. In the event: 'The final decision to go back was the result of a virtual coup by a 'soft left' current among NUM officials which crystallized during the course of the strike in opposition both to Arthur Scargill and to rank and file activists.'[64]

In this account – which is offered as an assessment of the relevant facts *after* the strike had been concluded – the material factors which contributed to the miners' defeat appear only as useful background information. All the emphasis is on the supposed conflict of interests between the NUM leadership and the rank and file. This is a curious procedure for Marxists who might be expected to situate the miners' defeat in the profoundly adverse context of year six of the Thatcherite offensive against the working class and the trade unions. The National Coal Board had eliminated around 41,000 miners' jobs in the three years before the strike began. Unemployment was some four million and a succession of trade unions had already been defeated since the formation of the first Thatcher government in 1979. Alongside this, Employment Acts designed to weaken the unions were introduced and a strategy to defeat the miners was conceived as early as 1978 in the Ridley Report. In accordance with this plan coal stocks were accumulated, legislation was introduced to cut the social security benefits of strikers and a so-called National Reporting Centre was created to provide a co-ordinated national response by the police against flying pickets. The government was also ready to use imported coal, oil-powered generators and non-union

haulage firms which together with the massive stocks of coal at
the power stations would ensure that any strike would have to
be a very long one if it was to have any chance of succeeding.
On top of this Cortonwood was selected as the first pit for
closure to provoke the start of the strike deliberately, nine
months before the next winter commenced.

The NUM leaders were also seriously handicapped by the
area incentive payment schemes which since 1977 had worked
to divide the union. Nottinghamshire – the second largest
coalfield – was in particular unlikely to respond to a strike call
over job losses. The miners in this coalfield, it will be recalled,
were fully behind the national strikes of 1972 and 1974. But
these were over pay. In 1977 they were among the most
militant opponents of the Social Contract – because it stood in
the way of bigger pay rises. A majority of them probably voted
for Arthur Scargill in the 1981 election for the NUM presidency. Thus this rank and file was second to none in the wage
militancy of the 1970s which the SWP applauded as proof of
class and socialist consciousness. But during the 1984–5
dispute over jobs they voted three to one against the strike and
around 5,000 of them elected to opt out of the political levy
which the union pays to the Labour Party. These facts dent
somewhat the SWP schema of a militant, politically radical
rank and file forever held back by trade union officialdom. On
the Nottinghamshire coalfield while most miners were
working, most branch officials and members of the area
council and executive were solidly in favour of the strike.
During the course of the strike there was a wholesale clear-out
of these left officials by the rank and file.

The SWP's analysis is no nearer the mark elsewhere. Arthur
Scargill is the example par excellence of a trade union leader at
least as left-wing as the rank and file. It was he who suggested a
strategy of strikes at selected highly productive pits with the
strikers financed by a levy on working miners. But this was
rejected by the NUM executive well before the strike began in
favour of winning the members' hearts and minds for a
national strike. In other words the executive placed its trust in
the solidarity of the rank and file.[55] Now Callinicos and Simons
– those advocates of the rank and file and critics of the NUM

leadership – might be expected to applaud this. But it seems
their faith has its limits: as soon as anyone proposes a ballot to
test the degree of commitment for strike action their trust in
the rank and file evaporates. 'Quite simply those who called for
a national ballot either before or at the NUM meeting on
Thursday 8 March [1984] did so because they didn't want a
strike.'[66] But this is quite simply wrong. Among those arguing
for a ballot on the union executive were left-wing *officials who
were personally against a ballot* but mandated by areas which
wanted one.[67] There is the sound of barrels being scraped
when we are told that the Left needs to be as pragmatic as the
Tories on the question of ballots: workers, it seems, are
reduced to passivity and isolation, the media would have
campaigned for a 'No' vote – and may have won!

But let the argument about ballots pass – NUM leaders
argued against a ballot on principle because it would allow men
to determine whether another's job survived or not – even
though five separate opinion polls between March and July 1984
showed that a majority for strike action existed. Let us return to
the leadership/rank and file dichotomy. Mick McGahey – one of
those allegedly softened by his alliance with the dominant Eurocommunist faction of the CP – was from the outset persuaded
that a ballot was irrelevant since the strike would sweep the
union by a 'domino effect' as one area after another came out.
The South Wales area – whose leadership is singled out by the
SWP as especially soft – was still 98 per cent solid after eleven
months of the strike and with not one man returned to work at
eight of the pits. None of the facts support the SWP's argument.

The miners' strikes in 1972, 1974 and 1981 were over within
weeks and days because they received the support of almost
the whole labour movement. In 1981 even the right-wing trade
union officials pledged their support and said that they could
not rule out a general strike. But by 1984 – with the notable
exceptions of the railwaymen, dockers and seamen – it did not
prove possible to summon up the rank-and-file support which
the *leaders* of the engineers and transport workers promised at
the TUC. Surely then, mass unemployment had something to
do with this? Of course bad leadership played its part –
conspicuously in the ineptitude of the Labour Party in allowing

'picket-line violence' and the issue of union democracy to hog the news reports on the strike. But the miners' strike demonstrates the limits of the SWP's obsession with the rank and file/trade union bureaucracy dichtomy. In reality the SWP is merely for the rank and file when it is militant and for the leadership when it is SWP.

Conclusion

When the rank-and-file strategy was belatedly abandoned in 1982 the logic on which it was based survived. The practical demise of the strategy is shown by table 4.1 which gives some indication of rank and file newspaper sales:

Table 4.1 Rank and file newspaper print orders

Newspaper	Orders (thousands)	
	1973	1982
Carworker	6.0	–
Collier	5.0	1.6
Hospital Worker	6.0	2.0
Platform	3.0	–
Textile Worker	1.5	–
Case-Con	5.0	
Journalists Charter	2.0	–
NALGO Action News	6.0	2.5
Rank and File Teacher	10.0	3.0
Scots Rank and File	2.0	–
Redder Tape	3.0	1.0
Technical Teacher	2.0	1.2
Dock Worker	5.0	–
GEC Rank and File	8.0	–
Building Worker	2.0	–

Predictably, traces of the rank and file groups remained among teachers, social workers and civil servants but there was none within the much more highly-esteemed industrial workers'

unions. Though the SWP leadership proved capable of a
degree of self-criticism this did not extend to the nub of the
issue – the contention that strikes are both the best index of
political consciousness among workers and its main cause:

> as soon as the National Rank and File Movement was
> launched at the March 1974 delegate conference the
> conditions which would have permitted it to flourish
> ceased to exist. The election of a Labour government took
> the political edge off wage militancy, which in any case
> collapsed thanks to the Social Contract. One sign of this
> was the collapse of most of our factory branches. In
> practice we abandoned the strategy, shifting to the Right
> to Work campaign. However when there was a revival of
> Rank and File militancy in 1977 we tried to relaunch the
> NRFM refusing to recognise the changes in the objective
> situation. This led us into ultra-left substitutionism.[68]

The problem, according to this account then, was the election
of a Labour government and its deal with the unions, the Social
Contract. Wage militancy had generated the necessary
political edge – the trouble was simply that conditions changed
and there was no longer sufficient wage militancy to sustain
the SWP's factory politics.

But if any of this were true the wave of wage militancy would
have brought enough activists into the SWP to sustain at least
the original 40 factory branches. As it is the erstwhile party of
socialist workers lost most of these factory cells and was forced
to fall back on the geographical branch. While it now admits
that it is 'quite simply too small and too marginal to influence
the direction of the Labour movement' it remains committed to
party building. The style of its politics – in particular the
single-minded concern to build the SWP in industry, the
reduction of all issues to class politics, the instrumental
attitude to other movements and organizations – remains
firmly Leninist. It is a dull Leninism content to admire and
repeat the master's words. In Cliff's case the emphasis is all on
the 'art' of leadership which we are told Lenin possessed to a
high degree and which manifested itself as a 'very keen

intuitive sense', a 'daring improvisation' and an ability to 'sense the mood of the masses'.[69] With Lenin, Cliff also evidently shares a 'readiness to bend the stick too far in one direction and then to go into reverse and bend it too far in the opposite direction'.[70] Tactics can thus be chopped and changed in accordance with the leader's special insight. But the basic ideology is immutable. Lenin's Comintern is still regarded as the highest expression of revolutionary organization and political wisdom – its faults residing only in the incapacity of the Western communists to fully assimilate the lessons of Bolshevism.[71] Accordingly the distinguishing characteristics of the Western democracies, as opposed for instance to dictatorship, can be dismissed as 'superficial differences of style and method.'[72]

5

The New Left and the Politics of the International Marxist Group

In this chapter I will examine the Trotskyist response to (and initiation of) political movements and campaigns which either originated outside, or were ignored by, the traditional mass organizations of the working class and their members. The emphasis so far has perforce been on the far left's pre-occupations with catastrophism, the Soviet Union, the communist parties, the Labour Party and the trade unions. In part this reflects the pre-war legacy of Marxist theory and political practice. But it also arises because the far left had virtually no other reference points during the 1940s, 1950s and early 1960s. By the late 1960s, however, the political situation was transformed as a great number of political campaigns and causes began to mobilize significant numbers of students, youth, women and ethnic minorities in Britain. As this was by no means confined to Britain and occurred in an increasingly explosive world political context the sections of the FI developed a political practice informed by the ISFI's thesis of 'the new rise in world revolution'. This period of FI history begins, however, with the re-unification of the ISFI and the American SWP, a process which began in 1956.

The re-unification of the Fourth International

The 1953 split in the FI, it will be remembered, was explained by the seceding organizations in terms of the ISFI's alleged 'liquidationist' tendencies and adaptations to Stalinism. The basis for these allegations was the optimistic analysis of the Malenkov reforms as proffered by Michel Pablo who, it was said, envisaged the self-reform of the Soviet bureaucracy. The tactic of entrism *sui generis* and the ISFI's mild condemnation of the Russian repression in East Germany were alleged to stem from Pablo's revisionist adaptations of Trotskyism.

However, the ISFI was more guarded when, in 1956, Kruschev's twentieth congress speech became known in the West. Though the secret speech was taken as confirmation of the bureaucracy's retreat in the face of 'pressure from the masses', the ISFI argued that the bureaucracy's self-reform could not be fully concluded unless 'the politicisation of the masses, going over to direct action, combines with a sharper differentiation, an actual break between the developing revolutionary wing and the more and more isolated thermidorean wing of the bureaucracy'.[1] In other words, the ISFI recognized the continuing validity and necessity of a 'political revolution' as Trotsky had posed it. The ISFI discounted the prospects of a return to the Stalinism of the Stalin era on the grounds that the international balance of forces made such a return 'impossible'. At the same time, the ISFI definitely excluded the possibility of the Soviet Communist Party (CPSU) becoming a genuine Leninist organization by a series of reforms from the top. It saw the Kruschev reforms rather as a bureaucratic self-defence: a return to Leninism would require a qualitative break involving whole sections of the CPSU rank and file.

Ernest Mandel was clear that 'the decisions of the 20th Congress favour the unleashing of . . . a violent movement of criticism and anti-Stalinist opposition', and he predicted the Hungarian revolution.[2]

When the Hungarian revolution finally erupted, the ISFI drew the lesson, yet again, that a revolutionary party was needed if such elemental upsurges were to lead anywhere. But the ISFI also used this occasion to produce its fullest statement yet on the necessity for a plurality of political parties in the post-revolutionary state as a precondition for realizing the original intent of Marx's 'dictatorship of the proletariat'.[3] It was Mandel, again, who wrote this statement. Beginning by noting that the ISFI's fifth world congress had reaffirmed its commitment to the 'freedom to organize all parties which place themselves within the limits of Soviet legality', Mandel proceeded to argue that:

> It is on this point that Trotsky, and ourselves still more clearly, go one step further than the fundamental documents of the Third International, and the Left Opposition. We believe that this step is justified by the Soviet experience. If the proletariat does not have the right to organise different parties, the tendency struggle inside the class party itself is inevitably stifled, for sooner or later this struggle threatens to end up by splitting the party. It is only if the revolutionary party honestly accepts the rule: all power to the workers' council, if it acts within the framework of these councils as an organized vanguard fighting for the triumph of its ideas, only then does the idea of the *dictatorship* of the proletariat take on its true meaning. Therefore, any other solution *ends up in bureaucratic arbitrariness* in which the party takes the place of the class, the Central Committee takes the place of the party and the secretary general of the Central Committee.

The ISFI did not limit itself to pedagogic productions either, since it did what it could to intervene through agitation in the Hungarian uprising via the distribution of propaganda within Hungary which expressed solidarity with the insurrectionists and called for a government of soviets. Both the theoretical and practical responses of the ISFI to the Hungarian revolt gave the lie to the ICFI's claim that the International Secretariat had become a liquidationist and Stalinist tendency. The analyses put forward by the American SWP and British SLL were substantially identical to those of the ISFI.[4]

Yet when, in 1957, the British Trotskyists moved a resolution on 'the situation in the world Trotskyist movement' it reiterated Healy's belief that there were two distinct wings – one orthodox (ICFI) and one 'Pabloite-Deutscher' (ISFI) – in the world movement.[5] The American SWP, however, had already re-established links with the ISFI via the good counsels of Leslie Goonwardene, a leader of the Ceylonese LSSP, the only mass Trotskyist party in the world. But the Healy organization had, if anything, hardened its attitude against the ISFI, maintaining that the latter 'could no longer be regarded as a trend within Trotskyism'. The Healy group reached this conclusion because of the ISFI's assertion that the epicentre of world revolution had shifted to the Third World. Healy's 'Euro-centrism' – another dispensable feature of his 'orthodox' reading of Trotsky – made him see this as the ultimate step in 'liquidationism'. For Healy, the ISFI had 'abandoned Lenin's and Trotsky's positions on independent working class actions and organisations, subordinating themselves to "progressive" nationalist leaders'. Healy's continued opposition to the ISFI was based on the latter's persisting commitment to entrism *sui generis* and its recent emphasis on Third World struggles. On the question of entrism *sui generis* the fifth congress of the ISFI had attributed the numerical strengthening of its national sections to the Pablo strategy. In 1961, the sixth congress argued that entrism *sui generis* had given the Trotskyists access to 'oppositional formations tending to organise themselves to carry out a tendency struggle' within crisis-ridden communist parties in the wake of 1956.

A more recent development concerned the ISFI's recognition in 1959 that the European working class was 'the *de facto* rearguard of the world revolution.'[6] The ISFI's attitude towards the Algerian and Cuban revolutions, in particular, was regarded by the SLL as final proof of its departure from Trotskyism.[7] Yet for the American SWP and the ISFI the Cuban revolution – or rather one's attitude towards it – became the 'acid test' for the re-unification of the FI. Having already agreed on the nature of the Hungarian revolution, its destruction and implications for revolutionary strategy, the ISFI and SWP had drawn close enough to regard agreement on Cuba as a final resolution of the differences of 1953. Even the SLL, sensing this convergence, proposed a parity commission which would begin talks on re-unification. But it also recognized that the differences of 1953 were being circumvented. Healy's response was to intensify his polemics against the

ISFI's alleged deviations from orthodoxy and chastise the SWP for 'treat[ing] . . . [Pabloism] as an accidental, theoretical deviation using wrong organisational methods. It [the SWP] is not able to give an account of the social and historical roots of this deviation.' In other words, for Healy the ISFI had become the representative of alien (that is bourgeois) class forces. Healy warned against purely organizational means for re-unification and desired that the parity commission discuss the differences between the ICFI and ISFI.[8]

However, the enthusiasm of the SWP and ISFI for the Cuban revolution swept the differences of 1953 to one side: in fact they even held out hopes for the conversion of Castro to a genuine (Trotskyist) socialist internationalism.[9] The isolation of the SLL was made complete as it adapted a position on the opposite extreme – regarding the Fidelistra as 'petty bourgeois nation-alists' who could not lead a socialist revolution because a Lenin-ist vanguard party was absent in Cuba. For the same reason, the SLL denied that a dictatorship of the proletariat existed in Castro's Cuba: 'the Castro regime is and remains a bonapartist regime resting on state capitalist foundations.' According to the SLL, the Castro regime was not qualitatively different from the Batista dictatorship. Castro's seizure of power was, for Healy, merely 'a political revolution which has transferred power from the hands of one class *to another section of that same class*'.[10]

The contrast between Healy's analysis and that of the parties to re-unification could not have been more acute since the SWP and the ISFI claimed that Castro had 'unconsciously' realized the programme of permanent revolution and had forged a revolutionary party in the process of revolution. On this basis the SWP and ISFI re-unified in 1963 to form the United Secretariat of the Fourth International (USFI). The SLL regarded this fusion as totally unprincipled and directly responsible for the capitulation in July 1964 of the LSSP which entered the bourgeois coalition of Mrs Bandaranaika in Ceylon. Though this move was taken against the instructions of the USFI and though the LSSP was promptly expelled from the International, Healy regarded the whole affair as symp-tomatic of the theoretical and political bankruptcy of the International leadership.[11]

It was certainly true, as Healy contended, that the re-unification talks between the ISFI and SWP did not confront the reasons for the split in 1953. What the re-unification did demonstrate, however, was the theoretically insubstantial nature of the original differences – differences which ten years later were patched over via agreement on the Cuban revolution. The sense of great expectations behind the re-unification of 1963 complements the sense of frustrated impotence which fuelled the split of 1953: the common element in both events was the desire to overcome the FI's political isolation, by short cuts.

Origins of the International Marxist Group

The split of 1953 left the ISFI without a section in Britain. It was for this reason that the Committee for the Regroupment of the British Section of the Fourth International was set up in 1955,[12] by sympathizers of the ISFI and several members of foreign sections of the ISFI who happened to be resident in Britain. Together these published a mimeographed journal called *Fourth International*. In 1956 the committee joined forces with the International Socialist Group (ISG) – an organization led by Ted Grant, Jimmy Deane and Sam Bornstein, who had all been members of the old RCP Majority. The new group became known as the Revolutionary Socialist League and worked within the Labour Party attempting an entrism which avoided the mistakes of Healy's Club. The fifth world congress of the ISFI in 1957 recognized the RSL as the British section of the International.

However this arrangement did not last long, for despite the fusion of the two groups, the ISG worked independently of the committee. Tactically the groups were confused, with entrism being conducted in the Liverpool and Glasgow Labour parties around the journal *Socialist Current* and independent activity elsewhere through the journal *Workers International News*. During 1958 and 1959 these organizational differences sprouted differences of a 'political' nature. The old ISG leadership opposed the ISFI's line on the colonial revolution and the danger of world war while the committee members supported it. The latter argued for united work with other entrists within the Labour Party and CND, while Grant's followers stressed perspectives of economic slump and political crises within the labour movement.

Of those who opposed Grant most left the RSL to join Healy's organization. Only six people, including Pat Jordan, withdrew from the RSL in 1961 to distribute a Fourth International journal called *The Internationalist* and it is from this group, based in Nottingham, that the later IMG can trace its history. In 1961 they called themselves the International Group and became the *de facto* section of the FI in Britain despite the fact that Grant's RSL continued to receive financial assistance from the American SWP. This confusion persisted until the USFI engineered their re-unification in 1964. Once again, however, the ostensibly fused groups worked independently with the former International Group members publishing *The Week*. This time the RSL did work with other organizations – most notably the *Socialist Review* Group – in joint entrist work organized by the journal *Young Guard* which they sold in competition with the SLL's *Keep Left* in the Labour Party's Young Socialist organizations.[13] Competition between the RSL and SLL is alleged to have caused the latter to use intimidatory methods in Wandsworth Labour Party Young Socialists. It was for this reason, according to Pat Jordan, that the RSL did nothing to assist the SLL when it was subsequently 'witch hunted' out of the Young Socialists in 1965. Certainly this occasioned the formation of a faction, which opposed the Grant leadership in the same year. Led by Jordan, this opposition became known as the International Marxist Group; but both this and the RSL were reduced to the status of sympathizers with the USFI by the eighth world congress in 1965, causing the RSL to sever all remaining links with the International. Thus the IMG remained the sole sympathizing section of the USFI in Britain, and consisted of those who had set up the committee of 1955, and who had subsequently formed the International Group. Since 1965 the RSL, which currently promotes the Militant tendency within the Labour Party, has had nothing whatever to do with the USFI.

The IMG tendency at first channelled its energies into the Nottingham City Labour Party where, according to Jordan, it 'won hegemony' and elected Ken Coates to the presidency. This was used as a base from which to launch national campaigns in the labour movement such as the Medical Aid to Vietnam Committee. According to Jordan, 'by this means we circulated the whole of the Labour Party and trade union movement with an appeal to give money to a fund which was linked with the NLF [National Liberation Front of Vietnam] . . . as a result dozens of contacts with sections of the Labour movement were made which were extremely useful in the early days of the Vietnam Solidarity Campaign'. Indeed, for such a small group of people obscurely connected with the FI the IMG tendency was extremely successful in promoting campaigns which drew widespread support from within the mass organizations of labour and won the sponsorship of notables in the movement.

The Week gained the support of Bertrand Russell, Ernie Roberts MP and Lawrence Daly, among others. The IMG's position in South Nottingham CLP enabled it to forward a motion calling for solidarity with the NLF, which *The Week's* editor Ken Coates championed at the Labour Party annual conference in 1965. Coates and *The Week* were also deeply involved from the beginning with the publication of *Voice of the Unions* and its offshoots which developed from an initiative by Ernie Roberts and Frank Allaun. In April 1964 the *Voice* news- paper promoted a conference on workers' control which won the support of Hugh Scanlon and Jack Jones. In addition to these activities the IMG emphasized Vietnam Solidarity work to which it had been directed by the USFI in 1965. In this the IMG members joined forces with the Bertrand Russell Peace Found- ation and the War Crimes Tribunal. Russell collaborated with leading IMG members in launching the Vietnamese Solidarity Campaign (VSC) in June 1966.[14]

Despite the prominence of IMG members in these public activities, the organization itself was still virtually unheard of as a consequence of its entrist status.[15] The perspective of *The Week* was that 'a mass left would arise in the Labour Party once Labour was in power'. Even after four years of the Wilson government the IMG's perspective remained unchanged. Yet during this same period the propaganda campaign which the IMG waged in VSC paid off in several respects. It succeeded in destroying the pacifist line of the Communist Party and the latter's vehicle (the British Council for Peace in Vietnam) and replaced these with its own slogan ('Victory to the NLF') and a mass campaign led by the VSC. The first VSC demonstration of 22 October 1967 mustered 5,000 supporters. In March 1968 25,000 were called on to the streets before the massive show of strength in October of the same year when over 100,000 marched under the slogan 'Victory to the NLF'. Most of those mobilized by the VSC were students and youth outside the Labour Party; indeed the trade union and labour movement – far from showing any initiative on the Vietnam issue – displayed, if anything, a waning interest. Labour Party conference agendas for the years 1965 to 1968 show amendments on Vietnam numbering 19, 51, 13 and *one* respectively.[16]

The strains between these two wings of IMG activity – its engagement with the traditional mass organizations versus its success in mass mobilization of a seemingly new vanguard – soon caused splinters within the group. The organization split in October 1967 when *The Week* supported an unofficial dock strike opposed by the TGWU leadership. According to Pat Jordan, Ken Coates favoured Jack Jones's stand against the strike. Because of the latter's importance to the campaign for workers' control, Coates is alleged to have temporized on this issue.[17] With Coates's subsequent departure from IMG, the latter lost its influence over the militants it had done much to mobilize in the workers' control conferences and since 1968 – when the conferences were formalized as the Institute for Workers' Control – the IMG has played no part in that movement. The fact that IMG failed to recruit even a handful of these trade union militants prior to the split must, in part at least, be attributed to its secretiveness as an entrist formation.

For the same reason the IMG gained fewer recruits from the VSC than the International Socialists. The IS was, like the IMG, at first connected with VSC through its involvement in the Labour Party Young Socialists. But unlike the IMG, the IS quickly withdrew from the Labour Party when it became clear that VSC supporters were, in the main, non-members of the

LPYS. It was the IS which wanted the VSC to orientate for working-class support while the IMG fought to keep it a single-issue campaign. In the event IMG won on this question and the logic of its commitment to the VSC forced it to give up entrism in 1969. By this time the IMG identified the student movement as its best field of activity and, in belated recognition of this, launched a youth organization – the Spartacus League – in 1970. The IS, which succeeded in gaining far more recruits from student campaigns, departed from the Vietnamese Solidarity Campaign in order to concentrate on the trade union struggle against *In Place of Strife*. In this way the IS was able to avoid becoming a purely student organization. Once again, the IMG only belatedly sought a similar route (during the miners' strike of 1972) and paid the price for its tardiness. But the IMG's major weakness in these years was part of the legacy of British Trotskyism which can be summarized as the view that any upsurge in working-class consciousness would automatically channel itself into the constituency labour parties and trade union branches. The concomitant error was the belief that any tendency struggle inside the Labour Party reflected an upsurge in workers' class consciousness. The IMG supposed, therefore, that protest struggles would be led by the working class. Though this was belied by the experience of VSC (and even, to some extent, CND) the IMG persisted in this mistake until the former became a spent force.

The new rise in world revolution

A *New Society* survey of 1968 showed that a majority of the VSC's rank and file had been active in CND.[18] Apart from personnel the two campaigns share a number of other characteristics which were to become typical of far left political interventions in the late sixties and seventies. Such movements tended to arise around single-issue campaigns of loose, *ad hoc* organization. They relied, for the most part, on the impact of mass demonstrations and appealed principally to the young. The political convictions of the 'membership' of these campaigns can best be described as liberal/libertarian. Within VSC, for example, Pat Jordan identified three tendencies, including those represented by IMG and IS. Since IMG and IS combined forces numbered no more than 1,000, it is instructive that the third tendency, according to Jordan, consisted of 'spontex' devotees imitating the American new left, i.e. believers in the virtues of spontaneous direct action. It is certain that the latter were more numerous than the Leninists among VSC's rank and file. Far from relying on the membership of the mass working-class organizations, these campaigns drew on new agencies of protest such as women, students, youth and ethnic minorities. The new rhetoric tended to be culturalist, anti-bureaucratic, idealist and anti-technological in content, rather than economistic. In complex ways these movements were connected with revived interest in alternative life-styles and even the fashion and popular music of the 1960s.

The IMG's involvement in such campaigns virtually comprised the whole of its independent activity after its withdrawal from the Labour Party. By 1970 its problem was how to relate the predominantly student base of its organiz-ation to the working class. The answer appeared to lie in the slogan 'from the periphery to the centre' – a slogan which echoed the USFI's conviction that revolutionary advance was proceeding from the Third World to the advanced capitalist countries. On this basis the IMG activists became preoccupied with campaigns on Ireland, racism, feminism, Vietnam, the organization of school students etc., aimed at immigrants, women, youth and the unemployed. By 1971 IMG had accumulated over 30 front organizations, approximately one for every eleven members of the organization.[19] The cost of this was an ultra-activism which reduced IMG to a federation of campaigns instead of a stable cadre.

The amount of political activity required of IMG members in these years can only be guessed, but it may assist the reader's imagination to note the following areas of activity expected of a member in 1978 (by which time activism had become 'normal' again and, therefore, typical of the far left as a whole). Assuming that the member is a teacher and female she might be expected to engage in the following three areas of work:

Activity related to work
(a) trade union activity (branch meetings, trades council, official positions)
(b) attendance of IMG teachers' fraction meetings (fortnightly)
(c) attendance of *Socialist Teacher* public meetings (monthly)
(d) *Socialist Teacher* sales campaigns among colleagues
(e) *Socialist Challenge* sales campaigns among colleagues
(f) sundry conferences, demonstrations, lobbies, etc.

Activity related to IMG (internal life and external work)
(a) branch meetings and 'aggregates'
(b) *Socialist Challenge* public sales (weekly)
(c) private study of journals (*International, Imprecor, Labour Focus on Eastern Europe*) and internal bulletins
(d) pre-conference discussions, literature and meetings (every two years for periods of three months)
(e) branch educationals
(f) sundry mobilizations for various campaigns

Special activities
(a) women's caucus within IMG
(b) feminist literature (*Socialist Woman*, etc.)
(c) women's movement (autonomous) meetings
(d) sundry conferences, campaigns, demonstrations, etc.

Such activism leaves little time for anything else and may account for high membership turnovers within the groups. It is also possibly both cause and consequence of the disproportionately student and recently ex-student compositions of the organizations. But, more importantly, the activism required of members – and even sympathizers – of the Marxist left underlines the 'otherness' of these organizations in the context of the British political culture. The commitment which is required of those transferring their political loyalties to 'revolutionary socialism' involves a change in political style which transforms aspects of the recruits' life-style. This undoubtedly acts as a barrier to the recruitment even of those who are further left than the Labour left. The high turnover of membership on the far left suggests also that even those who make the break with conventional politics have enormous difficulties in sustaining it (notwithstanding the strict selection procedure of groups like the IMG which operate a six-month candidate status for new members).

Both the IS and IMG had missed whatever opportunity for organizational and political advance CND might have afforded them. CND itself, of course, must be regarded as a failure, not simply measured against its own objectives but also by virtue of the fact that the call for disarmament was driven underground again for nearly two decades as the campaign petered out. Nigel Young pinpoints the cause of CND's demise in the absence of any theory of change or positive strategy, a failing which was 'reflected in and reinforced by the theoretical lack, and absence of strategic vision, in CND as an organisation'. It was this absence, argues Young, 'which enabled Marxist sects or organisations to successfully take over or supersede some of the offshoots of nuclear pacifism in the later 1960s moving into a vacuum of ideas and tactics'.[20] However, since the SLL mainly kept aloof from CND after its initial involvement and the CPGB only became involved three years after the movement began, it was the latter which was left in control of British pacifism as the campaign for nuclear disarmament fizzled out. By 1966 both the IMG and the IS had emerged to lead CND's past support successfully away from pacifism under the militant pro-Vietcong slogans of VSC.

From this development the IMG and the IS attempted to launch youth organizations which would win support for Leninist ideas. On the basis of the spontaneous student unrest of the late 1960s the IS launched a Revolutionary Socialist Student Federation in 1968 to rival the explicitly apolitical National Union of Students. In this the IS was supported by the IMG. Indeed the success of the French section of the FI – the *Jeunesse Communiste Revolutionnaire* (JCR) – in the events of May 1968 in Paris inspired the IMG to envisage a similar scenario in Britain which it described as 'toward the concept of Student Power'.[21] The desire to imitate the French events was present at the first conference of the RSSF which 'adopted an action programme around the Student Red Base concept'. The full measure of the IMG's preoccupation and enthusiasm for 'student power' is revealed by its support for the notion of universities transformed into 'red bases'. In the late sixties the organization projected an image and style of politics not dissimilar to the politics of 'extra-parliamentary opposition', which for a time took root in Germany. The IMG's collaboration with libertarians in the publication of *Black Dwarf* (between 1968 and 1970) and the Third Worldist and student emphasis of *Red Mole* after 1970 were symbols of a political practice which gave *de facto* support to the view that the European working class was no longer a revolutionary force. The political style of IMG at this time was suggestive of Marcuse rather than Lenin.

This political style was never, however, given theoretical justification. Indeed it was simultaneous with these practical orientations that the IMG launched a propaganda campaign to promote Leninism. The old *Black Dwarf* editorial board split because of the IMG's determination to create a Leninist youth organization – the Spartacus League – in 1970.[22] When *Red Mole* was launched it was a specifically IMG publication – its first – and it immediately promoted a Leninist line. The FI had developed an explanation of the student revolt which attempted to situate the phenomenon within an orthodox framework.

As early as 1965 Mandel had attempted to theorize an alternative strategy for socialism which escaped the bounds of catastrophist perspectives. He had argued that 'as far as economic crisis or catastrophe is concerned . . . there are strong reasons why this can be avoided by neo-capitalism for a considerable time to come'.[23] Mandel argued that while, 'for the next decade', catastrophic crises would probably be avoided in Western Europe, the system would periodically face other economic and social problems. Mandel instances high wages, automation, increasing alienation, income policies, 'managed' or provoked unemployment and so on as examples of the 'new' problems of capitalism. These would provide opportunities for a strategy of 'structural reforms' as advanced during the Belgian general strike of 1960–1. Such changes, he maintained, would be anti-capitalist in nature and part of a transition to socialism. The 'explosion' of May 1968 was, for Mandel, a vindication of this analysis.[24]

According to Mandel the role of students had been to 'detonate' a crisis in late capitalism by their fight to reform the system of higher education. This crisis had developed into a pre-revolutionary situation when the political and economic demands of 10 million striking workers were added to those of the students. For Mandel the May events had vindicated the central political positions of the Fourth International.[25]

Mandel explained the student revolt in terms of the insufficient material conditions and facilities of the institutions of higher education combined with the authoritarian structure of such institutions and the ideological bias of academic courses. This amounted to no more than a description of the students' avowed grievances; but to this, Mandel added an analysis of the long-term changes which the capitalist economy was beginning to place on the universities. He argued that this amounted to 'the demand for technically specialised labour and the demands of the swelling state apparatus'.[26] According to Mandel (and, for that matter, most of the revolutionary left) the universities were subordinating themselves to the requirements of capital and, at the same time, failing to expand fast enough to satisfy the burgeoning demand for higher education. The result, acccording to this analysis, was overcrowded campuses of disaffected students who were increasingly critical of the material and ideological shortcomings of their education. Mandel also stressed the proletarianization of post-graduate occupations and the disenchantment and alienation which resulted from it. He advocated that the 'revolutionary student movement' should use the university for the benefit of anti-capitalist workers' movements in need of information and research which would weaken the system. It is easy to see now that this analysis was almost wholly wrong but hindsight was not required to identify the childish political positions which were drawn from it.

The IMG echoed Mandel's conviction that the universities could become 'centres of opposition to the capitalist system'.[27] This faith was reflected in the RSSF's 'six point action programme' which demanded 'an end to bourgeois ideology . . . in courses and lectures'. Alongside this giddiness IMG reaffirmed the Marxist conviction that 'at present there is no perspective for the development of a mass revolutionary base outside the traditional working class movement'; and it spoke of 'our long term perspective for the emergence of a mass revolutionary party [which] remains a split in the ranks of social democracy involving, necessarily in Britain, a really significant section of the trade union movement'.[28] There was, however, a growing gap between such statements and the IMG's political practice. For despite its entrist status (which it terminated in 1969) the IMG was clearly preoccupied with movements and campaigns without significant connections to the Labour movement. The gap between the IMG's formal and actual policies was resolved in favour of its *de facto* practice when it became an independent organization and launched *Red Mole*.

The first issue of *Red Mole*, in 1970, declared its intention to help 'the student left . . . to generate a far greater self-consciousness', though it also spoke of a 'long-term aim' to create a 'revolutionary youth organization rather than a purely student one'.[29] The importance which *Red Mole* ascribed to its largely student readership was quickly attested by a proliferation of articles on the 'campus revolt' (the first issue carried articles on Lancaster, Oxford and Warwick Universities plus coverage of Jerry Rubin's trial and Japanese students' struggles). The second issue of *Red Mole* was entirely devoted to an exposition of a particularly ultra-leftist version of 'vanguardism'.

This latter took the form of a long article by Robin Blackburn entitled 'Let it Bleed'.[30] According to Blackburn 'the only principled course for revolutionary socialists during the coming election will be an active campaign to discredit both of Britain's large capitalist parties'. The FI's conventional wisdom which justified entrism by reference to the organizational ties between the trade unions and the Labour Party was specifically rejected. 'To say that the Labour Party is "organically" linked to the working class is thoroughly confused and confusing . . . because it has a totally bourgeois leadership [it is] *organically* linked only to the political institutions of the ruling class'.

For Blackburn, only the cash nexus linked the Labour and trade union bureaucracies. But, he argued, the significance of the Wilson governments lay in the fact that this experience had 'further weakened the hold of the Labour Party over the British working class and it is this fact that is of capital importance to any Marxist evaluation of this Party and the coming election'. Furthermore, says Blackburn, the Labour left, equally discredited, cannot, given the contraction of the economy, pose a serious alternative to the Tories. In these circumstances, he argued, there is no reason to suppose a Tory government would be worse than Labour.

Blackburn's article – supposedly a personal statement – is of interest here for the response it drew from the IMG leadership. Pat Jordan criticized some of its points but argued against a Labour vote just as Blackburn had. Later, with the election of a Tory government, *Red Mole* declared 'the old Tories are back' and Tariq Ali explained that

> For the workers the electoral victory of the Conservative Party represents a marginal set-back: marginal in the sense that it cannot be predicted categorically that the policies which the Tories adopt will be any different from those practised by Mr Wilson's government, but a set-back nonetheless because a Labour Party in opposition will once again be able to sustain the illusion that it is the only alternative to Toryism and in the absence of a real alternative it will not be easy to combat this illusion. For this reason alone a Labour victory would have been preferable.

In thus minimizing the differences between Labour and Conservative Ali, like Blackburn, argued as if the party's working-class constituency was merely the dupe and passive victim of an elaborate con-trick. There is no doubt that IMG's sectarian attitude to Labour (which it subsequently repudiated via Blackburn's and Ali's self-criticism)[31] was a manifestation of a wider ultra-leftism which affected the USFI in the early 1970s as well as groups such as the International Socialists.

As noted, the USFI, since its formation in 1963, had come to emphasize the importance of struggles for national liberation in the Third World.[32] The significance it attached to the Cuban model of revolution became clear through the FI's uncritical support of guerillaism in Latin America.[33] By its ninth congress, in 1969, it could declare that 'the only realistic perspective for Latin America is that of armed struggle which may last for long years.'[34] According to an international oppositional tendency led by the American SWP and some Latin American Trotskyist leaders like Hugo Blanco, this line, in practice, sanctioned kidnappings, ransoms, 'Robin Hood' redistributions by armed cliques and such like and stemmed from the FI's idolatry of Guevara's Bolivian adventure and the 'style' of 1968. This, they claimed, had infected the IMG since 'the same line of reasoning is apparent in the uncritical view taken of the use of terrorist tactics in Ireland, particularly those involving the Provisionals, the more extreme and less political wing of the IRA'.[35] The IMG's attitude to the Labour Party during the general election of 1970, then, must be viewed in this context. (During the 1970 election IMG members urged that Labour meetings should be broken up. At the same time the group talked a great deal about the coming 'armed struggle'.) The FI's ultra-leftist mood had developed, by 1973, to the point where it could claim that socialist revolution was approaching in Europe not just in broad historical perspective '. . . but even from a conjunctural point of view'.[36] Before pursing this, however, it is important to trace the development of the far left's attitude to Northern Ireland – especially that of the IMG.

Northern Ireland

The far left was as unprepared as any other section of the British political spectrum for the eruption of generalized political struggles in Northern Ireland in 1969. This accounts for the confused and shifting slogans and sympathies which these Marxist groups produced during the subsequent decade. An instance of this is the response of the IS to the anti-Catholic pogroms of 1969 in which it called for the intervention of the

British army to defend the minority. The IMG roundly condemned the International Socialists for committing the basic error,
in the Marxist view, of entrusting the coercive arm of the bourgeois state with the defence of the 'anti-imperialist' section of
the Northern Ireland community.

The IMG's response to the political crisis of the Stormont
regime was to declare 'Permanent revolution reaches UK'.[37]
The editorial of *International* however, recognized that 'a revolutionary leadership has yet to be built and no working-class
organisations have won any honours in the recent situation'. If
a contradiction exists in simultaneously proclaiming the existence of permanent revolution and the absence of a revolutionary party, the IMG ignored the problem by asserting that
'the left must support the right of the Irish people to use
whatever methods they think fit in the struggle for self-
determination' (my emphasis). From the beginning, the IMG
was aware that such support would include justification for the
armed struggle against B-specials, Paisleyites, and British
troops. Pat Jordan argued that apart from support for such
struggles as the Catholics felt fit to undertake in promotion
of their own interests, British socialists must regard as their
main task an agitation for the withdrawal of British troops
since the latter will 'inevitably be ... used against the
Irish people'.

During 1970 the IMG devoted much of its energies to the
education of its own membership and sympathizers on the
historical background to the Northern Ireland crisis.[38] As with
the rest of the organized left (excluding, of course, the Labour
Party), the IMG viewed the conflict as a crisis of British
imperialism. On this basis the IMG formed the slogans
'Self-determination for Ireland' and 'Withdraw all British
troops now'.[39] Otherwise as we have observed, the IMG had
resolved to support *any* tactics adopted by the Republican
movement and had reduced its role to that of a cheer-leader
for the Catholic minority. This became clear when the IRA
campaign moved from defensive to offensive postures.

In response to these developments the IMG began to publish
articles by Lenin and Trotsky in which the Bolsheviks had
taken a sympathetic view of terrorism. Despite the rather

exceptional nature of these extracts it is now clear that they were intended to prepare the IMG's supporters for a position of support for the Provisional IRA's terrorist campaign. In *International* the IMG's preamble to articles by Trotsky (on the murder of a Nazi official by a boy named Grynszpan) and Lenin (on Friedrich Adler's attempted assassination of the Austrian Prime Minister) warns against 'those who simply condemn terrorist actions out of hand and forget the obligations of Marxists to defend those who are struggling against exploitation and oppression even when those who are actually engaged in the struggle adopt methods which Marxists know will not attain the aims which are being fought for'. The question of classical Marxism's general attitude to terrorism was also dealt with in an article supporting the Quebec separatists.[40] By 1971 the IMG insisted that revolutionaries 'must unconditionally support the struggle of the IRA against British imperialism and its puppets'.[41] IMG's principal slogan was now 'Victory to the IRA',

Though, at first sight, the slogan 'Victory to the IRA' appears to be a logical extension of the IMG's initial 'unconditional support' (for whatever methods the nationalist Irish might choose to adopt) it in fact committed the IMG to a new political position. For it implied that victory *could* be achieved by terrorist tactics. This evolution in the IMG's 'understanding' of the Northern Ireland conflict was helped along by the USFI's enthusiasm for guerrilla warfare in the Third World. The IMG's relatively successful Vietnam Solidarity Campaign appears to have been the model for the Irish Solidarity Campaign, which it launched in 1970. 'Victory to the NLF' was replaced by 'Victory to the IRA'. And yet the IMG had earlier displayed an awareness of the political shortcomings of the Provisional IRA in so far as it recognized that 'Liberation for the North cannot be seen except in the *general* context of a republican movement throughout the country'.

The same article went so far as to claim that 'the fate of the Irish revolution in the immediate future will depend on the ability of the Irish revolutionary groupings to capture the leadership of the republican movement and to indivisibly weld together that movement with the struggle in the North'.[42]

As it became clearer that the Provo campaign was politically backward and confined to terrorist offensives in the North of Ireland so, paradoxically, was the IMG's support for this campaign increasingly uncritical. While, in late 1970, the IMG was still awaiting the 'constitution of the Irish revolutionary vanguard party', by 1971 it had seemingly discovered it in the Provisionals.

To some extent the change in political line may express the IMG's frustrated attempts to find alternatives to the IRA.[43] However the fact that these were also described as 'urban guerrilla' groups attests to the IMG's generally favourable view of that tactic. This was given some plausibility by the Provisional IRA's own early emphasis on *defence* of the Catholic ghettoes.[44] It may also have been that the IMG was unclear about the real situation in Northern Ireland. This is suggested by the statement that the Official IRA 'will play a much greater role in liberating Ireland than will the Provisionals'[45] At the same time the IMG's principal slogan ('Victory to the IRA') aligned it with the Provisionals – since it was they who promoted the military campaign. Furthermore all IMG statements on Ireland stressed the obligation *unconditionally* to support the IRA. Indeed the IMG castigated other far left organizations which distanced themselves from Provo terror.[46]

This was the situation, then, when the Provisional IRA extended its bombing campaign to London in 1972. The IMG had already isolated itself from the rest of the far left by its insistence on the centrality of unconditional support for the Provos. The refusal of the IS to go along with this logic made joint work on Ireland impossible. Despite the fact that the Anti-Internment League (AIL, set up by IS in the summer of 1971) also stood for 'Troops out now' the IMG stood apart from it: 'We would argue . . . that it is necessary to transform the present campaign against internment and for the withdrawal of British Troops into a campaign which is in active solidarity with those leading the fight against British imperialism. And in the meantime we will continue to build and support the Irish Solidarity Campaign.'[47] In practice this meant that in defence of its shibboleth of 'unconditional support' the IMG *was* the Irish Solidarity Campaign, and vice versa.

Occasionally the IMG's own statements demonstrated the illogic of its slogans on Ireland. Thus, according to *Red Mole* 'it is now clear that the split in the Republican Movement was the tragic and politically confused result of an attempt to graft a reformist programme on to the Republican tradition by the Officials'.[48] The same authors were equally clear that: 'the Provisionals . . . are bourgeois nationalists'.[49] Justification for the latter's bombing campaign was provided by the (spurious) argument that the Provisionals received mass support from the Catholics of Northern Ireland. According to Bob Purdie and Gerry Lawless (the IMG's authorities on Ireland) this meant that the campaign of bombings was 'not terroristic'.

It was this reasoning which prevented the IMG from supporting the AIL (which had proved capable of mobilizing 20,000 around its democratic slogans). In self-justification the IMG argued that 'we reject a campaign on self-determination and Troops Out because it can be very easily taken up and transformed into a "Bring the boys home" campaign based on *liberal* issues with only a negative impact'. It is difficult to take this argument seriously since both demands appeared among the six-point programme of the Irish Solidarity Campaign. Clearly it was the IMG determination to support the military campaign of the Provisionals which cut the organization off form all significant forces concerned with Ireland. Instead of fighting effectively against the conspiracy of silence on Northern Ireland by taking up specific issues (such as internment) the IMG's efforts were consumed in sectarianism.

The imposition of direct rule in 1972 took the ground away from the AIL. Strangely it was precisely at this point that the IMG entered the campaign. By now the AIL had degenerated to a political introversion obsessed with programmatic matters and, for what it was worth, was won over to the IMG's modified slogan: 'Solidarity with the IRA'. In 1973 the IS withdrew from the League. The IMG's 'Solidarity' slogan was put forward in recognition of the illusory content of its predecessor: that is, in belated recognition of the fact that the IRA campaign could not achieve 'victory'. The IMG continued, however, to be purblind concerning the Provos' use of terror. The AIL's 'Statement on the London bombing' makes this clear: 'We refuse to condemn *any* [my emphasis] action carried out in Britain by the IRA.'

Within the IMG there were voices of dissent from this policy -but they failed to change the leadership's line.[50] The members of 'the tendency' desired an orthodox Marxist line on IRA terrorism whch would put the IMG political position closer to that of the International Socialists. The latter regarded the IRA's bombing campaign in Britain as an instance of the contempt displayed by the 'middle class' Provisional leadership towards the working class of Britain. As for the IRA campaign in Ireland the IS had this to say:

> The attitude of socialists towards both wings of the IRA has to be similar: support for them insofar as they protect the Catholic population against the British troops and sectarian attacks, unconditional support for their right to throw out the British troops even if we do not agree with the tactics they use, but no illusion that 'Victory to the IRA' is possible in modern Ireland on the basis of the republican ideology.[51]

However, even this statement ignores the *indiscriminate* nature of Provo terror in Ireland itself during the early 1970s. It is this aspect of the IRA campaign of that time which renders the classical Marxist position on terrorism inapplicable.[52] This 'classical' line was largely developed in Tsarist Russia in relation to acts of violence against leading members of the governing class under political conditions in which legal politics was impossible. In this situation Marxists declared the futility of individual acts of terror and the impotence of terrorism as a method for achieving social change. At the same time their political sympathies were clearly with the oppressed who were driven to such acts of violence. But the Provisional IRA offensive in Northern Ireland during the greater part of the 1970s involved the bombing of bus depots, hotels, restaurants, public houses, and so on, and led to the deaths and maimings of people who could in no sense be described as 'the oppressors'. Thus even the IS's political line on IRA terror – in eliding the indiscriminate nature of the Provisional campaign

in Northern Ireland – was well wide of the mark. It thus
demonstrates the even greater political confusion of the IMG,
whose unconditional support for the IRA aligned it with an
organization which engaged even in openly sectarian killings.

Both IMG and IS began, from late 1973, to stress the slogan
'Troops out now' in their work on Ireland.[53] The 'Troops out'
movement was launched at Fulham Town Hall in October
1973 by individuals, acting on their own account, from IMG,
IS, Big Flame, and the CP. Ironically, it seems that the IMG
came to rediscover the potential of the 'Troops out' slogan only
after an army wife collected 46,000 signatures supporting this
demand which was posed along racist and chauvinist lines.
The press publicity received by the campaign did something to
raise the issue of British military involvement in Northern
Ireland – an issue chiefly ignored by the mass political
organizations.

In taking up the 'Troops out' slogan the IMG devoted less
time and space for discussion on the character of the Provo
campaign. Though its advocacy of 'unconditional' support for
the IRA remained formally intact, the London fire bombings of
August 1973 were described as 'tactically mistaken' by *Red
Weekly*.[54] Yet in reporting the second TOM conference nine
months later (May 1974) *Red Weekly* described the Marxist Fred
Halliday (a principal speaker at the conference) as a liberal for
publicly dissociating himself from the IRA's military campaign.[55] Any evolution towards a new position on IRA terror
was, therefore, rather *ad hoc* and empirical. The Birmingham
bombings in late 1974 drew an unequivocal condemnation
from IS while IMG continued to stress the exclusive culpability
of the British government.[56]

The first TOM conference (which attracted only 40
individuals) had decided to give priority to pressurizing left
Labour MPs to break with 'bi'-partisanship'. Jeff Rooker,
Maureen Colquhoun and Stan Thorne were among the first
successes of this tactic. By the second conference trade union
notables such as Mike Cooley and Dave Bolton (vice-president
of the Scottish NUM) had been won over. It was probably the
growing affiliation of trade unionists to the TOM which
eventually persuaded the IS to throw its weight behind the

campaign in the wake of the Ulster Workers' Council 'lock-out'.

Both IMG and IS (together with much smaller Trotskyist groups such as Big Flame and the Revolutionary Communist Group, RCG) have, since 1974, continued to stress the 'Troops out' slogan in their political work on Ireland. The RCG has since split and spawned the Revolutionary Communist Party which likewise supports terrorism if it comes from 'approved' organizations. Others, such as the Militant tendency[57] and the Communist Party, have backed campaigns like the peace movement and the 'Better life for all' campaign. The earlier excesses of the IMG and IS on the question of IRA terror have gradually given way to a more sober estimation, both of the Provisionals and of the Republican ideology.[58] At the same time the Provisionals themselves have moved away from their Catholic-Nationalist ideological legacy and this has been reflected in changed tactics and a stricter selection of 'military' targets. What is perhaps most significant about the IMG's and IS's political agitations on Northern Ireland was that they did genuinely attempt to find a revolutionary position in a context of enormous hostility. Apart from the ultra-leftism to which this attempt gave rise in the case of the IMG, it is perhaps even more disturbing that such efforts have occasioned an arrogant authoritarianism in groups such as the Revolutionary Communist Group and its offshoots which continue to proclaim that even *criticism* of IRA tactics is reactionary.[59] But this should not be allowed to detract from the invaluable role of the Marxist left in forcing the 'Irish issue' on to the British political agenda. This is a clear illustration of the need for independent socialists organized outside the Labour Party, since for most of the relevant period the latter collaborated in the conspiracy of silence on Northern Ireland. Only within the period since 1979 has the Labour left given this situation any of its attention and there is every reason to believe that this came about because of the persistent agitations of the Marxists demanding troops out.

Leninism and feminism

It has been remarked that the events of May 1968 gave rise to a 'great revival of interest in non-Leninist traditions on the left'.[60]

Yet we have seen that the International Socialists came to emphasize Leninism precisely because of these same events. Likewise the IMG, for all its youthful enthusiasm for 'student-ism', resisted the temptation of becoming a British equivalent of Lotta Continua. Throughout its short history the IMG has been an avowedly Leninist, vanguard organization. As we have seen, this certainly involved bouts of ultra-leftism but notably has never involved departures from the widest internal democ-racy. In part this may be attributed to the IMG's very recent origin as a mainly student, intellectual, organization expecting and obtaining high rates of political activity from its membership. In part, also, the IMG's democratic record is attributable to its connection with the Fourth International which may have learned the error of its own past mistakes in this field.[61]

It is more likely, however, that the IMG's commitment to a genuine internal democracy is the result of its formation during a period in which many important political struggles on the left were waged by militants deeply suspicious of all organizations on the grounds that organization necessarily involved conservatism and bureaucratism. Since the lead-ership of IMG was largely drawn from this same cohort it might be expected to be particularly sensitive to feelings on this issue.

Of all the new forces radicalized in the late 1960s the women's liberation movement (WLM) was both the most important and the most critical of traditional forms of organization. Of the two major objectives which the first conference of WLM set itself, the first was 'to develop an organisation that in its form and content would eradicate the relevant faults of the other preceding radical groups'.[62] Ideologically the WLM included elements drawn from 'the spontaneist methods of anarcho-syndicalism and the Situationists, the separatism of Black Power, socialist theories of the unity in struggle of oppressed peoples' and the psycho-politics of Laing and Cooper. Its organization, like its syncretic ideology, was a challenge to the orthodoxies of Leninism, emphasizing loose, non-hierarchical, grass-roots collectives and the necessity for all oppressed groups to develop their own autonomous organizations and 'their own understanding of their own situation'. The women's movement, from its inception, self-consciously resisted the leadership principle by promoting a pre-figurative politics which attempted to begin now (by strict application of the collective principle and 'consciousness raising') that which some socialists imagined would happen automatically *after* the socialist revolution.

Some organizations on the far left deride the women's movement as a middle-class pastime: this is the position of the WRP and the Militant tendency. The SWP, while recognizing the importance of women as an agency of revolution, sees itself as *the* nucleus of a revolutionary party to which all revolutionary forces must rally. Thus,

> a socialist feminist consciousness can only be created when there is a *fighting* organisation which has real roots among women workers and housewives. The women's liberation movement is not a fighting organisation. Because it puts the question of consiousness first, not the taking of power by the working class, it has its own distinctive structure: there is no clearly defined membership . . . no unified politics (it embraces women with very different views) and no centralised organisation . . . because of its politics, its structure and its middle class orientation the women's liberation movement can have little left to contribute in practice . . . our emphasis (the SWP) has to be on women workers.[63]

Accordingly the SWP's *Women's Voice* was concerned primarily with women as workers or strikers and with both in so far as they were potential recruits to the SWP.

The IMG, like the CP. was quick to recognize the value of an autonomous women's movement and its cadres played leading organizational and practical parts in campaigns which the women's movement mobilized for, such as the National Abortion Campaign. Its relationship with the women's movement has been described most clearly by IMG leader, John Ross.[64] According to Ross the Leninist party concentrates its energies and channels its forces in the struggle against the 'bourgeois state'. For Ross, the political is that which participates in or affects the affairs of the state: 'only if they are questions impinging on the state do they [personal relationships] . . . become specifically political as opposed to social'. Ross argues that it is here that the WLM errs – in conflating the personal and political – and it is this which leads some feminists to anti-Leninist positions. Just as a Leninist party would not attempt to take over the trade unions so, says Ross, it also recognizes 'the necessity of the *distinction* and organisational independence of the women's movement and the party . . . A party, and party members, can attempt to persuade or *urge* a course of action on the women's movement or a union but they must never be in a position to *impose* anything.' The IMG decided at a political committee meeting of July 1975 to inaugurate a written debate on the subject of internal caucuses for women, Blacks, and homosexuals. This resulted in the pursuit of a resolution, 'Women's caucuses within the revolutionary organisation', at the IMG's 1978 conference, which said:

> Sexism in society finds its reflection inside the IMG. It finds expression in a number of ways: inadequate educational development and integration into the leadership structures and insensitivity to women's level of development and confidence in their own abilities, fed by dismissive male assumptions and insensitive methods of debate and discussion; insufficient sensitivity to women comrades' responsibilities for children etc . . . caucuses of women comrades are therefore an important element in the steps taken by the IMG as a whole to understand and adopt measures to remove sexist barriers in the development and integration of women comrades.

In keeping with Ross's argument the same resolution also argues:

> It is not the place of a revolutionary organisation – or caucuses within it – to substitute for the WLM by structur-

ing discussions on . . . aspects of personal liberation, that is, *it is not* the place of a revolutionary organisation to structure discussions on how comrades should *conduct their lives* for example, discussions on comrades' personal relationships and attitudes to marriage, monogamy, children, etc.

However the resolution was forced to recognize that the distinction between the personal and the political is not always very clear, because it argues that where the former are 'a barrier to the development of a revolutionary organisation it is the responsibility of the whole organisation to structure discussions on these questions, with women's caucuses preparing contributions for discussion when it is necessary'. This, the most advanced position on the far left regarding the relationship between Leninism and feminism, is still regarded as unsatisfactory by leading socialist feminists.

Sheila Rowbotham, for example, complains that 'sexual relationships between men and women or between people of the same sex have been seen by Marxists as either decadent and diversionary or as personal questions outside politics'.[65] Against this,

Feminists have insisted that how we live, now, has a practical significance for how we organise. Such an assertion of subjectivity and the need to find organisational means to unlock structures of feeling as part of political practice is quite alien from the traditions of Leninism. Indeed Leninism was explicitly opposed to earlier social preoccupations with ethical questions and the new forms of life.

It is noteworthy that this critique of Leninism comes not from a radical feminist or a supporter of women's rights but from a socialist and ex-member of IS: as such it illustrates the estrangement of the women's movement from the politics of the far left. This follows from the WLM's preoccupation with prefigurative politics, since according to Rowbotham, 'Within Leninism there is no conscious commitment to struggling against the forms of relationship which are created by the division of labour under capitalism as part of the effort to make socialism. It is assumed that the existence of a revolutionary party itself can transcend the particular interests of sections within the working class.' Rowbotham's argument against Leninism was developed, in conjunction with Hilary Wainwright and Lynne Segal (both socialist feminists) to the point where it was claimed that, like Stalinism, Leninism deals in 'the manipulation of people' and assumes a superior knowledge. This arrogance is alleged to stem from a notion of the scientificity of Marxism held by Marxist organizations.[66]

Before taking up some of these issues it is worth examining the lengthy resolution, 'Socialist revolution and the struggle for women's liberation', which the Fourth International adopted at its world congress in 1979. This represents the first full resolution on the question of women's liberation ever discussed by the Trotskyist movement and certainly its most sophisticated attempt to deal with the relationship between Marxism and feminism. It begins by acknowledging the independent origins of the women's movement which forced the existing mass organizations of the working class to respond to its emergence. Arising in the context of 'the death agony of capitalism', the development of the women's movement has thus become an important factor in the political and ideological battle to weaken the hold of the bourgeoisie and its centrist, social democratic and Stalinist agents within the working class'.

The Fourth International – while warning of attempts to 'integrate the leadership of the women's movement into the accepted patterns of class collaboration' – envisages itself 'winning the leadership of the struggle for women's liberation'.[37] Yet the resolution clearly states that since the feminist struggle is not identical with the struggle of the working class 'women must wait for no one to show them the way' and 'even after the revolution the independent women's liberation movement will play an indispensable role in assuring the ability of the working class as a whole . . .to carry this process through to a successful conclusion.'[68]

The FI statement clarifies the relationship of its sections such as the IMG with the independent women's movement.

By independent or autonomous we do not mean independent of the needs of the working class. We mean that the movement is organised and led by women; that it takes the fight for women's rights and needs as its first priority, refusing to subordinate that fight to any other interests; that it is not subordinate to the decisions or policy needs of any political tendency or any other social group; that it is willing to carry through the fight by whatever means and together with whatever forces prove necessary. . . Our support for the work to build the independent women's liberation movement distinguishes the Fourth International today from many sectarian groups that claim to stand on Marxist orthodoxy as represented by their interpretations of the resolutions of the first four congresses of the Third International. Such groups reject the construction of any women's organisations except those tied to and under the political control of their party.[69]

The role of the Trotskyists *vis-à-vis* the women's movement is to contend for the support of the best socialist feminists 'in a framework of democracy' by arguing the Marxist analysis. The function of the revolutionary party is to time and formulate the raising of demands within the women's movement. Indeed the party is tactician and leader of the whole class and seeks to orient all facets of the class struggle to the abolition of capitalism. Armed with its superior understanding – enshrined in the Marxist programme 'that represents women and the working class' – the party seeks to overcome the deep divisions fostered by capitalism by synthesizing the experience and demands of all oppressed groups. The organizational norms of the Leninist party are derived from this programme. These incorporate the widest democratic rights but, it is argued, the formation of women's caucuses within the revolutionary party merely reproduces the divisions which the party seeks to overcome. Democratic centralism, on the other hand, can avoid the centrifugal dynamics implicit in the party conceived as a federation of interest groups. Thus the decision to allow women's caucuses within the IMG is specifically repudiated.

It will be noted that the case for democratic centralism ultimately rests on a conviction that the revolutionary programme of the Trotskyists, since it is based on the science of Marxism, is an actual synthesis of the multifarious interests and experiences of all the oppressed. But the objection of many socialist feminists, often Marxists themselves, is that 'a correct analysis of the subordination of women cannot be provided by Marxists unless Marxism itself is transformed'.[70] The Trotskyists seem blissfully unaware of even the possibility that the Marxist tradition to which they subscribe is inadequate for the task. Let us see how the Fourth International attempts to come to terms with the sexual division of labour and confront the specificity of women's oppression.

According to the FI the patriarchal nuclear family is one of the central pillars of class society; in other words it is 'rooted in private property'. For the bourgeoisie, we learn, the family provides for the transmission of private property between generations. But

> for the working class while the family provides some degree of mutual protection of its members, in the most basic sense it is an alien class institution, one that is imposed on the working class and serves the economic interests of the bourgeoisie not the workers. Yet working people are indoctrinated from childhood to regard it . . . as the most natural and imperishable of human relations.[71]

Several elements of this argument are worth noting. First, the Fourth International asserts that 'the family system is an indispensable pillar of class rule. It must be preserved if capitalism is to survive'.[72] In fact it is not at all clear that domestic labour, for example, is a functional prerequisite of capitalist production. To maintain that this and other aspects of the 'family system' are in some essentialist sense pre-given by the logic of capitalist development merely serves to deny that major advances towards women's liberation can be made within a capitalist system. As such it is just a more subtle way of claiming that women must trust in socialism if they are to achieve anything.

It can be further objected against this Marxist functionalism that it fails to see that the family and the sexual divison of labour as presently constituted are to a very great extent products of class and gender struggle. Such functionalism effectively ignores the conflict and choices which led to the present social arrangements. Moreover, the crudest instances of this logic purport to show that since the family is an effect of the economic causality of capitalism, feminists and socialists have identical interests best served by promoting the working-class struggle. This amounts to saying that all sectional interests can be aligned in terms of the labour–capital contradiction.[73] The FI does not explicitly draw this conclusion, unlike the SWP, the Militant tendency, and the RCG, but in linking the family system and capitalism as mutual dependents it promotes an all-or-nothing view belied by historical experience. After all, if the accumulation of capital were so dependent on domestic labour as the cheapest way of reproducing labour power, how could we explain the removal from the family of so much which formerly came under this heading?

The FI not only informs us that 'the family system is the institution of class society that determines and maintains the specific character of women as a sex': it is also argued that only the bourgeoisie has a material interest in the preservation of this institution. As we have seen, the FI attributes the support for the family within the working class to the pernicious influence of bourgeois 'indoctrination'. Thus the family, in this view, exists by virtue of false consciousness. It is not even acknowledged that the conventional male control over the family wage has normally provided a very solid basis for working-class sexism. The FI is too concerned to deny a male self-interest in the oppression of women and to insist that 'it is the capitalist class, not men in general and certainly not male wage earners, which profits from women's unpaid labour in the household.' This argument places the FI's analysis very firmly within the orthodoxy established by Engels's *Origin of the Family, Private Property and the State*.

Engels's argument stressed the coincidence of class and sex antagonism. His basic insight retains its validity in showing that as prehistoric, more egalitarian forms of society broke down in response to developments which created an economic surplus in society, classes and stable hierarchies emerged. Once class property was established, women's labour was privatized within the monogamous family in order to secure the inheritance of property. The subordinate position of women is thus attributed to their exclusion from socially productive labour. The clear implication of Engels's argument is that the liberation of women will coincide with their re-entry into socially productive work. Only the property-owning bourgeoisie has an objective stake in the preservation of the family, the site of women's oppression.

Indeed, in Engels's argument the social position of women is an effect of the family which is itself a product of private property. No wonder then that socialists impressed by this argument believed that the abolition of capitalism was synonymous with the liberation of women. The Fourth International has broken with this tradition in so far as it now recognizes the falsity of this conclusion. But it retains the economistic argument right up to this point before concluding that ideology – albeit, a false consciousness produced by indoctrination – plays a determining part in maintaining the working class's allegiance to the family. It is presumably the pervasiveness of this ideology which brought the independent women's movement into existence and which – together with the persistence of sexism in non-capitalist societies – has alerted the FI to the need for such an independent anti-sexist movement. However it should now be obvious that the Trotskyists regard this ideology as a product of the exploitation of labour by capital. This is an explanation in which gender plays no part at all. Such an analysis, argued Michele Barrett, 'can be of little use to feminist analysis'.[74]

This is because the position of women in any society is closely bound up with the gender constraint of wife/motherhood. To understand the oppression of women, therefore, it is necessary to use gender system as a basic category of historical analysis. But in the analysis of the Fourth International the concept of gender is not utilized at all. If we examine the FI's dissection of the 'family system' – which it makes the fundamental institution of women's oppression – we see that the burden of the Trotskyist analysis is uncomplicatedly economic. The five functions of the family system are:

Γ   a cheap method of maintaining labour power;
2   a mechanism for property inheritance;
3   the most inexpensive and ideologically acceptable mechanism for reproducing human labour;
4   the enforcement of a social division of labour in which women are fundamentally defined by their child-bearing role and assigned tasks immediately associated with this reproductive function. 'Thus the family rests on and reinforces a social division of labour involving the domestic subjugation and economic dependence of women';
5   the family is a repressive and conservatizing institution which 'fosters the possessive, competitive and aggressive values of capitalism' which are 'necessary to the perpetuation of class divisions'.

It can be seen that some concession to the importance of gender is made in point 4 but this is never developed while the values attributed to the family in point 5 are simply designated capitalist values. To have acknowledged the association of these values with masculinity would have undermined the FI's whole analysis which effectively confines the oppression of women to the material interests of the ruling class. Yet one can insist on masculinity as a problem without reducing the issue to a simple power struggle between the sexes, as in radical feminist accounts. If we reject the idea that the condition of women can be deduced derivatively from the economy, it is possible to analyse it as a complex structure of different elements – of which gender is one. This approach would dispense with the view which sees family ideology as a mere con-trick and give due weight to the importance of gender constraints in explaining the oppression of women.

The dominant gender system in any society provides authoritative versions of masculinity and femininity. And the sexual division of labour is presented as a natural extension of gender identity. This does not just apply to the rules of the family system:

The role they perform in conditions of legal-economic dependence as domestic labourers has followed women into industry reproducing the sexual division of labour on the larger terrain of socialised production, depressing their wages to a norm well below that of male labour, concentrating them within a narrow occupational range generally at the bottom of the job hierarchy and making them an easy prey for trade union opportunism.[75]

This being the case we are not simply talking about a division of labour between men and women but a division that places men in a superior and women in a subordinate position.[76] A material interest in the maintenance of this system extends far beyond the bourgeoisie. In the trade union concept of the family wage, for example, the ideology of familialism and the economic supremacy of men are both at work. The general failure of the FI's resolution on women stems from its refusal to recognize that the sexual division of labour is structured in such a way that relations between the sexes are relations of domination and subordination. In this respect its analysis remains 'sex-blind'.

It may be possible by emphasizing the role of ideology and thereby situating the problem of gender to understand the oppression of women within a Marxist problematic. For a number of reasons some of the most ambitious attempts to do this have sought to utilize psychoanalysis.[77] This is principally because it privileges the problem of gender construction and recognizes the profound nature of these identities. Psychoanalysis has thus been seen as a useful approach to understanding the deep hold of ideology on the individual and a method of investigating the nature of ideological representation. It is not our intention to advocate this particular approach to the union of Marxism and feminism, merely to emphasize that such a rapprochement is unlikely to develop within a Marxist tradition characterized by economism and an exclusivist insistence on the labour/capital contradiction. For it is the tendency of the Fourth International to reduce the political and ideological levels of the capitalist mode of production to mere mirror reflections or derivations of the economic base. This clearly emerges in its analysis of the family system and its hold on the working class. The Trotskyist approach is thus to trivialize the role of ideology just as most socialist feminists have come to emphasize it. In practical terms the functionalism of the Trotskyists points to little progress under capitalism (because the family is necessary for it) whereas leading feminists conclude that 'it is perfectly possible for feminism to make more intermediate gains under social democracy than it does in the first years of socialism'.[78] On the other hand, the Trotskyists are sanguine that the working-class family is in any case in process of dissolution while feminists observe the pervasiveness of familial ideology and conclude that this 'common-sense' is as in need of challenge within the working class and its institutions as it is anywhere.

This discussion shows the extent of the differences between the Trotskyist and socialist feminist analyses of women's oppression and indicates some of the practical ramifications of these varying approaches. In so doing it suggests some explanations for why even the most advanced far left analysis of women's oppression is unlikely to impress the current of socialist feminism within the women's movement. In particular, the posture of vanguard and the concomitant claim of the superior status of the Trotskyist programme will be treated with suspicion if the Marxist theory which underpins them is manifestly defective. Not only were the Marxists absent when the women's movement began its recent second phase; since then most Marxist groups have had little to say to people increasingly aware of the ideological and cultural dimensions of their oppression – be they women, gays, Blacks or youth. The social divisons which these new movements have drawn attention to, while expressing real material divisions in society, are not confined to the workplace or specific to capitalism.

While the Trotskyists have been prepared to champion the economic demands pertinent to these campaigns (equal pay, equal work, crêches, maternity/paternity leave) and take up less obviously economic issues (abortion) which have created mass mobilizations, they have not embraced the more difficult problems (of sexuality, pornography, domestic violence) which are, nevertheless, of central concern. This may to some extent reflect the narrowness of the Trotskyists' theoretical base and a failure to address (even recognize) its limitations. We have seen, for instance, that the Fourth International evades the problem of gender (and provides no convincing analysis of patriarchy). It may well be that in terms of its analysis of women's oppression the Trotskyist movement simply inherits the deficiences of classical Marxism which so conceptualized the field of production as to exclude women (and the production of the species and its labour power) from its central theoretical category.[79] But even so the mode of Trotskyist intervention in the politics of the new movements compounds these problems because this practice consists of importing externally-derived policy positions into the organizationally autonomous movements. The result is not simply that these interventions take on an alien, manipulative character, but that the Marxists thereby reduce their chances of enriching their theory by learning from the experience and politics of the mass campaigns. Thus when, for example, the elected leadership of Youth CND was suspended because of alleged irregulatities at its Manchester conference in July 1983 the Socialist League (alias IMG) was held responsible. Whether the specific charges are true or not, the very fact that the mode of operation of the Socialist League within these campaigns resembles that of entrists within the Labour Party creates an impression of duplicity and bad faith which leaves it vulnerable to charges of undemocratic practices. This practice owes a good deal to the widespread Trotskyist conviction that the main problems of theory have already been solved and that the task in hand is to apply the correct tactics and preserve the revolutionary strategy. We have seen that the FI (and, therefore, its British section) is characterized by this conviction and assumes a paternalistic attitude *vis-à-vis* the women's movement. However, it also needs pointing out that the Fourth International has made very real advances over other Trotskyist formations in this respect. If it is less doctrinally rigid than the others this owes something to its *international* character and the democratic conditions which now prevail within it.

The IMG organization

Ten years after 1968 the IMG membership stood at a mere 750, yet the organization was confident enough to launch a new youth organization, called 'Revolution'. The group had grown during the previous two years (from 650 members in 1976) and since the launching of *Socialist Challenge*, in 1977, paper sales had increased by 60 per cent; the paid sales stood at 5,500 with a print run of between 8,000 and 9,000. At this stage in its 'socialist unity' appeal IMG optimism seems to have been high. The self-imposed project of uniting the revolutionary left had attracted some small groups (such as Big Flame[80] and the Marxist Workers' Group[81]) to engage in joint work with IMG: the refusal of the SWP to enter the spirit of this initiative had yet to wreck it.

Despite these positive signs the IMG remained an organization confined to the student and white-collar sectors and almost wholly lacking in a working-class or industrial base. Its trade union work was, to practical purposes, only possible in the National Union of Teachers, the CPSA and NALGO. In industry it had achieved token visibility only at British Leyland (specifically in the Rover factory, Solihull). Even the group's penetration of larger *political* organizations was unusually feeble. By 1978 IMG members seem to have decided spontaneously that their column of entrists in the Labour Party and the Labour Party Young Socialists were wasting their time and such activity dwindled to nothing. While rebuking this, the group's central committee was forced to admit that 'the stranglehold of Militant is almost impregnable, especially when other small revolutionary forces . . . refuse to help us build a revolutionary alternative tendency'.

In fact IMG held the initiative only in respect of certain campaigns in the women's movement and in its socialist unity drive. Even in connection with the National Abortion Campaign and the Working Women's Charter, which it had done so much to sponsor, the complaint was heard that this activity did nothing to build IMG but only consumed its resources. The group's national 'periphery' (i.e. sympathizers) was estimated at just 500 – a poor showing for all the time it had spent promoting single-issue campaigns of wide appeal.

If the IMG was in any way sounder and more stable than the rest of the far left, it was in respect of the organization's internal regime. For throughout its existence the IMG has avoided the kind of internal disruption and authoritarianism which we have encountered elsewhere on the Trotskyist left. From its origins in the mid-1960s to the end of the seventies no factions were expelled from the IMG. The only exception to this pattern came in 1980–1 when a group of entrists were discovered to have created a faction with the purpose of splitting as large a section of the membership away from the organization as possible.[82]

The IMG sets high standards of political behaviour for its members. The rank-and-file is expected to be very active politically. New members must first endure a six-month period of candidate status during which member and organization can scrutinize each other. The group's norms insist that the recruit gives priority to party work, the only exception being when 'leave of absence' is granted on occasion of ill health or for purposes of vacation. While the IMG (as we have seen) does not attempt to structure the private lives of its members it clearly does expect the personal behaviour of members to accord with certain (ill defined) revolutionary principles. Certainly sexist or racist behaviour would not be tolerated. Indeed the group has taken measures designed to encourage 'oppressed layers' – such as by admitting a certain validity to the principle of 'positive discrimination', though not one based on quotas; these are firmly rejected as apolitical. For IMG no special status is attached to a members's social background but rather to his or her politics. Thus the organization positively discriminates in cases when the collective politics of the group are enhanced. This is why, as we have seen, women's caucuses were permitted within the organization but not as a replacement for the discussion of 'women's issues' at branch level. The IMG's commitment to measures designed to augment the collective nature of the group's politics also lies behind its guarantee of members' tendency, and even factional, rights.

The individual rights of IMG members command their own cost in terms of greater political activity. The model of participatory democracy which the IMG internal regime seeks to achieve exacts a price as can be seen from the following analysis of the group's 1978 conference.

The IMG conference is a two-yearly event spread over four or five days It is preceded by a three-month discussion period. During this time members are expected to conduct discussions at branch level around the dozen or so areas outlined by the central committee. They are also required to convene three regional aggregates at which these and other issues (suggested by individual members) are debated. Members are encouraged to write contributions to the discussions which are printed in internal bulletins. Of course the informed member needs to read these reports which average 32 pages each (approximately 20,000 words per bulletin). Only the technical capacities of the IMG national centre restrict the number of such bulletins to about thirty; otherwise this, and the 5,000-word limit per contribution, would undoubtedly be lifted. Bearing in mind that other activities are not suspended during the pre-conference discussion period, it is obvious that an enormous effort is required of individual members.

The right to form tendencies and factions increases this commitment of time and energy whenever it is taken up. On these occasions tendencies and factions produce reports and analyses of their own which are printed nationally and freely distributed throughout the organization. These, inevitably, prompt counter-arguments and alternative platforms. They also require tendency meetings, caucus activities and the co-ordinaton of supporters (which invariably involves travelling the country). Since the organization of conference is scrupulously fair, the right to form a tendency or faction involves the right to proportional representation of delegates. For every five members, a branch may elect one conference delegate so long as the members concerned have paid their subscriptions and the conference levy (which was £6,000 in 1978 or £9 per member).

The IMG conference is the sovereign political assembly of the organization though the norms of democratic centralism permit FI bodies to qualify this sovereignty. Conference elects a nominations committee which draws up a list of candidates for the central committee: the conference then chooses from this list and elects the central committee. Executive work is performed by a smaller political committee elected by the CC. Both these bodies may appoint subordinate committees: both are open to members of dissident tendencies elected on the basis of proportional representation.

Clearly these formal rights are extensive. Furthermore the IMG's political practice – which is relatively free from instances of authoritarianism – shows that these rights are real. We have already attempted to account for this in the previous section. Here it will simply be observed that the small scale of the IMG (IMG membership stood at 40 in 1968, 400 in 1972 and around 800 by 1978) and its intellectual composition are both congenial to the functioning of a participatory democracy. It must remain a matter for speculation as to how it would fare if either of these factors were changed.

To the Socialist League

The IMG's emergence in the late 1960s from the clandestinity of entrism together with its very success in VSC and among students ensured its character as an organization of the young and educated. Its distance from the struggles of the British working class – which reached new heights of militancy and innovation in the early 1970s – was perpetuated by the International's orientation summed up by the slogan 'from the periphery to the centre'. Once the student revolt had faded, the International Socialists sought a new orientation – the 'move to the class' – which marks the start of its attempt to construct a trade union base to the organization.[83] At the same time, 1970, the IMG's major initiative was launching the Spartacus League, a new youth organization which confirmed its status as a student formation. It was not until the miners' strike of 1972 that IMG made a serious attempt to intervene outside this milieu and even then it was confined to pamphleteering and calling for a general strike[84] (for which there was no resonance at all).

However, the IMG's isolation from the heavy industrial working class was not such a problem as traditionally depicted by Marxists. The ninth world congress of the Fourth International had after all justified IMG's withdrawal from entrism by reference to the recent upsurge in militancy among sections of the population outside the mass workers' parties and trade unions. It believed that a new opportunity had been created for the construction of a mass vanguard party capable of challenging the hegemony of the traditional workers' parties. In fact an anti-capitalist element could be perceived in many of the campaigns and movements which sprang up to the left of the Labour Party in these years. But it was extremely foolish and arrogant to suppose that the tiny and youthful IMG (with approximately 200 members by 1969) should act as vanguard to these groups. The chief ideological weakness of the IMG stemmed from its refusal to recognize that the Leninist model of a vanguard party deeply entrenched within the manual working class did not and need not apply to it. While there was no prospect of the IMG becoming a workers' party of this sort, it did have the chance to develop a close relationship with the new feminist, ethnic and student politics of the period. Together with these and other forces that had either rejected labourism or been neglected by it, the IMG had the opportunity to develop a socialist subculture through serious educational and agitational activities. Though at first confined to the periphery of British politics a Marxist group of this sort would have gained in influence as a variety of vanguardist illusions elsewhere on the left were shattered and confidence in the Labour Party repeatedly depressed. Already, by 1970, it was becoming apparent that (as Miliband has expressed it) '"organised labour" must now be taken to include a vast number of people in teaching and other forms of communication: here is to be found, for the first time in British history, an "intellectual proletariat" which is insecure and often disaffected. Its contribution to the political culture of labour is already considerable and is likely to grow further.'[85]

Unfortunately, the IMG in common with all other Trotskyist groups was wedded to conceptions which prevented it from too close an identification with these forces. The underdeveloped

state of Marxism in relation to sexism has already been noted.
A similar barrier disposes the Trotskyists to think of most
white-collar workers as either middle class or strategically less
significant than other wage earners. Both assessments are
wrong. But it is common for such workerism to downgrade all
struggles and agencies at one remove from the industrial
militancy of the traditional proletariat. Thus, although the
IMG is by no means the worst exponent of such notions, it
strove to rid itself of an embarrassing non-proletarian image.
In this respect the development of the International Socialists
(via the struggles against the Industrial Relations Act) into a
bigger force with an industrial base was looked upon as a
model to be imitated. Dissatisfaction with IMG's performance
in the recruitment of manual workers led to the removal of Pat
Jordan and Tariq Ali from the leadership in 1972; both were
closely associated with the perspectives of 1969.

Though this change was intended to help IMG gain a
foothold in the manual trade unions, in practice it led to a
sterile campaign for a general strike and the election of a
Labour government with a socialist programme. In fact the call
for a general strike was a completely futile pose but the fact
that it was thought credible within the IMG is attributable to
the re-emergence of catastrophism within the Fourth International.

For the general line adopted at the ninth congress of the FI
argued that the downturn in Western economies was the
context in which 'the political positions of Trotskyism, not
merely against social democracy and Stalinism, but also
against all centrist deviations within the vanguard, will be
strikingly re-affirmed.'[86] Of course, this was not to be a mere
academic vindication of Trotskyism but was expected to have
very tangible results. The period is characterized as one of
political victories (starting in Vietnam) that have turned the
balance of forces decisively against imperialism and though
defeats occur (as in Chile) they run counter to the general
tendency. The world situation is described as exactly the
opposite of 1923–43 when the general picture was one of
working-class defeats. As for Britain, the IMG concluded that
in effect the economic preconditions for the post-war consensus

no longer obtained. Its analysis was given substantial support by Mandel's *Late Capitalism* (1972) which predicted a long recession in the capitalist economies rooted in the preceding 25-year boom.[87]

Thus initially the 'new rise of world revolution' was described in very general terms. But by the early seventies the FI was sure that the approach of socialist revolution in Europe could be identified 'not just in broad historical perspective . . . but even from a conjunctural point of view'.[88] Within IMG, however, a series of shifting tendencies, alignments and re-alignments developed after 1972 as the militants tried to fashion tactics appropriate for those perspectives. Internationally the FI was split between tendencies based in the Americas (the Leninist–Trotskyist faction) and in Europe (the international majority tendency) partly over the pros and cons of guerrilla movements. The IMG debate – at times very fierce – revolved on the claims made for united fronts on single issue campaigns (on the model of VSC) versus the leadership's rather abstract faith in a general strike. As already mentioned this general strike line was pursued by those desirous of emulating the International Socialists' 'turn to industry'.[89]

In fact despite the explosion of industrial militancy under the Heath government the IMG was not able to establish an industrial base comparable to that of IS. In some measure this was no doubt due to the IMG's overwhelmingly student composition which, despite Narodnik-style forays into factory work, was always unlikely to appeal to trade union militants. Moreover the IMG's style of politics was still informed by its experience of the late sixties. One important feature of this was the abiding conviction that a significant cohort of militants, organized in a variety of radical campaigns outside the Labour Party and trade unions, was the raw material of a future Marxist party. Despite its so-called 'industrial turn', a large proportion of IMG members preferred an orientation aimed at those already breaking with Labourism. As the IS's industrial strategy unfolded in the mid-seventies and it became increasingly apparent that rank-and-filism actually amounted to little more than a prolonged celebration of wage militancy, those in IMG concerned to avoid such economism

were even more disposed to emphasize the importance of
political consciousness.

By 1977 the project of gathering together all those prepared
to fight on a platform of class struggle gained majority support
inside the IMG. One aspect of this orientation – and perhaps
an aspect that was over-emphasized – was the conviction that
the myriad Trotskyist groups could be won over to a unified
revolutionary organization.[90] It was now argued that the
doctrinal differences dividing these groups were not of sufficient importance to justify separate organizations. Indeed the
IMG was clearly prepared to include the 'state capitalists' of
the SWP in this category of potential unifiers. However, the
very fact that the International Socialists had become the
Socialist Workers *Party* was symptomatic of that organization's
determination to regard itself as the core of any future revolutionary organization. That this was an entirely sectarian attitude is evinced by the refusal of the SWP to field candidates
under the banner of Socialist Unity as proposed by IMG in a
number of by-elections in the seventies. This not only resulted
in the SWP candidate standing against Socialist Unity, but
also permitted the National Front to beat both in the Hull and
Newham contests. And in the Ladywood by-election of August
1977 the Socialist Unity candidate polled almost four times the
SWP vote.

However, these experiences did nothing to bring the SWP to
a revaluation of its position and the IMG unity initiative only
succeeded with much smaller groups like Big Flame. Ironically
by 1979 it had become apparent that both the Socialist Unity
initiative and the SWP rank-and-file strategy had failed. But
the IMG and SWP drew different conclusions from this mutual
failure. As we have seen the SWP recognized the need for
ideological consolidation while remaining an independent
organization. The IMG, on the other hand, came to stress the
importance of the Benn campaign to democratize the Labour
Party and increasingly submerged itself in entrist activity.
Finally, the organization – by now completely absorbed in
entrism and CND – re-named itself the Socialist League and at
the start of 1983 brought out *Socialist Action* to replace *Socialist
Challenge*.

Conclusions

By the mid-sixties the Fourth International had acknowledged
the *de facto* rearguard position of the Western working class and
increasingly emphasized Third World struggles as the
epicentre of world revolution. The IMG's politics were formed
around this time and the growth of the organization coincides
with the exodus from the Labour Party and the explosion of
extra-parliamentary struggles of the period 1965–70. From the
time of its emergence as an independent organization in 1969,
the IMG's political orientation was towards students,
feminism, Third World solidarity campaigns, Northern Ireland
and other 'peripheral' causes and groups. The very fact that
these struggles were regarded as in any sense peripheral was,
of course, attributable to the conviction that serious revolutionary work must ultimately be based on factory cells and the
industrial working class. But IMG was singularly unsuccessful
in establishing an industrial base despite resort to several
'turns to industry' such as that of August 1983 which resulted
in politically motivated sackings at British Leyland's Cowley
plant. In practice IMG politics were bound up with the 'new
left' of 1968.

For the political milieu in which IMG operated, from the
moment it abandoned entrism, was heavily influenced by the
anti-bureaucratic thrust of the women's movement, student
radicalism, community politics, the squatters' and claimants'
movements. IMG's greatest success was in helping to catalyse
single-issue campaigns like VSC, NAC and the revived CND.
But it sought to build a Leninist party from its involvement in
these mass mobilizations and that it emphatically failed to do.
Instead its attempts at channelling diverse organizations in the
same direction resulted in the IMG becoming an ultra-activist
group championing more issue campaigns than it had members.
A feature of the organization's politics was its tendency to react
to radical causes such that consistent, patient work was mostly
out of the question. Instead the group was more likely to take up
an issue once it had become the focus of attention only to drop it
when the mood passed.

This practice eventually led the IMG, now called the Socialist League, back into the Labour Party in pursuit of the same radical forces that it had failed to organize independently. The decay of the Labour Party which occasioned the withdrawal of IMG from entrism in 1969 now, more advanced, took it back in 1982. By 1986 the print order for *Socialist Action*, once 6,000, was down to 1,400. Bearing in mind that a high percentage of any far left paper typically remains unsold this suggests a pitifully small circulation and an even smaller membership. Perhaps these are the real reasons why a so-called International Group split from the Socialist League early in the same year.

6

From Stalinism to Eurocommunism

Although the first quarter-century of British communism had been replete with tactical shifts and changes in its attitude to all manner of things, its basic conception of politics was consistently crude and mechanical. The party was no nearer to an appreciation of the importance of the institutions of liberal democracy than the delegates at the original communist unity convention in 1920. Here parliamentary democracy had been described as a 'superstition' which communist propaganda would eradicate. Parliament itself, according to Tom Bell, was simply controlled by 'high finance' and 'so far as the working class were concerned there was nothing to be hoped for from that chamber.'[1] Participation in elections was merely an 'opportunity for propaganda' which also acknowledged the 'psychology' of the working class.

These theories were repeated in the *Manual of Party Training* of 1924 which was the nearest thing to a programme that the party possessed in its early years. The capitalists, we are told, use parliament as a gauge of how far they can go against workers' interests. Any 'concessions' registered here are understood as in some way functional to the end of securing an effective prop for the capitalist conspiracy. There is no suggestion that they could have intrinsic value – indeed the party stressed that its more immediate demands 'are merely a means to our end and not an end in themselves'.[2] Just as the party saw the state primarily in terms of its coercive power, so it saw its own role defined by the need to mobilize a working-class counterforce. The inevitability of a big showdown between these physical forces was only emphasized by the alleged propensity for the state's coercive powers to grow and for the dictatorship of the bourgeoisie to become 'more apparent'.[3] Insofar as the party ackowledged a role for ideology and politics in all this, it was confined to a logomachy between capitalist propaganda pumped through the schools, church and press and communist attempts to expose the fraudulence of democracy and to secure vantage points from which the ruling class might be harried in local government, parliament and industry. The party believed that a sufficient explanation of the generation of consent in liberal democratic Britain was contained in talk of the workers' 'psychology', capitalist propaganda and treacherous leaders within the workers' organizations.

The party thus put itself at a disadvantage. It could only seem indifferent to those democratic gains already won and was strongly inclined to the view that they could not last for very long under an increasingly authoritarian capitalism. Not until the popular front period did the party act as if democracy under capitalism was worth defending. But it never established itself as the champion of democracy – its own propaganda and blatant subordination to the Stalin dictatorship prevented that. Instead by 1945 the enemies of socialism had an easy task in depicting the CP as the foremost opponent of democracy.

For as long as the wartime alliance held fast the CP was an enthusiastic exponent of the 'national cause' and campaigned vigorously for increased production and industrial peace. With the election of the Attlee government in 1945 the party was briefly euphoric. Its own electoral showing was better than ever before – two MPs and 256 councillors – and its membership was swollen to 45,000. Just as the party could now envisage unity between the USSR and the USA in mutually beneficial plans for post-war reconstruction, so it imagined a role for itself in British politics alongside the Labour Party. By 1947 Pollitt was able to stress the party's role in reconstructing Britain and specifically denied the validity of the Russian experience for the British road to socialism.[4] In the same text it was asserted that 'it is possible to see how the people will move towards Socialism without further revolutions, without the dictatorship of the proletariat.'[5] So without ceremony, internal debate or theoretical innovation, the British communists calmly dropped their commitment to the cornerstone concepts of Leninism. What had happened?

Major changes had been in progress for some time but the CPGB was, as ever, not the initiator. The strategic turn to popular frontism in 1935 was perhaps the beginning of the process which enabled the communist parties to discover their own national roads to socialism. However, it is a measure of the CPGB's innocence of this that it adopted its first full programme, *For Soviet Britain*, in the same year and this pledged the party to the Bolshevik route to socialism. Thus the British party continued to talk like old-fashioned Leninists even as the popular front strategy was developed. The 13th congress of the CPGB declared in 1935 'that the building of a mass CP within an all-inclusive united working class front is the sole path to the advance of the working class struggle . . and the victory of the working class revolution in Britain and the establishment of workers' dictatorship on the basis of Soviet Power.' Later that year Pollitt told the seventh congress of the Comintern (which adopted the popular front) that 'The Communist Party does not believe that Socialism can be achieved through Parliament and will always state this standpoint in its agitation and propaganda.'[6] Such statements indicate that the popular front was merely a useful tactic and any strategic significance was only discovered later. What we can say for sure is that the popular front was developed as a means of overcoming communist isolation after the sectarian Third Period. By promoting the unity of all anti-fascist forces the popular front sought to overcome working class isolation too. It was both a method for combating fascism and, in communist calculations, a preparation for socialism.

The pre-war record of popular front governments in France and Spain was dismal. But after the war such governments spread to Austria, Belgium, Norway, Italy and Denmark as well as France and the so-called People's Democracies. Thus, by 1947 Pollitt had this success as well as the evidence which the war afforded of collaboration between Russia and the capitalist states to suggest that some sort of working relationship with the Labour Party might enable the CP to discover a peaceful parliamentary path to socialism in Britain. There was also the fact that the end of the sectarian Third Period had come as a great relief to Pollitt and company and the CPGB had then been able to recruit more members than ever before, conclude electoral pacts with local Labour parties and sell relatively vast quantities of communist literature. As I observed in chapter 2, weekend sales of the *Daily Worker* were from 1935 sometimes as high as 200,000 while pamphlet sales exceeded a million copies in the years 1935–7.[7] Communist influence had spread like never before so it is not surprising that the party leaders preferred to continue the methods that seemed to generate it. Stalin's decision to liquidate the Comintern in 1943 may also have opened the way for the CPs to devise their own roads to socialism. Certainly Stalin is on record to the effect that socialism is 'possible even under the English Monarchy',[8] and according to Kruschev it was Stalin who *advised* the CPGB to pursue a parliamentary road to socialism.[9]

It is doubtful then that Pollitt's *Looking Ahead* had developed from the accumulated wisdom, gained from experience and theoretical reflection, of the British communists. There was simply no debate to reorientate the party – the least evidence required to merit such a conclusion. Yet by 1951 the CP had produced a new programme – the *British Road to Socialism* – which took up Pollitt's reflections and calmly asserted that only 'The enemies of Communism accuse the Communist Party of aiming to introduce Soviet Power in Britain and abolish Parliament. This is a slanderous misrepresentation of our policy.'[10] Following Pollitt the programme argued that the People's Democracies demonstrated the possibility of national roads to socialism. The prospect for Britain, it argued, is the transformation of parliament so that it becomes 'the democratic instrument' of the majority will, the essential condition for which 'is the building up of a broad coalition or popular alliance of all sections of the working people'.[11] It is difficult to resist the conclusion that all this 'democratic', 'peaceful', and 'parliamentary' talk was some sort of *ruse de guerre* or, as E.P. Thompson called it, the Russian way 'done into English'. John Gollan alluded to just such a motive when he referred to Pollitt's plea for the need to dispense with the bogey of bloody revolution.[12] Everything else that we have said points to rank opportunism rather than a genuine reappraisal of Leninism as the reason for the change.

So far as the British communist leaders were concerned, the new outlook had no implications for their relationship with the USSR. Pollitt may now assert the democratic credentials of the CPGB but he was quick to reaffirm the infallibility of the Soviet party, 'for me these . . people could never do nor ever can do any wrong against the working class.'[13] It was just as well that he thought this way because Stalin created the Cominform to prosecute an ultra-left offensive just as Pollitt was looking forward to a co-operative relationship with the Labour left. From 1947 the CP became the Labour government's severest critic principally because the Attlee administration played a leading part in fomenting the Cold War and bringing the US into 'the defence of Europe'. The CP campaigned against the Marshall Plan on the grounds that its purpose was to 'weld Western Europe into a war bloc'. It campaigned for industrial militancy to break the austerity regime which, it argued, Marshall Aid imposed.[14] The party saw the real aggressive implications of the Truman Doctrine and agitated against the establishment of NATO and SEATO. It was an early opponent of British nuclear weapons and campaigned fiercely against America's British bases. There was much truth in what it then said. Pollitt argued that the financial sector of British capital pursued policies at variance with the needs of manufacturing industry, and this same sector supported the policies which the US imposed on Britain to guarantee American free enterprise access to British markets. Britain itself was becoming an aircraft carrier and bomb base for American imperialism.[15]

But the CP's blanket support for the USSR made its double standards so obvious that the force of its anti-American arguments was considerably weakened if not nullified altogether. The party's credibility was not helped by the fact that it dressed up this anti-Americanism in a patriotic language and nationalist imagery while plainly prostrating itself before the USSR. Thus the American military presence represented an 'army of occupation': American policies threatened the 'national interest'. But according to Pollitt 'Since November 8 1917 . . . the Soviet Union has never once formulated a policy that was not in the interests of the common peoples of the whole world.'[16] None but the true believers could be expected to swallow this. It was easy to demonstrate, however, that when the CP proposed ' a close association and friendship' with the socialist countries, it was tantamount to surrendering British interests to the Russians whose policy it believed to be synonymous with those of ordinary people everywhere.

The party was therefore as pro-Soviet as it ever had been but, as the Cold War began, opinion leaders in Britain were fast becoming zealously anti-Soviet. Communist opposition to Marshall Aid – which was hailed as the saviour of the British economy in almost every other quarter – was an excuse to intensify the anti-communist campaign in the trade unions. Those unions dominated by the Right were especially inclined to see the communists behind every grievance. Without producing a shred of evidence to support the allegation for example, Arthur Deakin denounced a dispute on London's docks in 1948 as the 'politically motivated work of communist agitators'. Indeed the Labour Cabinet, most employers and right-wing trade union leaders 'tended to identify *any* industrial stoppage with communist subversion'.[17] This 'became almost an obsession' in the 1940s and early 1950s.[18] And within the unions and the Labour Party it was possible to define dissent as so many manifestations of the communist project to subvert the government and the national economy. A notable instance of this procedure was Hugh Gaitskell's claim that as many as one-sixth of the constituency party delegates at Labour's 1952 conference were either communists or communist-inspired.[19]

The CP certainly had some strength in the trade unions by the 1940s. Communists had risen to leadership positions in USDAW, the AEU, NUR, and TGWU. But this was not the same as real industrial strength, as the mineworkers' union illustrated. Here the president was communist but the union always backed the Labour leadership and official TUC policy. Nevertheless, the CP managed to get nine of its members on the 34-strong executive council of the TGWU – a position squandered by the party's intransigent opposition to NATO, wage restraint and Marshall Aid which it combined with an equally intemperate pro-Sovietism. The union right, including Deakin, Vic Feather and Vincent Tewson, campaigned to forbid office to communists and succeeded to this end within the TGWU. By July 1949 the nine party members were removed from its executive council and Bert Papworth was removed from the TUC general council. The issue was defined by the Right as a defence of democracy against communist subversion. One can only suppose that the CP had accumulated so many ideological deficits on this issue that the bureaucratic and authoritarian proclivities of Deakin and company were 'forgotten'.

The campaign against communists in the trade unions commanded the zeal of so many trade union leaders because they opposed anything that endangered the Attlee government. Communists seemed hell-bent after 1947 on proving that social democracy could not work. It was all the more galling to face the CP in a militant mood having seen it pass during the previous twenty years through alternating phases of ultra-leftism, popular frontism, the double volte-face over the war and, most recently, the super-patriotism of 1941–7. It was all in such bad faith – the only consistent factor was that the preferences of Moscow dictated the pattern. For the conservative Labour and trade union establishment, with its simple-minded reverence for the national interest, the defeat of European fascism had left but one threat to Britain – the USSR. Stalin's brutal and blundering foreign policy succeeded in persuading even the Labour left – fellow-travellers excepted – that this was so. So it was in this context that the TUC withdrew from the World Federation of Trade Unions in July 1949 to break free from its communist majority and a war against communism was waged in particular unions in Britain. Even the London Trades Council was expelled from the TUC in 1952 because communists were prominent in the leadership.

But the CP dominated only small unions such as the Foundry Workers and ETU. Elsewhere the focus of its activity after these early anti-communist onslaughts was on the shop floor. Membership of the party by 1952 was already, at 35,124, ten thousand down on the figure for 1945. Was the shrinkage due to the Cold War? Did full employment throughout the 1950s undermine the communist project? Or was the communist project already so incoherent that only a diminishing cadre found it supportable? The invasion of Hungary was yet to come but let us not forget the bizarre and demoralizing campaign against Tito which culminated (in the case of the CPGB) with the publication of James Klugman's mendacious diatribe *From Trotsky to Tito* in November 1951. Then there was the Slansky trial at the end of 1952 as the purge of Titoists in the People's Democracies reached its climax in a repulsive imitation of the Russian purge trials of the 1930s. Stalin died in March 1953 before the Russian party could begin another major purge around the so-called Doctor's Plot. In June 1953 an uprising in East Germany was suppressed by Soviet tanks – further proof if any was needed that all was not well in the People's Democracies, the ostensible model for the CPGB's new socialist vision. At the end of the year Beria, the head of the KGB, was shot along with his associates as the Russian party tried to sort itself out. In May 1955 the new Russian leadership visited Tito, the former 'fascist-Trotskyist-spy'. By now the monolith was well and truly cracked but the real shocks to the communist movement were still being prepared.

In February 1956 the CPSU held its 20th Congress. On the last day of the conference, Kruschev made the secret speech exposing some of the crimes of Stalin. Not until June was the full text available in the West but well before then a debate, mainly subterranean, had been provoked within the CPGB. On the same day that Kruschev's speech was published, E.P. Thompson wrote to the *Daily Worker* arguing for a genuine internal debate within the party. By now many were hopeful that a more democratic party regime would emerge from the report of the commission on inner-party democracy which the CPGB leadership had conceded after the party's April congress. Major doubts about the Stalin period, the real nature of the People's Democracies and the honesty of the CPGB leadership, had been stirred by the

Kruschev revelations. Palme Dutt smugly conceded apropos the Stalin dictatorship that yes 'there are spots on the sun'. This complacency merely stoked the fires of discontent within the party. Rioting began in Poznan, Poland at the end of June and marked the beginning of yet another crisis in the communist bloc. By mid-summer some of the CPGB dissidents took the bold step of publishing a faction paper called *New Reasoner*. They were instructed to desist and then suspended from membrship. But any hope of holding back the wave of discontent was extinguished when the Hungarian uprising began in October.

The crisis thus provoked within the CPGB resulted in more than just an 'exit of the intellectuals' though many who resigned from the party were nationally-known figures such as Doris Lessing, Hyman Levy, Paul Hogarth and Rutland Boughton. The party also lost many individuals who subsequently played a major part in the New Left – E. P. Thompson, Ken Coates and John Saville among them. Others, such as Cliff Slaughter, Tom Kemp, Bob Pennington, Brian Pearce, Brian Behan, and Peter Fryer joined the Trotskyists. But the bulk of those who left were working-class members, including prominent trade unionists such as Lawrence Daly and Les Canon and industrial militants such as Bill Jones who had been prominent in the famous London busmen's struggles of the 1930s. In all CP membership fell by 10,900 between June 1956 and March 1959. This represented about 32 per cent of the 1956 membership while the situation was even worse in the Young Communist League, which lost around half of its smaller number.[20]

It was probably the invasion of Suez, overlapping the Hungarian revolution, which prevented the exodus from the CP resulting in another phase of disenchantment with socialism. The collusion of the British and French governments with Israel in an attempt to overthrow Nasser reminded everyone of the enemy at home which disillusionment with communism may otherwise have obscured. The socialist humanists grouped around the *New Reasoner* were opponents both of the degraded socialism which supported dictatorship and the degraded democracy which supported imperialism. They were quick to point out the contradictions in a Communist Party claiming fidelity to democracy and a parliamentary road to socialism in Britain – the section of its programme dealing with civil liberties was even 'amended and strengthened' after Kruschev's speech – yet supportive of the Russian and East European dictatorships. The attachment of the CP to liberty, concluded one ex-member, was as weak as Labour's attachment to socialism.

CND was born in 1957. It was significant that for the first time in post-war Britain a spontaneous and radical mass movement could emerge independently of either CP or Labour patronage. It seemed that the crisis of 1956 had helped to create a Left free from the stultifying orthodoxies of labourism and official communism. The CP was multilateralist and actually boycotted the first two Aldermaston marches of 1958 and 1959. In accordance with Soviet predilections the party agitated for summit talks and international agreements and argued that the unilateralist demand was misguided as well as incapable of arousing mass support. The party's anti-war propaganda via its front organization, the British Peace Committee, pursued the issue of American bases in Britain, German rearmament and the need for diplomatic agreements between the superpowers. In short, the party was out of step with opinion in CND even though individual communists threw themselves wholeheartedly behind the campaign. Not until 1960 did the line swing abruptly behind unilateralism and away from an emphasis on purely communist preoccupations such as British recognition of the German Democratic Republic.

When Stalin died in 1953 party leaders fell over each other to eulogize his unimpeachable record – this Antaeus who consistently renewed himself 'by direct contact with the masses', this 'architect of the rising world of free humanity' and so on and so on.[21] Doubts were allowed to gestate in the three years which followed, however – no doubt because no clear line was coming from Moscow, where the party leadership was in turmoil. But once the tanks had rolled into Budapest, a clearer vision returned to the CPGB leaders and the doubters were silenced or removed from the party. Nevertheless, permanent changes had taken place and there could be no return to the old Stalinist certainties. Cominform was dissolved in April 1956. The different national roads to socialism were not only still intact – Togliatti, leader of the Italian party, announced the necessity of this 'polycentrism' and thereby implied a denial of Moscow's leading role. The myth of Russian infallibility had been exploded by Kruschev's revelations and socialism had been saved more than once by timely military repression of the East European working class. Already the comrades would observe that British socialism 'will be different'.

Since 1951 the party had been committed to the view that British socialism would depend on the creation of a popular alliance of all sections of the working people. The objective basis for this alliance, which would go well beyond the ranks of the working class, was supposed to rest on the emergence of state monopoly capitalism. According to this thesis real power now rested in the hands of a tiny minority of finance capitalists. Finance capital, it was argued, 'is built into and controls the entire government and administration of this country for its own profit and against the wider interests of the nation'.[22] Thus the national interest and the interests of specific sections of the population coincided in an anti-monopoly movement. From 1951 the CPGB argued that such an alliance required a united Left. But here was a problem. It was all very well to argue that the Labour left – ideologically unsound, heterogeneous and badly organized – needed the CP as much as the CP needed the Labour left (the latter was in truth very often dependent on the communist press and communist organization, as for instance in the various solidarity campaigns with nationalist movements overseas which the two often ran together). But how could the Labour left be expected to forget the CP's perfidious record of Moscow-dictated policy reversals? *The British Road to Socialism* seems to have been written in the hope that all this would be forgiven or forgotten.

In the 1940s *Tribune* made it clear that the CP's past record could not be forgotten. Under the Attlee governments the Labour left was in any case strongly inclined to support its party's belligerent imperialist policy while the CP was equally keen to oppose it. Foreign policy remained a CP preoccupation in the early 1950s and most of its 1951 programme was concerned with one or another aspect of it. Until the mid-1950s the CP was extremely suspicious even of the Bevanite left on account of its equivocal attitude to the USSR, its courting of Tito and its often positive appraisal of American policy. By 1953 however, Cominform propaganda was substantially toned down and the CP became generally supportive of the Labour left. Indeed the unions where the CP was strong were invariably supporters of Bevanite positions at Labour's annual conference. But by then Labour was consumed by internecine quarrels between the Gailskellite and Bevanite wings and confined to opposition for thirteen years. These were not propitious years for the Left by any reckoning but a united Left such as the CP imagined was a complete non-starter after its support for the Russian invasion of Hungary.

From those who broke with the CP in 1956/7 an independent Marxist left slowly developed while the communists resumed their post-war drift. New drafts of the *British Road to Socialism* appeared in 1958 and 1968 but the party simply ignored the major theoretical and historical issues which it had side-stepped in 1951. It was given to the new left to examine Gramsci's Marxism though many years later the CP would use his ideas as theoretical support for their long-standing orientation to a broad anti-monopoly alliance seeking socialism through peaceful, parliamentary change. But this was for the future. At no time did the party confront the legacy of Leninist and Stalinist politics and its own history of subordination to Soviet socialism. Significant changes, of course, took place in spite of the amnesia and aversion to ideological change of the party leaders.

We have already noted some of the events which gradually corroded unquestioning support for the Russian party. The Sino-Soviet dispute added another fissure to the erstwhile monolith of international communism in the early 1960s. In 1963 a small split occurred in the CP when a group of Maoists led by Michael McCreery left the party to form the Committee to Defeat Revisionism for Communist Unity.[23] The party may have seemed otherwise unconcerned with such ideological

differences. But in most years after 1963 it lost members.
While it may have become irrelevant to the USSR the latter
was slowly beginning to be seen as a burden to Western
communism. Furthermore the most successful representative
of communism in the liberal democracies was also an
ideological innovator – the Italian Communist Party (PCI).
The electoral successes of the PCI stood in complete contrast
to the declining fortunes of the CPGB. The British party's
shrinking membership was forced to compete by the 1960s
with a growing ultra-left and radical extra-parliamentary campaigns had long since ceased to be CP-dominated affairs. To
many of these militants the CP was a despised relic of the
Stalinist past but it was precisely now and perhaps in some
measure because of this challenge on the far left, that the party
began to make adjustments in the old relationships.

In 1968 the party joined with most other West European
communists in denouncing the Soviet invasion of Czechoslovakia. This demonstrated not only a measure of independence from the USSR but also an alignment with and
recognition of, the need for 'socialism with a human face.'
Anti-bureaucratism, anti-centralism and an emphasis on the
virtues of direct action and prefigurative politics were very
much the themes of the student and feminist radicals now
setting the agenda of left politics in many Western countries,
including Britain. Most of the Marxist organizations saw these
'new social movements' as potential growth points for their own
factions. The CP was no exception. The proliferation of these
radical movements and causes took place in the period of the
first two Wilson governments, when individual membership of
the Labour Party plummeted by a quarter of a million and 'the
active Constituency Party organisations shrivelled to a skele-
ton.'[24] The Labour left was thus of little consequence as the
activists deserted the party or allowed themselves to be led by
the Marxists who initiated most of the radical causes from
Vietnamese Solidarity to the Troops Out Movement. The
Labour government pursued policies diametrically opposed to
the decisions of annual conference and disillusioned activists
by its support for the USA in Vietnam. Wilson also instigated a
bitter clash with the trade unions in an attempt to reduce shop

steward power. All the evidence suggested an improvement in the CP's fortunes if it could establish itself as the champion of the unions and the new feminist, student and community politics radicalism. Had it not, since 1951, envisaged the emergence of a very broad coalition of anti-monopoly forces?

The parallel 'discovery' of Gramsci provided the theory which the 1951 programme had lacked and the new social movements seemed to require. The party was in possession of a programme which had been put together for tactical, pragmatic and opportunistic reasons. Yet in committing the party to a long revolution which was to be peaceful, parliamentary and popular, the programme could not be justified on Leninist grounds. The party had dropped the dictatorship of the proletariat, was no longer bent on smashing the state, had discovered the virtues of parliament and was avowedly dependent on alliances with reformists. But where Lenin had analysed bourgeois democracy as a mere sham and the capitalist state was an exclusively coercive machine by which one class oppresses another, Gramsci had argued that the hegemony of the bourgeoisie is constituted in civil society – the realm of 'private' associations. In so doing he had stressed all those facets of class rule especially germane to Western democracies which Lenin had ignored – cultural forms, the generation of consent, the role of ideology etc. A class which wants to re-form the nation must first establish its supremacy here in civil society it could now be argued. To achieve hegemony the working class must exercise intellectual and moral leadership since, as Gramsci observed, class power rests on this basis as well as open coercion. Such intellectual and moral leadership requires that the real interests and aspirations of innumerable and diverse social groups and classes find expression in and are transformed by the programme of the hegemonic class.

But the party was not yet ready to orientate to the new radicalism fully. Indeed it was temporarily by-passed when these movements first appeared but a number of factors enabled it to recover some of the lost ground. The party's annual Communist University was by the mid 1970s the spearhead of its recovery among students. It was undoubtedly aided by the vogue for Althusser and his co-thinkers which dominated leftist debate in the universities during the 1970s. Together with the work of Gramsci with which it coexisted uncomfortably, the Althusserian corpus enhanced the Party's intellectual credibility in student circles and contributed to the recruitment of a new generation less reverent of the old idols than their elders. This also helped to turn the tables on the ultra-left which could get no further than Trotsky in the search for authoritative Marxist analysis. Moreover after 1968 the International Socialists, International Marxist Group and Socialist Labour League vied with each other as the exclusive vanguard party of the working class though none of them could claim more than two thousand members. The CP, on the other hand, in accordance with its alliance strategy was able through a broad left with Labour students to dominate the National Union of Students for most of the 1970s and into the 1980s.

As we saw in chapter 5, the Trotskyist left was also handicapped by its determination to fit all social phenomena into the categories of classical Marxism. In practice this amounted to a preoccupation, particularly from the early 1970s, with industrial disputes.

The Trotskyists – too puny to exercise any real influence – played the part of principal cheer-leaders of the strikers with *Socialist Worker* and the SWP's theoreticians in particular persuaded that mounting wage militancy could under recessionary conditions add up to a political challenge to capitalism.[25] Communist intellectuals were far less sanguine though not until the late 1970s did it become clear that the inflationary wages scramble had actually weakened the Left and exposed the absence of a credible socialist alternative. The first half of the 1970s, in the judgement of one leading communist, had witnessed a new syndicalism but one devoid of the vision and strategy of the original version.[26]

Nevertheless there were important exceptions to this pattern and in one – the Upper Clyde Shipbuilders occupation – communist shop stewards played the leading role. Communist industrial strength was still evident in the 1970s and far greater than that of its Marxist rivals though far less pervasive than Harold Wilson alleged when he raised the communist bogey in 1966 in an attempt to discredit the seamen's strike.

Bert Ramelson, the CP's industrial organizer, was on that occasion ludicrously dubbed 'the most powerful man in Britain'. A powerful communist leadership did, however, make the UCS dispute of 1971 a national media event and one which directly inspired around 190 factory occupations and work-ins between July 1971 and December 1975.[27] Here the communist stewards Jimmy Reid and Jimmy Airlie managed to keep united the workforce of four shipbuilders' yards faced with closure by taking physical control of the premises and launching an appeal for support from the whole labour movement. Leaders of the Labour Party and TUC were forced to declare their support and the Heath government made a dramatic U-turn by reprieving the yards from the liquidator. One of the principal ideological gains of the experience – albeit a temporary one – was that the work-in tactic dispelled the image of the workers as strike-happy and selfish disrupters. In weakening the government's resolve the dispute also paved the way to the victory of the NUM, in 1972 (in which another communist, McGahey, was made the bogey) and, in the same year, the effective abandonment of Heath's Industrial Relations Act. To this extent it also represents the origin of the Thatcherite rebellion within the Conservative Party.

The CPGB also played a leading role in mobilizing militants against the Heath government's general assault on trade union power. It revived the Liaison Committee for the Defence of Trade Unions (LCDTU) – originally set up in 1966 to focus oppositon against the Wilson government's prices and incomes policy – and campaigned from 1970 to pressurize a sluggish TUC to take general strike action against the Industrial Relations Bill. At its conference of February 1972 over one thousand trade union delegates attended while over 3 million stopped work on March 18 1971 in answer to its call for a one-day general strike. The LCDTU also organized mass demonstrations under the slogan 'Kill the Bill' before the TUC was prepared to defy the government. In December 1970 some 600,000 took strike action and mass demonstrations took place in most of the major cities.[28] Two communists were among the five dock workers imprisoned in July 1971 and a communist was one of three building workers imprisoned for 'conspiracy' in 1972.[29]

No communist would doubt that the party played an honourable role in defending basic trade union rights in these years. Divisions were appearing, however, on the question of its assessment of the strike wave and the issue of how its industrial work related to the party's programme. By the mid-1970s a definite Eurocommunist element among the membership was demanding something far more positive than the promotion and defence of strikes. Such militancy in defence of 'working class interests' was the traditional reflex response of the old guard among whom trade union militants, the party's working class cadre and most of the leadership were prominent (though not exclusively so). When the Wilson government announced in 1974 its intention of implementing a Social Contract negotiated with the TUC, Bert Ramelson, the CP's Industrial Organiser, denounced it as a 'con-trick'. Here the party announced its opposition to all wage restraint while demanding all manner of public expenditure increases on benefits, housing, pensions, health and so on in accordance with the Alternative Economic Strategy (AES).[30] The AES was elaborated by the Left from the late 1960s and variants of it were incorporated into the Labour programmes of 1974 and 1983. Until the advent of 'Thatcherism' the CP agitated for a strong version of the AES which included selective import controls, withdrawal from the EEC and a programme of nationalization designed to implement central planning.

This kind of programme lacked credibility in the view of those 'Gramscians' in the organization who argued that if there was to be a socialist solution to the British economic crisis it had to address real problems in such a way that the labour movement began immediately to operate as a leading force. This could not done by making general propaganda on the merits of socialism. Actual possibilities had to be assessed in conjunction with the reorganization required to realize them. Since there was no escaping the conclusion that inflation was indeed the result of wage militancy – it was 'the only consistent explanation for the emergence of *persistent* · inflation as the major economic problem of modern capitalism'[31] – no useful purpose was served by blind opposition to wage controls. Instead the organizations of the working class should construct their own incomes policy as a bargaining device for greater say in economic decision-making. Thus as a quid pro quo for wage restraint the trade unions could demand a decisive say in the allocation of the investment resources so released. The merit of such a general approach, for which this instance serves merely as an exemplar, is that it practically advances the political sophistication of the working class and represents the starting point for a counter-hegemonic strategy of the sort Gramsci insisted upon.

The same or similar themes were taken up – mainly by the party's economists – in the pages of its theoretical journal *Marxism Today* from the mid 1970s. Here it was argued that

> what above all characterised the decade from 1966–75 was that the ruling class was unable decisively to impose a new strategic course on the working class whilst the working class . . . failed to advance beyond the bounds of corporate defencism to mount an offensive political struggle around a credible alternative economic programme of its own.[32]

Once again it is argued that the incoherence and implausibility of the Left's own programme stemmed from its desire to plan everything *except* wages. But it is also pointed out that the demand for large-scale extensions of nationalization achieved the same undermining effect. Although the wages-inflation issue undoubtedly rankled the fundamentalists in the organization it concealed for a while a much bigger ideological gulf between sections of the party which would soon be at war with each other.

For those inspired by Gramsci and the modern PCI were embarking on an altogether different enterprise from the one which for over four decades had made the CPBG a purely oppositional party. The modernizers wanted recognition of the need to change habits, practices, values and institutions *now* in order to make socialism something more than propaganda They reasoned that the social order rests on consent and a social practice that serves to reproduce the class system. Only because this social practice often embodies principles of action which anticipate an alternative social order is it possible to challenge the hegemony of the dominant group. But for this to happen organized socialists must assist in unlocking the socialist potential in actually existing movements and social forces. In this view the party does not act as a Leninist vanguard or the paternal custodian of other people's interests but in the spirit of a conscious section in a pluralist movement of self-emancipation. This view therefore rejects the Leninist mode of organization and insists on the need for real democracy in working-class organizations – whether trade union, Labour or communist.[33]

Equally rejected is the dismissive idea of 'bourgeois democracy' as something exclusively fashioned in the image and interests of one class. Meaningful reforms *are* possible and suggest a strategy something like Rudi Dutschke's 'long march through the institutions', but only if socialists avoid mere propaganda and initiate specific policies in specific areas designed to bring about structural changes. Revolutionary change, in this view, does not take place because of a moment of dislocation any more than progress can be measured by increases in private wealth. Socialists must champion that opinion and those movements which since 1968 have shown potential for the subversion of capitalist values and bourgeois hegemony – specifically the demands of conservationists, the revival of 'community' and nationalist movements, demands for direct democracy and women's liberation – 'in essence . . . all socialising movements'.[34] Finally it is argued that left unity is a victim of the sectarian origins of the CPGB, the total acquiescence of the party in Stalinism and its continued inability to sever the link with Moscow as well as the Cold War and the hostility of social democrats.

When in the 1970s such arguments began to be produced by members of the CPGB they were not only confined to a small minority of (mainly) intellectuals but they seemed to have no vigorous support among the party leadership. Some measure of the peculiar nature of the transition then taking place can be gauged from the retiring general secretary's assessment of 'socialist democracy' on the twentieth anniversary of Kruschev's secret speech.[35] While unable to go along with the idea that the 'personality cult' could explain the criminal abuses of power in the USSR Gollan was simply incapable of improving on Kruschev's 'explanation'. Thus according to this view the Red Army proved by its defeat of Nazism 'that the basic socialist foundations of the Soviet Union were unshaken despite the crimes in the period of Stalin's leadership'.[36] Since 1956, we are told, the superiority of the socialist system has been demonstrated not simply economically but, 'with power in the hands of the working class', also in terms of 'the widest satisfaction of human economic, social and cultural needs'. Its problems are essentially problems of growth whereas the heyday of 'bourgeois demoracy' is past since, as Gollan argues, it is under 'increasing threat' of authoritarianism.[37] In this way Gollan opened a debate in the party's theoretical journal which merely served to illustrate the great variety of positions on this crucial issue among the membership, ranging from those who saw the origins of degeneration in Lenin's time and policies to those who could see no problem and wondered what all the fuss was about.[38]

The frustration of the Eurocommunist element can be imagined. Gollan was succeeded by Gordon McLennan who showed no interest either in driving out the old-fashioned authoritarians or in embracing the new mentality. Nevertheless the energies of these opposing forces went into the creation of a new draft of the party's programme which appeared in February 1977 and was debated publicly until the 35th congress of the party in November of the same year. With the exception of a group of around 700 who resigned to form the (Stalinist) New Communist Party, the new programme seemingly managed to accommodate all shades of opinion within the CPGB. Since 1951 the organization had been talking of a socialist transition without civil war and by means of a socialist parliamentary majority supported by mass extra-parliamentary struggles.[39] The 1978 edition inserted the idea of a broad democratic alliance where once the programme had spoken of an anti-monopoly alliance. In the new version the 'new social movements' are used frequently to illustrate the old arguments. More emphasis is given to the party's democratic commitments but this is quite in keeping with the original identification of monopoly capital as the enemy of virtually everybody else: hence the need for a broadly-based coalition, left unity, tolerance of diversity and systematic democratiz-ation of society. But the party also asserts the superiority of actually existing socialism over capitalism and of the ideology of 'Marxism Leninism',[40] the need for democratic centralism as well as the 'key and decisive responsibility' of the Commun-ist Party. In all these respects the fundamentalist element got its own way while making one or two verbal concessions.

Thus the working class is described as the 'leading force' of the alliance. At its 'heart' are workers in extractive industries, manufacturing and transport although the programme allows that professionals and non-manual workers are also members of the working class which is in any case not static in composition and structure. In this way every conceivable position is cobbled together. A similar attempt at compromise is made on the question of democratic centralism which is needed, so we are told, to realize internal democratic norms. Yet soon after this doubtful proposition the programme argues that the party's inner life 'needs enrichment' to make it more democratic. By itself of course this is only feeble evidence that attempts were being made to deal with the legacy of Stalinism. But no sooner was the programme adopted than a further lengthy period of introspection was begun when a Commission on Inner-Party Democracy was set up – proof in itself that the modernizers were having an effect. Two more years elapsed before a report on this matter was brought to the party's 36th congress in November 1979.

In the event the proposals actually adopted by the congress convey the impression of a rearguard action by defenders of the status quo trying to beat off criticism with purely verbal amendments to the time-honoured formulae – rather in the fashion of the last report on this issue in 1957.[41] This time, however, six of the 16 members of the Commission produced a minority report which argued that 'part of our heritage is those bureaucratic, anti-democratic, distorting practices which have come to be known as Stalinism'.[42] Both in the election and exercise of leadership, they argued, the party is out of step with its programme. The CP does not yet permit and encourage its branches to take political initiatives. It is too centralized for that and this rigidity, they observe, is augmented by the rarity with which mistakes are openly recognized and the leadership is seen to learn from experience. This leadership is largely a self-recruiting elite since the executive committee is able to nominate its successors by means of a recommended list. The executive committee, in turn, is dominated by the political committee. Promotions are based on 'sponsorship' and genuine democracy is stymied by the refusal to allow different trends of opinion within the party to express themselves via the circulation of written papers in pre-congress periods. It is argued that barriers exist which restrict such 'horizontal communication' between branches and regions while dissident members of the executive are not allowed to explain to the ranks and report back the reasons for disagreement with party policy. In short, the minority report recommended far-reaching changes designed to open up the organization to the more recent and more dynamic elements of the membership at the expense of the entrenched cadre. Roughly speaking such changes would have had the short-term effect of bringing the party closer to the 'new social movements' and 'Eurocommunist' vision of the modernizers.

One of these, Martin Jacques, was already editor of the party's theoretical journal *Marxism Today* where he announced his intention to open its pages to non-communist contributors and encourage a British focus on topical issues aimed at a much wider audience.[43] All of this was achieved and *Marxism Today* became the party's one success story. While membership, trade union and electoral influence continued to fall, *Marxism Today* became the acknowledged forum for left debate with a circulation (12,500) bigger than the number of party members. The *Morning Star*, on the other hand, firmly under the control of the party's 'Marxist Leninist' wing, catered for its stagnant readership with an unrelenting diet of trade union news informed by militant postures which were soon exposed as complacent and ill-informed.

It wasn't simply that in the general election of 1979 trade union militancy was widely regarded as a cause of the downfall of the Labour government or that the Tory victors had won with a manifesto containing promises of an attack on trade union powers. The Thatcher victory also seemed to expose the ideological weaknesses not just of Labour but of Labour in both variants – left and right – as well as the communists and the far left. In usurping the language of individual rights and liberty, by championing anti-statism and an array of cultural issues on which the fundamentalist left in particular had virtually nothing to say, Thatcher's victory had the incidental effect of strengthening the position of those socialists long since dissatisfied with the statist and paternalist forms of socialism. These were also the socialists who had learned from Gramsci that the socialist project had to relate to the cultural life of the mass of the population where a vast array of ruling-class ideas had to be combated. In 1979 the dominant discourse of the Left was virtually devoid of this insight and on many basic issues – law and order, freedom of choice, home ownership and so on – the rhetoric of the Right encountered no resistance in spite of decades of social democratic consensus. This underlined, of course, the extent to which the post-war consensus had left untouched values inimical to socialism and how little by way of a socialist morality and value system had been created.

The pages of *Marxism Today* were devoted to understanding the meaning of Thatcherism and creating an agenda for the recovery of the Left. But the debate was really begun by Eric Hobsbawm's Marx Memorial Lecture in 1978 when the CP historian asked if 'the forward march of Labour' had been halted. The very posing of this question at a time when Labour still held power, trade union membership had reached a post-war peak and the Labour left had grown (and included a sizeable entrist faction in the Militant tendency) reveals the gulf in perceptions between the small but innovative left, loosely Eurocommunist, and the much larger traditional left on the brink of challenging for the Labour leadership and per-suaded that once this was accomplished the last barrier to socialist government would be overcome. In contrast Hobsbawm talked of a thirty-year crisis of the labour move-ment characterized by a decline of the manual working class, a growth of sectionalism at the expense of class solidarity and a long-term fall in the Labour vote and membership of socialist organizations. While Hobsbawm specifically drew attention to the largely sterile economistic militancy of the period 1970–74 his opponents in the debate which followed asserted that the labour movement had never been stronger and that 'wage battles . . . will through militancy challenge contemporary capitalism.'[44]

Just before the May general election of 1979 bore witness to Hobsbawm's central argument Stuart Hall argued forcefully that Thatcherism represented something more than just another reactionary Tory political trend.[45] It represented instead an authoritarian populism bent on a radical reversal of the post-war drift of British society which sought to shift the terms of political debate on the basis of a new, reactionary common sense. Its rise was predicated on the decline of Labourism utilizing the internal contradictions of the social-democratic consensus and those elements of popular consciousness either abandoned or absent from Labourism. It had occupied the terrain of ideology – 'mere ideology' in the perception of the hard left – and had harnessed a range of fears (on race, education, trade union power, crime, statism, etc.) for a great assault on collectivism. From this analysis and its development into the 1980s, with the experience of the Thatcher government on hand to invest it with urgency and immediacy, the argument concluded that while the decay of Labourism was an opportunity for the Left 'the most crucial task' is to concert the anti-Thatcher forces and create 'the broadest possible set of alliances'.[46]

Most of the Marxist and quasi-Marxist left (the latter and much of the former by 1979 grouped around Tony Benn in the Labour Party) thought otherwise and concerted their forces in campaigns to change the Labour Party constitution and win the deputy leadership for the hard left. This was a credible step in the direction of socialism for so many communists because for decades the CP had argued – the most recent programme still does – that no advance was possible until the right-wing usurpers of the Parliamentary Labour Party were removed from influence and the organization adopted a genuinely socialist programme. The constitutional changes which the Benn campaign actually obtained together with the defection of right-wingers to form the Social Democratic Party actually paved the way for the adoption of a programme in 1983 radical by the standards of traditional leftist criteria. Moreover the fundamentalists in the CPGB perceived that behind the common talk of broad democratic alliances which they shared with the Eurocommunists lay completely different priorities. The latter were all doubts and questionings on the very basics of socialist theory (and East European practice) and pursuant of every radical and liberal trend that raised its head. The spectacular defection of a 'Eurocommunist' member of the party executive and former communist president of the National Union of Students to the Council for Social Democracy highlighted the lack of ideological rigour and cohesion in an organization which for the fundamentalists had opened its doors to anybody but was incapable of inducting recruits and formulating, let alone enforcing, a party line. Naturally the Marxist-Leninists in the party were also alarmed at its continued slide into obscurity – one useful index of this being that CP candidates in local elections were now regularly beaten by candidates from other peripheral organizations. Thus in 1978, for example, the fascist National Front surpassed the CP in 26 out of 29 common contests while the Trotskyist 'Socialist Unity' candidates beat the CP in five out of seven.[47]

But it was this same remorseless decline which eventually forced the party's leadership around Gordon McLennan to choose between its warring factions. On one side were the innovators who had taken the ideological initiative and whose doubts on the efficacy of industrial militancy were well advanced by 1979. These were the people who also questioned the desirability of 'actually existing socialism' – whether Soviet or home-spun. On the other side were the party's traditionalists fearful that the orientation to the new social movements actually entailed the surrender of class politics and the corrosion of the party's original virtues – in particular its discipline, unity, ideological self-sufficiency and selflessness for the cause. Both sides were imperfectly represented by the party's principal journals, *Marxism Today* and the *Morning Star*. Even now it is not certain why the party leadership threw its weight behind the modernizers but it is surely connected to the successes in 1979 and 1983 of the Thatcherites which provided a major boost to revisionist forces all along the left spectrum. Whatever the causes, an alliance of *Marxism Today*, the party leadership and members loyal to one or both of these was in command of the organization by the early 1980s.

These divisions within the party surfaced in August 1982 when the private dispute went public when the *Morning Star* attacked the policy of *Marxism Today*. It should be clear by now that this was not the start of the CPGB's crisis but merely the most recent episode in a crisis which began over thirty years ago. The party has even now not come to terms with its Leninist and Stalinist past while drifting since 1951 with a programme which has united Stalinists and those who eventually sought to break free from much of the legacy of 1917. When the party's 38th congress convened in November 1983, delegates were presented with a faction paper *Congress Truth* through which the forces led by the *Morning Star* took the unprecedented step of providing an alternative recommended list of candidates for election to the executive committee. The challenge was soundly defeated and congress voted for the removal of the editor and deputy editor of the *Morning Star*. However they could not be removed until the AGM of the People's Press Printing Society (PPPS) met in June 1984 since this body actually owns the newspaper. But though 3,000 shareholders were mobilized for this event the meeting re-elected the editors 'sacked' by the party.

By November 1984 oppositionist majorities were returned to the district leaderships of the CP in London and the North West. At the North West district congress eleven of those on the recommended list for district committee were defeated by candidates broadly sympathetic to the *Morning Star*. The legitimacy of these elections was denied by the party leadership on grounds of violations of the norms of inner-party democracy (i.e. factions). Factions such as the North Manchester Marxist Forum and *Morning Star* Readers' Associations did by now openly exist in support of the opposition. The party's general secretary then attempted to dissolve the London district congress to pre-empt another success for the opposition but 125 delegates refused to follow him out of the congress hall. Founder members of the party Robin Page Arnot and Andrew Rothstein denounced the leadership in the pages of the *Morning Star* under headlines declaring 'CP Executive Wrecking Action' and 'Eurocommunist Opportunism'. The party was ridiculed for 'currying favour with the more "advanced" spokesmen of capitalist society' and by January 1985 was described as an 'outside body' by its own newspaper. The CP was forced to launch an alternative called *Focus* (since replaced by *Seven Days*) which at a cost of £30,000 was distributed free to all party members in the mistaken belief that a quick mobilization for the next AGM of the PPPS could defeat the opposition. Meanwhile the opposition enlisted trade union leaders such as Arthur Scargill and Moss Evans to their cause.

Expulsions began in January 1985 and a special congress was called for May when the leadership was able to secure two to one majorities for all its policies. But in June, AGMs of the PPPS held in Glasgow, Manchester and London voted by a convincing three to two majority for management committee nominees chosen by the *Morning Star*. At these meetings the CP was attacked by industrial militants for its lukewarm support for the miners' strike and Arthur Scargill denounced *Marxism Today* and the party's industrial organiser for respectively 'compromising with the class enemy' and 'vilifying' the NUM. By now the *Morning Star* was more closely associated with non-party socialists such as Benn, Scargill and even the Trotskyists of the Militant tendency than it was with the CP. These were all united in their abhorrence for *Marxism Today* and in their conviction that the socialist ideas and electoral support required for the defeat of Thatcher were ready to hand if only a clear lead was given by a united, militant left. A variety of factional journals propounded variants of this thesis inside the CP but those identified as supporters of *Straight Left* and the *Leninist* were effectively expelled from the party when whole branches were dissolved and required to re-register. Perhaps as many as two thousand members were dealt with in this way though many oppositionists remain in the ranks. On the outside now a Communist Campaign Group has been formed to win back the CP to Leninism. But the real problems exist on the inside. It is not yet clear why the 'machine minders' of the leadership finally backed *Marxism Today* in this dispute. Was it simply to support a success story or does it represent a genuine shift towards Eurocommunism by those who dragged their feet when such perspectives were originally advanced in the 1970s? Either way this trend will not be consolidated until it can reverse the decline in membership which now stands at a mere 11,000. The role of think-tank for the Left may have its attractions for some of the party's intellectuals but it is anathema to many communists who remember the days when the CP actually led the sort of campaigns its programme now makes so much of.

7

Militant and Entrism

Entrism

The tactic of infiltrating rival political organizations – entrism – was a feature of Bolshevik politics inside Russian social democracy after 1905[1] and on Lenin's recommendation acquired routine application by communists 'in every last organisation' of the working class.[2] The CP, repeatedly frustrated in its attempt to affiliate to the Labour Party, accordingly conducted entrism therein for the first twenty years of its existence as the British section of the Comintern. But by 1940 the tactic was dropped. Obviously the wartime electoral truce rendered such activity irrelevant as constituency politics withered away. Once the war was over, as we have seen, the Labour Party took measures to extinguish communist hopes of affiliation and so the principal *raison d'être* of the CP's entrist campaigns was removed. Even so, had entrism even been an efficient method of exercising influence and gaining recruits we may be sure that these considerations would have weighed heavily in the balance. The fact that systematic communist infiltration actually came to an end suggests that the party's long experience of covert work inside the Labour Party was an unhappy one.[3]

After all, entrism is based on duplicity and deceit: no matter how persuasive the entrists' arguments the members of the host organization will not take kindly to being hoodwinked. Trotsky and his followers recognized this problem in the early 1930s but since they could be counted in tens rather than tens

of thousands independent party building was a futile project
for them. The so-called 'French Turn' of 1934 signalled
recognition of this reality and thereafter the tiny groups of
Trotskyists entered parties of the left just as their comrades
had done in France and Britain. Of course it was impossible to
bring off this expedient without occasioning 'principled' splits
among the faithful – some of whom declaimed against 'liquidationism' and the abandoning of earlier rhetoric concerning the
construction of independent mass parties. Trotsky, as always,
was compelled to write essays of advice, persuasion and
exhortation. A good deal of this cajolery amounts to no more
than the 'fatuous trivia' he once complained of though this has
never deterred contemporary Trotskyists from invoking it to
support current 'theory'. What is clear, however, is that the
organizations which the Trotskyists entered in the 1930s were
faction-ridden parties generally moving leftwards, at least in
terms of the rhetoric and demands employed. These 'centrist'
organizations were unstable, perhaps likely to collapse or be
'hi-jacked' by the communists. Trotsky hoped that by entering
them his followers would act like a 'little lever' turning the
organizations towards Trotskyism. If at the end of the process
the growth of the Trotskyist entrists should contribute to the
destruction of the host organization – so much the better, an
'obstacle' has thereby been removed.[4]

On the other hand, communists and Trotskyists also occasionally held out the prospect of completely transforming the
larger party rather than simply destroying it or detaching a
section of its membership. In Britain the returns from entrism
have been so derisory that until the publicity which attached to
Militant in the 1970s this prospect was always thought incre-
dible. In the 1940s the Healy group advocated entrism in the
Labour Party on the eccentric reasoning that less than two
hundred Trotskyists, most of them in London, could by virtue
of a major economic and political crisis so intervene in its
internal afairs that they would emerge as leaders of a mass
revolutionary movement. This was the stuff of fantasy but it
had an authority among most Trotskyists because it was
Trotsky who dreamed the original scenario in the 1930s –
precisely along these lines. Nevertheless even in the 1940s we

have seen that Healy's Trotskyist opponents eventually came over to the entrist tactic for the exact opposite reason. Haston, Ted Grant and company envisaged years of sectarian isolation in trivial groups at the margins of political life *unless* their small band took shelter in the Labour Party. Here years of waiting would be required before circumstances became more propitious for growth and revolutionary politics.

Almost twenty years after Healy embarked on full-time entrism his faction, on the eve of '1956', amounted to less than 100. By then he had parted company with the Fourth International and the latter was concerned to establish an official section. A Committee for the Regroupment of the British Section of the Fourth International was set up in 1955. In this chapter we will consider the evolution of that portion of it which thirty years later became better known as the Militant tendency.

Origins of Militant

The search for an official section of the International in Britain inevitably led to a regroupment of those members of the old RCP who had opposed Healy in the 1940s: these now once again had something in common with the FI. Ted Grant and Jimmy Deane resumed contact. In January 1955 Grant told Deane that Liverpool was to be the base from which their tiny group would spread its influence 'in Lancashire, then London, and nationally'.[5] From the beginning of their restored favour with the FI, Grant and Deane were wary of committing themselves to an organization whose leaders had destroyed the RCP. But they recognized the advantages that would accrue from some sort of working relationship with the International – at least it would then be possible to finance a theoretical journal for instance. This would be an enormous gain for a group of twenty individuals scattered in different branches of the Labour Party. Outside London, Liverpool was the only place where several reliable members could be found. Here Deane was active in the Walton branch of the party and this was where he had joined the Workers' International League in

1939. Along with his brother Brian, Paddy Wall and Terry
Harrison – who joined the group in 1958 – Jimmy Deane
managed to make the Walton constituency party a secure base
for the Revolutionary Socialist League (RSL) which he co-
founded with Ted Grant. In June 1957 the RSL staged its first
national congress. At the start of 1958 it began publication of
Socialist Fight.

At this early stage the tiny RSL had the resources of the
International to assist it. Grant and Deane were also on good
terms with Eric Heffer but differed on the question of tactics.
Heffer's Socialist Workers' Federation refused to throw in its
lot with total entrism and would go along with the RSL on this
question only as far as maintaining an entrist fraction.[6]
Amazingly, since no one noticed the fact, the RSL also had the
assistance of the Labour MP for Wolverhampton North East,
John Baird, who must be counted the first Trotskyist MP. But
the RSL's inaugural congress documents testify to the group's
firm conviction that only an economic crisis would enable the
group to achieve its ambitions:

> Both in the Wards and in the trade union branches, a
> convulsive shake-up under these conditions would be
> inevitable. The Right Wing would find itself isolated . . .
> the Ward and Constituency organisations will be vibrant
> with life . . . the youth . . . will be revitalised and pushed
> towards the radical left . . . the crisis of the Labour Party
> will be far-reaching and deep. . . A really strong and
> organised Left Wing would come rapidly into existence:
> the possibility of a split in the event of the Right Wing
> retaining control of the Party apparatus would be present.
> It is however more likely that the Left would gain the
> majority and transform the Labour Party into a mass
> centrist organisation. . . In either case the work of the
> revolutionary Marxists in the period ahead must be
> largely the preparation and training of a cadre with such a
> perspective in view. The intervention of a disciplined
> group of Marxists, politically educated in the Trotskyist
> method, steeled in struggle and imbued with a capacity to
> intervene in the mass movement without sectarian reserv-

ations will yield ready results in a broad movement ready as never before, to receive and assimilate the revolutionary programme.[7]

This was for the future; the immediate prospect was one of 'slow methodical and persistent agitation'.

From the outset the RSL was careful to rationalize its Labour Party work so that responsibilities of a routine character or activities devoid of political weight were avoided like the plague. But the most important organizational imperative was to establish separate groups of trusted militants:

> These groups will meet and decide tactics and work before Labour Party meetings etc. They should be centrally linked by a committee which should give the responsibility to someone to organise this work, setting model resolutions, keeping a record of members and contacts, organising the articles for the Labour Party journal, initiating local area meetings and conferences to discuss work and programmes, development of the fight against local and national bureaucratic restrictions and impositions on Labour Parties.[8]

Of course it is pointed out that the RSL's journal 'should become a voice of these groups and be used as a medium of discussion, information and initiating of this work'. For entrists the newspaper is absolutely central. Its very title will change to denote tactical shifts, realignments and political perspectives. Changes of format, frequency and content invariably communicate changes in the group's politics. If a split in the organization occurs – such as the 1986 division within the Socialist League – we may be sure that the group publishing *International*, for example, is the one which has maintained its connection with the FI. If a paper changes its name from *Labour Worker* to *Socialist Worker*, say, this may well denote an intention to abandon entrism.[9] These considerations should be borne in mind when we come to discuss the politics of *Militant*.

An interesting light is cast on the politics of the RSL when the group is considered from this organizational angle. So

concerned with their own security were they that this tiny,
ineffectual and unnoticed group created a committee to ensure
that documents circulated for discussion would bear no evidence of authorship lest they fell into the wrong hands. Thus
'all the texts for internal discussion must be published through
this committee.'[10] Clearly this entailed a degree of centralism
unconducive to the formation of factions or indeed any 'horizontal communication' between different groups of RSL
members. Since these were disadvantaged anyway by the conditions of entrism – to the extent that the groups were not
supposed to exist at all – it is not surprising that the Fourth
International eventually complained that the RSL lacked an
'internal life'.[11] The truth is that the RSL and its offspring
Militant were always extremely centralized groups and for this
reason the leadership never had the difficulties encountered in
other far left groups with opposition factions and tendencies.

The RSL constitution, in common with those of other
Trotskyist groups, permits the formation of minority platforms
within the organization and allows them the right to use internal bulletins for the dissemination of opinions opposed to those
of the leadership. But as in all Leninist groups real power is
vested in the higher committees and 'all decisions of the governing bodies are binding upon all members and subordinate
units'. Naturally the entrist group insists that 'all members
holding public office, paid or otherwise, shall come under the
complete control of the party and its organs . . . all members of
the Revolutionary Socialist League are required to enter the
mass organisations of the working class under the direction of
the party organs for the purpose of fulfilling the aims of the
party.'[12] It was always customary in Leninist parties for elected
representatives to provide the leadership with a letter of resig-
nation which could be invoked the moment the MP or councillor offended against the party. If the over-riding allegiance is to
the party this is because 'The basis of all work within the mass
movement is the construction of the revolutionary party for the
overthrow of capitalism. Work in the Labour Party, trade union
branches, Trades Councils, Co-operative organisations, Young
Socialist branches and local government authorities is subor-
dinated to this fundamental task.'[13]

There is no question of the Leninist party subscribing to parliamentary democracy:

> Unlike the reformists, centrists and stalinists the Marxists reject decisively the theory of the Parliamentary road to socialism and stand four-square on the revolutionary necessity of constructing a combat party of the Fourth International for the replacement of capitalist membership by a workers' state. The Marxists, therefore, do not accept the view that it is possible, within the framework of Parliament or the existing structure of local government to achieve Socialism. The Parliamentary system has to be replaced by the soviet system. This applies on a local as well as a national level. The Marxist concept of local government is seen to be part of the concept of a soviet workers' council system based on the nationalisation of the commanding heights of the economy.[14]

These strictures on local government, although composed in 1961, were not entirely academic even then since both Pat Wall and Brian Deane became councillors in Liverpool soon afterwards. (The author was Ellis Hillman himself a GLC councillor in years to come.) At this relatively early stage in its development the RSL argued that 'the base of reformism both historically and as far as local Labour Parties are concerned rests in local government.' It was here in local government – an arena traditionally neglected by British Marxists – that the RSL urged the need for special work.

> To lift the horizon of the local parish-pump politicians on to the broader national and international field – this is the first task of the revolutionary Councillor . . . Marxists also reject the reformist view of Council work as a 'thing in itself' . . . it is necessary within the Labour Groups and in open council to point out the limitations of particular struggles and reforms and show how (in theory and practice) reformism (nationally and locally) cannot resolve the contradictions of capitalism.

Finally these 'Notes on Council Work' spell out the policy later associated with *Militant*: 'Marxists oppose all rent and rates increases on the grounds that the burden of these increases should not be imposed on the class which is least able to afford them but on the class whose system is responsible for the pressure on local government, for high rents and high rates.'[15]

It was during the talks on unity between the RSL and the International Group to which I alluded in chapter 5 that the suggestion was first made to name the 'entrist propaganda paper' '*The Militant*'.[16] In June 1964 a sub-committee of the RSL executive voted three to one in favour of the title *Militant: for Labour and Youth* with Ted Grant in the minority.[17] Later the same month Peter Taaffe complained to Deane that 'it is imposssible for me to do the Secretary, local and National (Youth) jobs as well as be an effective editor of the paper.'[18] From the first issue of *Militant* Taaffe was put in charge. There can be no doubt, therefore, that the newspaper *Militant* was launched by an entrist organization called the Revolutionary Socialist League. The present editors of the paper have always denied any knowledge of the RSL and no doubt hoped that the group's security precautions would suffice to maintain the cover-up. In fact all the documentary evidence was eventually provided by the group's co-founder Jimmy Deane. Among his voluminous papers there is even one which contains the rare mistake of an attendance list in which the full names of committee members are given: these include Peter Taaffe, Pat Wall, Doug Holmes, Terry Harrison, Harry Dowling and Tony Mulhearn.[19]

By 1965 the RSL numbered around 100 members. An important base was established at Sussex University. This was big enough to produce two local journals – *Spark* and *International Perspectives* – and a number of future leaders such as Clare Doyle, Lynn Walsh, Alan Woods, Roger Silverman, Bob Edwards and Pat Craven. 1965 is significant also as the year when the RSL ended the years of pseudo-collaboration with the Fourth International. But it is more important for the fact that it was then that the Labour Party Young Socialist (LPYS) organization was created. In the previous years Transport House had fought a running battle against Healy's SLL and the latter finally wrecked the Young Socialists in the process of building its own youth organization. When the LPYS was set up the surviving entrist groups endeavoured to use it as the 'little lever' of their own ambitions. But since the International Socialists were from this time withdrawing from entrism the battle for control of the LPYS was really between the RSL and their even smaller erstwhile comrades in the International Group. Within two years a member of the RSL was elected to the LPYS national committee. By 1970 it had secured a majority and most members of the LPYS national committee were full-time organizers for the entrists (who had prudently stopped referring to the RSL in the wake of the expulsion of Healy's followers in 1964). With the IMG also withdrawing from entrism in 1969 the rise of Militant (as it was now known) was made that much easier. The Labour Party also helped by providing the LPYS with *Left* in 1967 – a journal which duly propagated the Militant line. In 1972 Militant was also given the place on Labour's NEC allotted for youth: since then Peter Doyle, Nick Bradley, Tony Saunois, Lawrence Coates and Steve Morgan – all members of Militant – have held this position.

The politics of Militant

In 1973 Militant talked of the beginning of the crisis which its leaders had been predicting since they joined the Trotskyist movement in the 1930s. The key feature of this crisis was supposed to be a 'ferment in social democracy' and the rapid emergence of 'the revolutionary tendency' within it.[20] Grant had explained in 1959 – in response to impatience with the entrist tactic – that the end result of the crisis would be the transformation of the Labour Party into 'a revolutionary party.' Thus there had never been any question on this reasoning of using entrism to make short-term membership gains for the purpose of building an open rival party to that of Labour. According to Grant 'the historical justification for the policy of entrism' was to transform Labour itself. This is consistent, at least, with the Militant thesis that both reformism and parliamentarism are attributable to the work of a politically corrupt (read middle-class) leadership based on the aristocracy of labour:

> Relying on the double exploitation of workers in the colonies, British capitalism was able to buy off a small, skilled section of the working class by conceding above average living standards to them. It was upon this section, plus the growing members of trade union officials and middle class 'Lib-Labs' who found their way into the leadership of the Labour Movement, that the ruling class were to depend to hold the movement back.

Thus once the middle-class leadership is ousted all will be well with Labour: 'Then as now it was the lack of a clear Marxist leadership, prepared and determined to draw together the separate strands of industrial and political struggle to achieve a definite solution to the destruction of the moribund capitalist system and the building of a socialist society.'[21] The problem, then, is one of leadership, as Trotsky insisted in the 1930s: the analysis has even older roots – in Lenin's *Imperialism* of 1916.

Militant is proud of the ancestry of its argument and boasts of the legacy of Lenin and Trotsky, the first four congresses of the Comintern and the foundation documents of the Fourth International.[22] 'Correct ideas' amount to no more than the faction lore of Grant's tendency within the Trotskyist movement since 1938 and the Workers' International League. As for the Fourth International itself, Militant is persuaded that 'Even to dignify this tendency by calling it centrist would be a compliment . . . twenty five years . . . has indicated that they are organically incapable of transformation organisationally and politically in the direction of Marxism.'[23] This accurately captures the contempt which Militant feels towards its fellow Trotskyists. There is therefore no question of collaboration between Militant and the FI. Instead it has sought to 'develop and broaden . . . work among contacts, groups and even individuals that we can reach in other countries.' Militant's dominance of the LPYS after 1970 enabled it to use Labour's money and organizational resources to make these contacts. By these means Andy Bevan, Peter Doyle, Tom Aitman, Alex Wood and Brian Monaghan were able to attend conferences of European youth organizations to make contacts for Militant. By 1975 Militant boasted brother parties in Spain, France, Greece, Sweden, Ireland, West Germany, Belgium, Canada and Sri Lanka. Only the last mentioned, however, was of any significance. The Irish section in 1975, for example, numbered only 31.[24] Crick reckons that Militant now dominates the youth section of the Irish Labour Party (3,000 to 4,000 members) but observes that elsewhere – again with the exception of Sri Lanka – its sympathizers are insignificant.[25]

We may be sure that Militant's friends abroad pursue identical positions and causes. Militant is completely intolerant of those who dare to disagree and reserves its fiercest scorn for near-neighbours such as 'the anti-Marxist sects'[26] i.e. rival Marxist groups. These are swept aside as the work of false prophets with a 'middle-class' disdain for the proletariat. In fact this only betrays Militant's conviction that the real stuff of socialist politics takes place inside Labour and trade union organizations and consists of the agenda which these bodies set: other priorities – feminism, ecology, peace, etc. – are merely the effete concerns of the 'middle class'. Thus any group which actually takes these issues seriously is necessarily inept. All the other Marxist organizations qualify for Militant's contempt because they have dared at one time or another to build open parties and in so doing have courted students, feminists and peace campaigners.

Militant's disdain for its rivals is no stronger than the hubris with which it describes itself: 'What guarantees the superiority of our tendency – the tendency of Marxism – from all others inside and outside the labour movement is our understanding of all the myriad factors which determine the attitudes and moods of the workers at each stage. Not only the objective but the subjective ones too.'[27] This was probably written by Grant or Taaffe but it represents more than the pathetic self-delusion of one person: it represents the conviction that to qualify as a genuine Leninist party it is necessary to possess a monopoly of truth and prescience. Undoubtedly this dubious idea is to be found in the writings of Lenin and Trotsky. It is chiefly from this source that Militant has learned to assert without blushing that 'our organisations are alone in upholding the banner of Marxism . . . we repudiate every sectarian fragment appropriating the name of Fourth International.'[28] In practice it has meant that Militant abjures contact between its supporters and 'the sects.' It argues that 'experience has shown that the task of re-education especially of their middle class elements takes so long and is such an exhausting process that it is not worth the effort.'[29] This insularity serves the useful purpose of protecting Militant members from dangerous contamination from ideas. Militant's absence from campaigns initiated by the other Marxist groups has the same useful side-effect as does its disdain for the 'new social movements'. It is noteworthy that Militant is weak where the socialist tradition is strong, as in Scotland, and relatively well-established where alternative socialist ideas have only feeble roots, such as in Liverpool.[30] All this – together with the fact that Militant's growth in the Labour Party coincided wth the absence of its Leninist rivals – suggests that it has protected itself by sectarianism and created a following only where competition was absent.

Certainly we look in vain if we try to find the causes of Militant's later growth in its ability to set the agenda of left debate and initiative. In fact the 'tendency' has confined itself to the advancement of its members through the labyrinth of Labour and trade union machine politics. It has to be said that Militant has proved itself a much more serious student than the other Marxist groups in learning the basic lessons of this game. To get one's members selected as Labour candidates for council or Westminster it is necessary first to prove their worth by diligent and conscientious work on behalf of the party. This means zealous pursuit of the party's objectives rather than campaigns for an alternative set of priorities. Where Militant differs from Labour is in terms of the amount demanded (the nationalization of 200 rather than 25 monopolies for example) rather than the goals themselves. Generally it has been loath to upset the applecart by taking on issues which have been controversial or uncongenial to the Labour mind. It ignored the National Abortion Campaign until it received official TUC backing. It kept quiet about the Falklands War until eventually adopting the pious view that once the 200 monopolies had been nationalized

> British workers and Marxists will be able to wage a war against the Argentine junta, to help the Argentine workers to take power into their own hands. But only a democratic socialist Britain could have clean hands. A Labour government committed to socialist policies would probably not need to wage war, but could issue a socialist appeal to the Argentine workers to overthrow the monstrous junta, take power and then organise a socialist federation of Britain and the Argentine in conjunction with the Falkland Islands.[31]

This amounts to an admission that Militant is not really interested in politics. Not only are 'middle-class' issues such as community politics and feminism foreign to it, Militant really does not want to bother with anything beyond 'the basic needs of working people' (to coin a phrase). If the issue lends itself to this type of economic reductionism Militant is interested: if not the issue will suffer the fate of those concerned with women: as Pete Duncan observed, 'the first 267 issues of *Militant* up to 1975 contained four articles on women.'[32] While the radical left campaigned vigorously against the Corrie amendment to the 1967 Abortion Act, Militant maintained an Olympian detachment until the TUC took up the issue and rendered it respectably 'proletarian'. Likewise Militant stood apart from the Anti-Nazi League. Here again the justification was that 'only the Labour movement mobilised on a socialist programme is capable of eliminating those conditions which breed racialism and fascism and can combat this poison.'[33] Of course these sentiments served as a pretext for abstention from a campaign which on occasions brought as many as 80,000 people into political activity. In this way Militant refused to acknowledge that the 'anti-Marxist sects' could ever be right. But the most absurd argument was the one which was found to justify Militant's disdain for CND:

> the capitalists do not wage war for the sake of waging war but in order to extend their power, income and profit . . .

to destroy the working class which nuclear war would mean would be to destroy the goose that lays the golden eggs. Consequently it is only totalitarian fascist regimes, completely desperate and unbalanced which would take that road.

No doubt the comrades were reassured to learn that 'a war between Russia and the capitalist West . . . is completely ruled out in the foreseeable future.'[34]

Militant is quite as persuaded as the WRP ever was that the Day of Judgement is at hand. Grant has even referred to the present economic crisis as a vindication of Trotsky's pre-war prognoses.[35] Britain's 'irreversible decline', it would appear, is all part of the scheme of things described by Lenin in 1916. In particular Militant assures us that

> On a world scale capitalist economies not only find themselves in a crisis they find themselves ensnared in an epoch of crisis, stagnation and decline . . . short-lived, half-hearted booms followed by downturn and recession in an ever tightening cycle – these are the characteristics of the new period of general decline of world capitalism . . . the search for lasting concessions and lasting reforms is now as futile as the search for flesh on an ancient skeleton.[36]

Again and again Militant insists that reforms are not only useless and unattainable but involve a perspective which is entirely reactionary: 'The 'reformist' alternatives of the leaders of the trade unions and Labour Party are attempts at . . . shoring up decrepit and decaying capitalism. They do not see that by doing so, they are merely prolonging the death-agony of the system and lending it a more violent and convulsive character.'[37] Of course this casts quite a different light on the motives of Militant members on the Liverpool Council. If reforms are unattainable and a perspective of reforms merely prolongs the life of an unsupportable system, what could be the purpose of the confrontation with the Tory central government in 1984–5? The policy of 'no cuts, no rent or rate rises' was on Militant's own reasoning bound to fail. The 'strategy' therefore was to inflict a painful lesson on the people of Liverpool: these were supposed to deduce the need for a socialist system from the 'inability' of 'capitalism' to make the required concessions.

For Militant there 'are no capitalist solutions to the problems of world capitalism let alone to the acute difficuties facing the British capitalists'.[38] That is, the present crisis will

> end either in the greatest victory of the working class achieving power and the overthrow of the rule of capital with the installation of workers' democracy or we will have a military police dictatorship which will destroy the labour movement and kill millions of advanced workers' shop stewards, ward secretaries, Labour youth, trade union branch secretaries and even individual members of the Labour movement (sic).

Like the WRP, Militant's insight on the shape of things to come allows it to predict in the same document that the whole of the above scenario will be concluded within ten to fifteen years of the time of writing – 1977.[39] This is quite on a par with the 'apocalyptic ravings' which Ted Grant once found so obnoxious about the 'anti-Marxist sects'. As such it raises interesting questions about Militant's bias towards economistic issues. For while it completely neglects to mention the ideological and institutional props of sexism, for example, Militant insists that 'the big movements among working class women will . . . be economic issues – low pay, prices, rents, nursery facilities and the like.'[40] It is on this basis that the comrades are instructed that 'the liberation and emancipation of women and the main sector with which we are concerned, working class women, lies in struggle . . . within the framework of the organised trade union and labour movement.'

But we know already that Militant holds out no hope of extracting economic reforms from moribund capitalism and disparages the leaders of the trade union and Labour movements for sowing illusions on this score. What then is the point of raising economic demands on pay, rents, nursery facilities and housing and insisting that these are pursued to the exclusion of all else? The answer is that these demands are conceived as transitional demands. Once expectations are aroused on these issues the failure of the system to meet the people's demands will result in anger and a lurch to the left. Here the masses will find Militant explaining that further progress depends on the complete abolition of capitalism. As we have seen, Militant shares the capacity for 'correct' leadership with nobody. It does however regard the function of leadership as the indispensable prerequisite for socialism. The success of a campaign can be judged by the extent to which it has built Militant influence and membership. The day will come when Militant is the leadership of 'the best elements' in the Labour movement and through this vanguard controls the rest. Once this happens the road to socialism is broad and straight. A Militant parliamentary majority would be able to usher in socialism by an Enabling Act. With a Militant leadership the trade unions 'could assume power peacefully'.[41] With so much in the balance then why it is obvious that everything has to be geared to bringing members of Militant to the fore in the Labour Party and trade unions.

Progress of the organization

The hysteria about Trotskyist infiltration of the Labour Party began in the late 1970s. We were told that the party had become the victim of 'creeping Marxism' and *The Times* asserted that the party was 'infiltrated to a terrifying degree by crypto-communists and fifth columists'. Of course this served the interests of Tory propaganda very well and renegades were available to testify to 'a growing emphasis on class war and Marxist dogma' and predict the coming of an 'openly ultra-left' Labour government.[42] Some pundits were even prepared to attribute the campaign for constitutional changes in the Labour Party to the Trotskyists[43] and even those who knew better referred to 'the extraordinary revival of Trotskyism in Britain'.[44] This was all very flattering to Militant but a long way removed from the truth.

It required ten years of entrist activity before Militant could boast 100 members in 1965. By 1970 it was at most 200 strong and the Trotskyist group least affected by the events of 1968. Militant's growth began in the mid-1970s when student politics and the attempt to build independent vanguard parties were discredited. By the end of 1975 Militant reached 1,000 members and drew the attention of Reg Underhill, Labour's general secretary, who compiled his first report on entrism in that year. But Labour had already done away with the list of proscribed organizations in 1973 and there was no desire to return to the purges of the past. Militant's growth continued – especially after the ignominious demise of the Labour government in 1979. From 1,800 members Militant grew to 4,700 in 1983. By 1986 it was claiming over 8,000 members.

Militant's growth should be seen in the context of the growth of the constituency left in the Labour Party since the nadir of 1968. In that year Labour's council representation was massively reduced. There is evidence that this helped to clear away a certain type of entrenched boss politics and provide the opportunity for a new cohort of Labour councillors next time.[45] These were often people with some prior experience of socialist politics outside the Labour Party who were strongly influenced by the attitudes and priorities of the new left. Disillusion with the Wilson governments was of course much more widespread. A stronger left emerged in the trade unions and the Parliamentary Labour Party. During the years of opposition, Labour's NEC prepared the most radical yet of its election manifestos while the massive wave of industrial unrest under the Heath government – with its repeated States of Emergency and three-day week – did much to bring the attention of the left back to the politics of the Labour movement. As we have seen, the various schemes for building significant Leninist parties were in obvious disarray by the late 1970s. At the same time another Labour government had reneged on many of the radical policies adopted in 1974. When Thatcher was elected in 1979 the scene was set for another exodus of left activists from the party but they had nowhere to go.

Moreover this time the broad left had built up sufficient strength within all three sections of the party to make the running and enforce a greater degree of control over the PLP than anything known before in Labour's history. As early as July 1975 Newham North East had de-selected Reg Prentice, the sitting Labour MP. This bitter and protracted affair came about not because of conspiratorial entrism but because the constituency activists were no longer prepared to tolerate a representative whose right-wing views ran counter to official party policy. This was a warning shot presaging bigger battles to come and was only finally resolved when Prentice joined the Conservative Party. Militant had long predicted the defection of the Labour right. For years its leaders had talked of an economic crisis which would expose the intellectual bank-ruptcy of the party's Keynesian liberals. By 1976 this was fully accomplished. For years Militant had insisted on the centrality of Labour and trade union politics rather than the 'middle-class' distractions of feminism and student politics. Again the events of 1970–80 seemed to vindicate their exclusive concern with the advance of the left (read Militant) in the Labour Party. Obviously these factors are likely to have boosted Militant's credibility in some circles.

But the shift to the left within the Labour Party was not caused by Militant any more than it initiated or played a leading part in the constitutional changes after 1979. For the first time in Labour's history the rank and file was in wholesale defiance of the parliamentary leadership. There was now no evidence of that deference and instinctive solidarity which had kept the constituencies behind the leadership even in the 1930s. The cohesion of the past was gone, in part because the socialist vision which had sustained the faithful up to and beyond the Attlee years was now in tatters – thanks mainly to the performance of successsive Labour governments. The 'betrayal' of the Callaghan government and the election of the Tories under a leadership determined to take the offensive was the last straw: a majority of party members were now desperate to believe that changes to the party's organization could retrieve the situation.

The bulk of Militant's growing membership were culled from the LPYS which became its private fiefdom after 1970. No special talent was required to achieve this hegemony: Labour's youth section invariably falls to the biggest Marxist group determined to take it over. With all the other sizeable Trotskyist groups elsewhere Militant had the field to itself. The LPYS was to be the 'little lever' of Trotskyist influence. From 1972 its LPYS dominance secured Militant a seat on Labour's NEC. Its control of the LPYS also allowed it to foster international links as we have seen. Invariably it was Militant which agitated to set up LPYS branches where they did not already exist. Another advantage was that Militant secured by this means two places on the general management committee of the local constituency party.

Likewise in the early 1970s Militant was the best-organized faction within the National Organisation of Labour Students (NOLS). Most students professing Marxist convictions then held the Labour Party in supreme contempt. Militant briefly took over NOLS in 1974 but it is a measure of the anger that this event aroused in Labour student circles that within one year the Militant majority was overturned by a broad coalition of leftists calling itself Clause Four. While Clause Four could do nothing to challenge Militant's hegemony within the LPYS it is significant that Militant made no impact in the National Union of Students. Here Labour students were generally in alliance with the CP in the so-called Broad Left. Everything suggests that Militant's ideology was far too threadbare to exercise any persuasion within the student left and it was in any case openly dismissive of campus politics. Nevertheless Militant accounted for about 40 per cent of the NOLS membership though in practical terms its control of the LPYS was far more important. Militant's importance among Labour youth was underlined in 1976 when one of its prominent members, Andy Bevan, became National Youth Officer.

In the wider party Militant's growth and new-found infamy depended on several factors. Firstly, by virtue of its low profile and patient and continuous entrist activity over many years, some of its members were in contention as Labour parliamentary candidates. No other Trotskyist group has ever beavered away on this enterprise for so long. By the mid-1980s some of Militant's leaders had belonged to the Labour Party for 30 years or so. Secondly, Militant's long-standing concentration of supporters on Merseyside began to make an impact in local politics. Finally the growth of a much bigger Labour left and the successful campaign for constitutional changes within the Labour Party helped to attract a new wave of leftist recruits to the constituency parties after 1979. Militant initially benefited from this leftist movement and was able to exploit organizational changes such as mandatory reselection of MPs which the Bennite left had won.

On Mersyside Militant's predecessor the RSL had managed to get the Walton constituency to select Ted Grant as its parliamentary candidate as early as 1959. Peter Taaffe, Keith Dickinson, Pat Wall as well as Jimmy Deane had all been active here at one time or another. Elsewhere in Liverpool the Labour Party was for many years the victim of sectarian prejudices and the penchant of the Braddocks for a Tammany Hall-style machine politics. The latter helped to keep Labour Party membership purposely low while sectarianism deprived it of council power until the mid-1950s. If a precondition for Militant ascendancy is the existence of a small, largely inactive, local party membership, the Liverpool constituencies would seem to have fulfilled this requirement. Liverpool was also cursed by a disproportionate number of Labour MPs who either defected to the Social Democratic Party – Richard Crawshaw, Eric Ogden and Jimmy Dunn did this in 1981–2 – or who were otherwise completely out of touch with party and public opinion, for example, Sir Arthur Irvine. This experience – which lived up to Militant's predictions – together with the appalling problems of unemployment and poverty and the physical decay of the city paved the way for the emergence of Militant councillors and parliamentary candidates. In the approach to the 1983 general election Terry Harrison (Edge Hill), Tony Mulhearn (Toxteth), Terry Fields (Kirkdale) and Derek Hatton (Wavertree) looked set to stand as Labour candidates although in the event only Fields did so and secured a seat. Other Militant candidates fought Bradford North, Isle of Wight and Brighton Kemptown but apart from Fields the only other success was the election of Dave Nellist in Coventry South East.

In the local elections of 1983 Labour won its first majority for ten years on the Liverpool council. Of the 51 councillors in the

Labour group only 16 were members of Militant but by effective caucus activity this self-disciplined minority was able to exercise considerable influence just as Militant was able to control the general committee and executive of the district labour party by virtue of the greater activity and unanimity of its members. There is no doubt however that the Labour group on Liverpool council were united around policies of job creation, mass housing projects and cuts in council house rents. Though it was evident from the beginning that this policy would bring the council into a head-on collision with the government's stringent financial controls on local spending, this course was not dictated by Militant's narrow factional ends. The Militant slogan 'No cuts, no rent or rate rises' was adopted in 1982 but the policy was dictated by the terrible housing problems and unemployement in a city faced with a declining population and therefore diminishing rate revenues. So whatever Militant's ulterior motives this was a policy which the entire Labour group stood for. Nevertheless Militant's belief in the efficacy of 'transitional demands' – that is demands which no capitalist government would concede – emboldened it to expect a private success from the confrontation whatever the result from any other angle. Crick observes, for example, that its membership on Merseyside rose from 180 in 1983 to 354 in the summer of 1984. During this period of unprecedented publicity Militant's national membership rose by one third.[46]

We have already observed Militant's scorn for the rest of the Left. It regards all other Marxist organizations, including the 'Stalinist' CP, as the 'anti-Marxist sects'. This attitude is perfectly in keeping with the Leninist credentials of the Militant leaders. Being steeped in this tradition they have learned to regard rival organizations, especially those closest to their own ideological positions, as dangerous obstacles to socialism. It goes without saying that the Militant leadership is utterly derisive about the Tribunite left as well as the so-called 'Neanderthals' of the Labour centre and right. Other radicals are dismissed as 'middle class' if they beg to differ from Militant on the best ways of promoting peace, sex equality and race equality. Not surprisingly then, Militant's arrogance, narrowness of vision and manipulative approach to socialist campaigns – not to mention the duplicity and deceit associated with its entrist status – were bound to win the organization more enemies than friends on the left. But these antagonisms did not come to the fore nationally for as long as the Left believed that major advances were possible via the campaign for constitutional changes in the Labour Party. Militant was involved in a minor way within the Rank and File Mobilising Committee formed in May 1980. Later that year Labour's annual conference introduced mandatory reselection of MPs and a new electoral college for electing the party leader. During the first half of 1981 Benn focused attention on the deputy leadership battle against Denis Healey.

Real differences within the left began to emerge in 1983. In February Michael Foot managed to obtain the NEC majority needed to expel five members of the *Militant* editorial board – Taaffe, Grant, Lynn Walsh, Clare Doyle and Keith Dickinson. But it was Labour's defeat in the general election which caused the biggest rift. For decades the far left had diagnosed Labour's ills in terms of the absence of radical policies on state ownership and defence. When Labour lost the election in a context of mass unemployment these policies did nothing to prevent the rise of the 'moderate' Alliance and the maintenance of a high working class vote for Thatcherite 'extremism.' It was Labour's worst performance for fifty years and yet many on the left were inclined to 'explain' the disaster in terms of media bias and divisions within the Labour leadership. For these people there was no need to rethink socialist theory and policy – the policies were on hand waiting merely for a forthright leadership which would expound them clearly. This analysis was rejected by the leadership of the Communist Party, as we have seen. Naturally the new Kinnock leadership in the Labour Party was indisposed towards the 'hard left' argument but so were many of those who had formerly backed Tony Benn, such as the Labour Co-ordinating Committee and the municipal innovators such as Ken Livingstone and David Blunkett. The result was that Labour's defeat encouraged a realignment on the left. On one side were those who saw the main problem as timidity and equivocation over socialist fundamentals – Benn, Scargill, the Trotskyists and the CP opposition took this view. On the other side were those who believed that Thatcherism had succeeded partly because of the blind spots in socialist theory and policy.

In Liverpool Militant used its position on the council to set up and control a central support unit concerned to propagandize on behalf of council policies. It also provided the leading figures in the personnel committee and the joint shop stewards' committee. It also controlled the executive committee of the district labour party by packing the latter with delegates from pro-Militant branches of the TGWU and GMBATU. Within the Labour Party Militant was opposed by the Merseyside Labour Co-ordinating Committee and *Merseyside Labour Briefing*. These opponents did not question the need for a programme for jobs and services. They did however point to the limitations of the urban regeneration strategy as well as the disastrous conse-quences of the ultra-left rhetoric of refusing to countenance rate rises. In the first place the £350 million urban regeneration strategy was an entirely centralist affair which while uniting Labour paternalists and Militant vanguardists alienated independent groups of tenants and housing co-operatives. Indeed the antagonism of the council to the decentralizing initiatives taken by other municipal socialists was vividly illustrated by the way it treated the city's black community.

In October 1984 Sampson Bond, a Militant supporter and quantity surveyor, was appointed principal race relations advisor to the fury of Liverpool's Black caucus which refused to deal with a man of such limited experience. Militant's response was to set up its own Black front organization – the Merseyside Action Group. It also abolished the race relations sub-committee of the council. By November 1986 Militant was accused by the Black caucus, in a report published by the Runnymede Trust, of 'wrecking race relations' in the city. Here it was alleged that the council had done nothing to alter its own racist employment policies which restricted Blacks to one per cent of council jobs though they represent seven per cent of the city's population. It had, however, cut off grants to Black groups (except the Merseyside Action Group, which received £7,000) and frozen appointments to race relations posts.[47]

Militant's selective use of patronage also brought opposition from council unions and the Liverpool Labour Left group, which was formed to fight Militant within the party in October 1985. Just as it had antagonized NALGO by the Sampson Bond affair so it alienated NUPE by fostering a special relationship with the Militant-dominated branches of the GMBATU and TGWU. These unions were given nomination rights for relevant job vacancies with the council while NUPE was excluded from the deal. Likewise a policy of creating sabbatical positions for student unions in further education colleges was used to *nominate* members of Militant for these positions, which allegedly resulted in the organization gaining five additional full-time organizers financed from the rates.[48]

But these were minor irritants compared to the consequences of Militant's local economic strategy. The illegal budget deficit adopted in March 1984 set the scene for the city's bankruptcy. By the end of the financial year 5,000 redundancies or a rate rise of 170 per cent were threatened. Nevertheless the elections in May 1984 saw Labour maintain its 46 per cent share of the vote and increase its seats by seven thus allowing the deficit budget to go through. At this stage only the NUT among the council unions opposed the illegal budget, and there is no doubting that local problems and the local chauvinism encouraged by the council played a big part in setting the course for confrontation. But it should not be forgotten that in 1985 sixteen other Labour-controlled rate-capped councils also announced that they would not set a rate, believing themselves the loyal instruments of Labour policy as determined at the 1984 annual conference. A majority here had supported the call for defiance of the rate-capping law. Even Liverpool, however, abandoned this stance in June 1985.

But the nine per cent rate rise which was then adopted was both insufficient and belated having been delayed for eleven weeks during which time the city lost £106,000 in interest on government payments and it was for this that the auditors pressed for surcharging and disqualifying the councillors. A bigger blunder was made in September when the council announced 31,000 impending redundancies in the hope that the shock would galvanize trade union support and force the government to make concessions. In the event NALGO pick-eted to prevent the council from sending out redundancy notices and the NUT tried to achieve the same objective by taking the council to court. It was the spectacle of GMBATU stewards distributing the redundancy notices in 30 taxis specially hired for the purpose which symbolized the degener-ation of the campaign for jobs and services: now jobs and services were being threatened in the hope that the campaign could be saved. The workforce was divided and in November 1985 the council announced that it had negotiated a loan of £30 million from Swiss bankers. But even this was a final piece of brinkmanship since the deal had been 'on the table' for months.

These events brought about an investigation of the Labour Party in Liverpool which from the outset showed every indi-cation that the Kinnock leadership would require the expulsion of leading members of Militant. By the time the NEC inquiry reported back in February 1986 nearly forty constituency par-ties had independently expelled *Militant* supporters and the number would have been higher had not Walworth Road feared successful court actions to reinstate those expelled. The Labour left, the Communist Party and even some Trotskyist groups could now no longer be expected to rally behind Militant automatically, so widely disliked had its authoritarianism become. The inquiry recommended charges against sixteen party members from Liverpool suspected of membership of Militant. By June 1986 seven of these had been expelled including Derek Hatton, deputy leader of the Liverpool council, Tony Mulhearn, president of Liverpool district labour party and his vice president, Terry Harrison. Further expulsions followed but the Liverpool party continued to recognize those expelled and Derek Hatton remained deputy leader of the council until November. By the end of the year it was clear that the problems of the Liverpool labour party could not be solved by expulsions.

The one thing that does emerge clearly from the Liverpool affair, however, is the similarity of Militant's methods and policies with those of the people most determined to expel it from the party – the Labour right. Militant's corrupt use of

patronage and exclusion of rank-and-file community groups
from the decision-making process has an obvious affinity with
the city boss politics long established on the Labour right. Far
from seeking to 'smash the state' Militant did a great deal to
increase the powers and augment the centralism of local
political institutions. A similar trend was reproduced within the
local party. The district labour party (DLP) was controlled by
Militant by virtue of the simple device of over-representing
oganizations controlled by Militant and under-representing
others. Hence the GMBATU and TGWU could send 85 delegates to the DLP while the wards and constituency organizations had to make do with 75. The DLP then usurped the
functions of wards and constituencies and acted as a general
and binding parliament on the local party. According to the
Merseyside Labour Co-ordinating Committee, Militant also
manipulated the DLP local government panel to prevent opponents within the party from becoming candidates in winnable
seats. They further allege – and what we know of Militant's
attitudes would support this – that Militant was 'responsible for
creating a climate of intolerace and hatred of political opponents'.[49]

It is arguable that thirty years of entrism – successful
entrism at that – have exacted a price in that Militant became
exclusively preoccupied with the sort of policies which could
make headway in a Labourist milieu. Certainly Militant's talk
of Enabling Acts to introduce socialism – as if such a change
could come about by decree – is strikingly similar to the
rhetoric of Cripps, Attlee and Laski in the 1930s. Likewise its
opposition to Black sections in the Labour Party, and disdain
for feminism and CND (until 1983) as 'middle-class' issues are
in the traditions of mainstream Labourism. So is its passionate
support for mass housing schemes in Liverpool and obstinate
opposition to small-scale community housing projects. Its
high regard for nationalization – nothing less than the top 200
companies will do – suggests that like *Tribune* in the 1940s and
1950s Militant sees state ownership as a panacea. One way or
another Militant is stuck in a time warp and the changes of the
last thirty years or so seem not to have touched it at all. Its
ideological sterility guarantees that it will play no part

in advancing the case for socialism and its utter dependency on entrism ensures that it will continue for a while as a declining force in the Labour Party.

8

Conclusion: The Alchemists of Revolution

The Communist International was created to overthrow capitalism, not to debate socialist theory. Its founders were disposed to regard Marxism as a finished system of thought and Lenin's theoretical rationale for the establishment of the Comintern purports to characterize the imperialist *epoch* not just the conjuncture of 1914–18. By the mid 1920s Leninists were entrenched in the conviction that the communist movement possessed a monopoly of truth and insight within the working-class movement. The fact that the European revolution, so keenly awaited in the period 1918–21, had not materialized did not occasion a major rethink of Leninist assumptions. The theory remained intact as the communist parties made the tactical adjustment of the united front. Leninism remained intolerant of alternative socialist standpoints including other variants of Marxism which were depicted as the most insidious misleaders of the working class. Leninists continued to see themselves as uniquely qualified to deliver the working class into socialism.

Other Marxist thinkers were marginalized or interpreted through the Leninist lens. Invariably the latter entailed explanations of disagreements between socialist parties or indeed within the Leninist party as expressions of contradictory class interests. In this way the guilt or error of opponents is 'proved' without reference to their actual arguments. A corollary of this was the habit of thinking and acting as if a single proletarian party was all that was required to represent the 'interests of the working class'. Leninist groups persist in this error and fail to see that the socialist project is too complex for it to be the monopoly of one organization. Such a monopoly would hardly square with the pluralism required of any democracy worth the name. As for Leninist parties claiming to represent a higher socialist democracy this is only plausible on the Leninist assumption that the interests of the working class are identical to those of the party. There is no basis for such a far-fetched assumption. But if major disagreements, conflicts and hard choices are an inevitable feature of any politics, the tolerance, open-mindedness and the spirit of co-operation required to make socialist democracy work are almost entirely absent on the Leninist left.

These groups are as preoccupied with doctrinal orthodoxy as the Bolshevik leadership of the Comintern was when the organization was first set up. Well before the ascendancy of Stalin the communists had become accustomed to following policies fashioned by the Bolsheviks though the latter were often ignorant of the political conditions in other countries. Inestimable damage was done to the communist cause when the International finally became an instrument of Soviet foreign policy. The resulting twists and turns of Comintern politics eventually made communism synonymous with mendacity and duplicity. For a while Trotsky seemed to offer an explanation of this degeneration but it is the reproduction of these 'Stalinist' practices within the ranks of his own followers that points to a common source in Leninism – the body of theory and practice of which Trotsky became the most zealous theorist and practitioner. Thus the reflex to conserve Leninism is ever more deeply entrenched among the Trotskyists – who as it were volunteered for the role of defender of the faith. In contrast, the Stalinists became increasingly pragmatic. This helps to explain the paradox that it was from within the ranks of official communism rather than 'principled', 'revolutionary' Trotskyism that doctrinal change and new, more democratic political practices began to emerge from the 1960s. Because Trotsky founded a movement, a stillborn movement moreover, on the myth of Lenin's infallibility, this tradition has done little to advance knowledge on the problems of socialism, for all its preoccupation with the nature of the Soviet Union, the degeneration of the October revolution and related problems of bureaucracy and the like. To this day Trotsky's followers display all the features of this original myopia. The 'spotless banners' of Leninism continue to be counterposed to those of the Stalinists, centrists and reformists – all of whom are treated as forms of political corruption. The mechanical Marxism of Lenin, with its neglect of the actual aspects of bourgeois domination continues to serve as the infallible guide.

Similarly the Bolshevik revolution remains the model which Trotskyists seek to imitate. They continue to 'explain' contemporary events by reference to phases in Russian politics of very dubious analogy. Like the first Leninists they reduce socialist politics to a question of tactics. In dealing with upsetting innovations they habitually turn to the Russian directory of political phenomena. Thus Lenin's attitude to the Jewish Bund in 1903 determines the Trotskyist line on women's caucuses within 'the party' in 1983. Lenin's attitude towards individual terrorism as practised in Tsarist Russia is used to justify a stance on the IRA. And so on as if there really is nothing new under the sun and all political questions can be resolved liturgically.

The Trotskyist tradition even more than that of official communism has pre-empted the development of socialist political theory by its emphasis on the economic collapse of capitalism as the guarantee of socialist revolution. This catastrophism pervades every line of the resolutions of the first four congresses of the Comintern and characterizes Trotsky's thought, especially after 1933. Inevitably the epigones made this apocalyptic vision the principal tenet of revolutionary socialism in the 1940s and 1950s and prophesies of the final crash recur at regular intervals thereafter. In every case these predictions have served to establish the close proximity of the socialist utopia. Nevertheless this has not caused these prophets to concern themselves with the actual shape of socialism, since any speculation on this score is deemed 'reactionary'. Marx's strictures on the reactionary nature of blueprints for the future are always invoked by our conformists to stop any such inquisitiveness in its tracks. Instead Trotskyists have developed a number of stock responses, mostly in relation to the USSR, which serve to cover the whole problem. Thus the problems of economic planning, for example, were explained entirely in terms of 'bureaucracy' which 'workers control' would put right: the problems of socialist democracy would be solved by the restoration of political power to the Soviets; and so on.

The field of what is taken to be legitimate and necessary political enquiry is hardly any broader when it comes to Trotskyist analyses of the present. There is hardly anything on socialist strategy save ritualistic references to October 1917. The rest is tactics and it is here that the little Lenins of the far left fall out with one another and find the causes of innumerable splits, tensions and regroupments. In these hands 'revolutionary' politics is a gnostic reading of the texts in search of the appropriate lesson from the writings of Lenin or Trotsky. Absent is any tradition of analysis of the specificity of particular liberal democratic systems which may have helped in the emergence of relevant Marxist politics. Dependence on perspectives of economic collapse and the alleged propensity of bourgeois democracy to succumb inevitably to authoritarianism has also obstructed the analysis of positions 'mid-way' between reform and revolution. Indeed the posing of the question 'Reform or Revolution?' – which both Leninist and Labourist politics were comfortable with – has functioned to suggest that a 'third road' is a mere chimera. Yet in Britain it is not too much to say that the dominant currents within the labour movement have offered neither reform nor revolution. Just as the Labour Party is not committed to the eradication of capitalism by means of systematic incremental reforms, the 'revolutionary' politics of the far left turns out to be mere sentiment.

The failure of any of the 'revolutionary' groups to establish viable political parties has been the spur for numerous attempts to square the circle by means of entrism. But the history of this particular form of manipulation shows that, by any standards of serious politics, it has not been very successful. Against the dubious achievement of promoting the parliamentary and municipal careers of individuals who otherwise might not have risen so high we have to set the fact that entrism does not promote and cannot promote a political tradition which challenges the assumptions of Labourism. Nor does it greatly advance organizations in terms of recruitment and the promotion of particular causes. Any balance sheet of entrism would have to conclude that this tactic has been counter-productive, as anyone familiar with Marx's remarks concerning the 'alchemists of revolution' might have guessed. It is simply an attempt to conjure a mass movement by means of conspiratorial manipulations. But I have argued that Leninism today in Britain is indeed all about who possesses the correct formulae for transforming the base metal of small sects into the pure gold of a Bolshevik mass party. This explains the frequency with which we meet the voluntarist assumption that progress in party terms will follow once the right line on this or the analysis of that has been discovered. The current vogue among Trotskyist groups for the study of their own history is but a variant of this procedure. In spite of everything these organizations will persist because they answer a need – the need for militancy which demands action against an unjust system. But of these organizations it cannot be said that 'theoretically they have over the great mass of the proletariat the advantage of clearly understanding the line of march, the conditions, and the ultimate general results of the proletarian movement.'[1]

If it is characterized by anything at all, the Leninist left is unanimous in not even recognizing the existence of a problem in any of these respects. The Communist Party on the other hand is now at least trying to get beyond the mechanical and monopolistic politics of Leninism. It is too early to say if it has emerged from the crisis of the last thirty years. The innovators may simply have become masters of a sinking ship. Certainly there is now a question mark against the very survival of the 'Modern Prince', though the future of socialism is still likely to be bound up with communism – if only negatively.

Notes

Preface

1   John Callaghan, *British Trotskyism* (Oxford: Blackwell, 1984).

Chapter 1   Communist Ideology

1   B. Lazitch and M. Drachkovitch, *Lenin and Comintern* (California: Stanford, 1972) p. 6.
2   P. Anderson, *Lineages of the Absolutist State* (London: New Left Books, 1974) pp. 353–60. T. Skocpol, *States and Social Revolutions* (Cambridge: University Press, 1979) p. 207.
3   L. Trotsky, *History of the Russian Revolution*, vol. 1, (3 vols, London: Sphere Books, 1969) p. 28.
4   Quoted in A. Besancon, *Intellectual Origins of Leninism* (Oxford: Blackwell, 1981). See also N. Berdyaev *Origins of Russian Communism* (Glasgow: Geoffrey Bles, The Centenary Press, 1937).
5   See D. W. Lovell, *From Marx to Lenin* (Cambridge: University Press, 1984).
6   Victor Serge, *Memoirs of a Revolutionary* (London: Writers and Readers, 1984) pp. 374–5.
7   Lenin, *Collected Works (CW)* (Moscow: Progress 1966) vol. 31, pp. 21 and 31.
8   Lenin, *CW*, vol. 29, pp. 310–11.
9   Lenin *CW*, vol. 31, p. 64.
10 Ibid. pp. 84–5.
11 B. Hessel (ed.) *Theses, Resolutions and Manifestos of the First Four Congresses of Comintern* (London: Ink Links, 1980) p. 35.

12 Lenin, *CW* vol. 23, p. 116.
13 Ibid., p. 118.
14 Hessel (ed.) *Theses, Resolutions and Manifestos*, p. 93.
15 Ibid., p. 134.
16 Ibid., p. 1.
17 Ibid., p. 8.
18 Lenin, *CW*, vol. 28, p. 107.
19 Ibid., p. 107.
20 Ibid., p. 245.
21 Lenin, *CW*, vol. 29, p. 502.
22 Lenin, *CW*, vol. 31, p. 193.
23 Ibid., p. 194.
24 Arthur Rosenberg *A History of Bolshevism from Marx to Lenin* (London: 1934) p. 72.
25 R. Lowenthal, 'The Bolshevisation of the Sparticist League' in D. Footman (ed.) *St Anthony's Papers Nomos IX* (London: Chatto and Windus, 1960).
26 J. Degras (ed.) *The Communist International Documents*, (3 vols, London: Frank Cass, 1956) vol I, p. 250.
27 L. Trotsky *Writings on Britain* (3 vols, London: New Park 1974) vol. 2., p. 57.
28 R. Luxemburg, *The Russian Revolution and Leninism or Marxism*, B. de Wolfe (ed.) (Michigan: Ann Arbor, 1961) pp. 103–6.
29 E. J. Hobsbawm, *Revolutionaries* (London: Quartet, 1977) p. 4.
30 F. Claudin, *The Communist Movement* (London: Peregrine, 1975) p. 106.
31 Hessel (ed.) *Theses, Resolutions and Manifestos*, p. 75.
32 F. Borkenau, *The Communist International* (London: Faber, 1938) p. 200.
33 J. Braunthal, *History of the International 1914–1942* (London: Nelson, 1967) vol. 2, p. 190.
34 Lenin, *CW* vol. 31, pp. 187–8 and 189–90.
35 Hessel (ed.) *Theses, Resolutions and Manifestos*, pp. 68–9.
36 Lenin, *CW*, vol. 31, pp. 191.
37 Quoted by R. Jacoby, *Dialectic of Defeat* (Cambridge: University Press, 1981) p. 65.
38 E. H. Carr, *The Bolshevik Revolution 1917–23* (3 vols, Harmondswoth, London: Penguin 1953) vol. 3, pp. 389–91.
39 A. Davidson, *The Theory and Practice of Italian Communism* (London: Merlin, 1982) pp. 105–10.
40 Lenin *CW*, vol. 26, pp. 379–80
41 See A. J. Polan, *Lenin and the End of Politics* (London: Methuen, 1984).

42 See Oscar Anweiler, *The Soviets* (New York, Random House, 1974) and Skocpol, *States and Social Revolutions*.

43 R. Luxemburg, *The Russian Revolution*, p. 69.

44 S. Smith, *Red Petrograd* (Cambridge: University Press, 1983) pp. 216–18.

45 R. Luxemburg, *The Russian Revolution*, p. 79.

46 Lenin, *CW* vol. 27, p. 269.

47 C. Sirianni, *Workers' Control and Socialist Democracy: The Soviet Experience* (London: New Left Books, 1982) p. 253.

48 Ibid., pp. 279–80.

49 Lenin, *CW*, vol. 31, pp. 41.

50 L. Trotsky, *Terrorism and Communism* (Michigan: Ann Arbor, 1961) p. 109.

51 Victor Serge, *Memoirs*, p. 350.

52 Ante Ciliga, *The Russian Enigma* (London: Ink Links, 1979) p. 217.

53 L. Trotsky, 'Germany What Next?' in *The Struggle Against Fascism in Germany* (Harmondsworth, London: Penguin, 1975).

54 L. Trotsky *Writings of Leon Trotsky 1938–9* (New York: Pathfinder, 1974) p. 340.

55 Ibid., p. 234.

56 L. Trotsky, *Documents of the Fourth International 1933–40* (New York: Pathfinder, 1973).

57 L. Trotsky, *The Transitional Programme* (New York: Pathfinder, 1973) pp. 72 and 94.

58 Trotsky, *Writings 1938–9*, p. 32.

59 See for example Ernest Mandel, *Revolutionary Marxism Today* (London: Verso, 1979); Duncan Hallas *The Comintern* (London: Pluto, 1985); Donny Gluckstein, *The Western Soviets: Workers Councils Versus Parliament 1915–20* (London: Pluto, 1985).

Chapter 2   British Communism Between the Wars

1 Stuart McIntyre, *A Proletarian Science: Marxism in Britain 1917–33* (Cambridge: University Press, 1980) p. 69. See also Jonathan Ree *Proletarian Philosophers* (Oxford: Clarendon Press, 1984).

2 Walter Kendall, *The Revolutionary Movement in Britain 1900–21* (London: Weidenfield, 1969) pp. 398–9.

3 Harry Pollitt, Looking Ahead (London: Communist Party, 1947) pp. 41–3.

4 Martin Durham, 'British Revolutionaries and the Suppression of the Left in Lenin's Russia 1918–24', *Journal of Contemporary History* vol. 20 (1985).

224   *Notes to pp. 29–38*

5   Martin Durham, 'The Origins annd Early Years of British Communism 1914–24', (unpublished PhD., Birmingham University, 1982) pp. 174–6.

6   Raymond Challinor, *The Origins of British Bolshevism* (London: Croom-Helm, 1977) pp. 253–4.

7   Hugo Dewar, *Communist Parties in Britain* (London: Pluto, 1976) p. 25.

8   James Hinton and Richard Hyman, *Trade Unions and Revolution: The Industrial Politics of the Early British Communist Party* (London: Pluto, 1975) pp. 14–18.

9   In James Curran (ed.) *The Future of the Left* (Oxford: Polity, 1984) pp. 94–5.

10   *Second Congress of the Communist International, Minutes of the Proceedings* (2 vols, London: New Park, 1977) vol. 2, pp. 1983–4.

11   See Dave Priscott, 'The Communist Party and the Labour Party', *Marxism Today*, January 1974.

12   See, for example, Leon Trotsky, 'Where is Britain Going?', *Trotsky's Writings on Britain* (3 vols, London: New Park, 1974) vol. II, pp. 57. and 118.

13   E. H. Carr, *Socialism in One Country* (London: Macmillian, 1964) vol. 3, part I, p. 72.

14   Ibid., p. 522.

15   H. Dewar, P. 41

16   Noreen Branson, *History of the Communist Party of Great Britain 1927–41* (London: Lawrence and Wishart, 1985) p. 5.

17   S. McIntyre, *A Proletarian Science*, p. 231.

18   L. J. McFarlane *The British Communist Party* (London: McGibbon and Kee, 1966) p. 104.

19   The debate between Dutt and Murphy is in *Communist International*, nos. 8, 9, 12, 13, 1925.

20   E. H. Carr, *Foundations of a Planned Economy*, (London: Macmillan, 1976) vol. 3. part 2, p. 315.

21   R. Palme Dutt *Socialism and the Living Wage* (London: CPGB, 1927).

22   Branson, *History of the Communist Party*, pp. 31–52.

23   See *Labour Monthly*, May 1929.

24   *Communist Unity Convention*, (Pamphlet London: Communist Party, 1920) p. 11.

25   *Manual of Party Training: Principles and Organisation* (1924) (pamphlet, London: Communist Party, 1924) p. 26.

26   The New Line: Documents of the 10th Congress of the Communist Party of Great Britain (London: CPGB, 1929) p. 7.

27   William Gallacher *Mondism and MacDonaldism* (London: CPGB, 1928) p. 9.

28 Stuart McIntyre *Imperialism and the British Labour Movement in the 1920s: an Examination of Marxist Theory*, Our History pamphlet 64, (London: CPGB, 1975).

29 H. Branson, *History of the Communist Party*, pp. 58–61.

30 Ibid., pp. 231–2.

31 Ibid., p. 191.

32 Ben Pimlott, *Labour and the Left in the 1930s* (Cambridge: University Press, 1977) p. 43.

33 Reg Groves, *The Balham Group: How British Trotskyism Began* (London: Pluto Press, 1973).

34 Quoted in E. H. Carr, *The Twilight of Comintern 1930–35* (London: Macmillan, 1982) p. 226.

35 Sam Bornstein and Al Richardson, *Against the Stream: A History of the Trotskyist Movement in Britain 1924–38* (London: Socialist Platform, 1986) pp. 140–1.

36 Jonathan Wood, 'The Labour Left and the Constituency Labour Parties 1931–51', (unpublished Ph.D., Warwick University 1982).

37 Ibid., p. 67.

38 Ibid., p. 97.

39 James Jupp, 'The Left in Britain 1931–41' M.Sc. dissertation, University of London, 1956, p. 182.

40 Quoted in Jonathan Wood, The Labour Left, p. 256.

41 Ibid., p. 259.

42 See, for example, Eugene Varga, 'The Imperialist Struggle for a new Redivision of the World', *Labour Monthly*, 22, 11 (1940) pp. 578–89.

43 J. R. Campbell, 'The Labour Movement Discusses the War' *Labour Monthly*, 22, (1940) 2 pp. 108–9.

44 J. R. Campbell, 'The Workers and the British Totalitarians' *Labour Monthly*, 23, 3 (1941) p. 138.

45 H. Pollitt, *How to Win the War* (pamphlet London: CPGB, 1939).

46 Sam Bornstein and Al Richardson, *Two Steps back: Communists and the Wider Labour Movement 1935–45* (London: Socialist Platform, 1982) p. 63.

47 Ivor Montague, 'Stand by the Soviet Union!' *Labour Monthly*, 23, 7 (1941) p. 304.

48 Quoted in Robert Black *Stalinism in Britain: A Trotskyist Analysis* (London: New Park, 1970) p. 149.

49 James Hinton, 'Coventry Communism: A Study of Factory Politics in the Second World War', *History Workshop Journal*, 10, autumn 1980, p. 97.

50 H. Pollitt, 'Teheran in Deeds', *Labour Monthly* (1944) p. 232.

51 J. R. Campbell, *Labour on the Eve*, Labour Monthly (May, 1945) pp. 144–5.

52 J. Callaghan, 'The CPGB and Local Politics in B. Szajkowski (ed.) *Marxist Local Government in Western Europe and Japan*, (London: Pinter, 1986).

53 R. P. Dutt, 'Notes for the Month', *Labour Monthly*, 16, 12 (1934) p. 724.

54 Ibid., p. 725.

55 H. Pollitt, 'The Communist Party and Unity' *Labour Monthly*, 18, 2 (1936) pp. 98–9.

56 Ralph Fox, *Communism* (Oxford: Bodley Head, 1935) p. 53.

57 H. Gallacher, *Mondism and MacDonaldism*, p. 3.

Chapter 3 Apocalypse Now: The Politics of 'Orthodox Trotskyism'

1 See L. Trotsky, *Writings of Leon Trotsky 1939–40* (New York: Pathfinder, 1973) pp. 104–5, 221–2, 253–9, 321–2, 333–5.

2 Peter Jenkins, *Where Trotskyism Got Lost: The Restoration of European Democracy after the Second World War*, (Pamphlet 49, Nottingham: Spokesman, n.d.).

3 RCP, Perspectives in Britain', 6 June 1945, pp. 1–6.

4 RCP, The New Imperialist Peace and the Building of the Parties of the Fourth International', 1946.

5 G. Healy, 'Against the Politics of Stagnation', 1947.

6 E. Germain (Mandel), 'From the ABC to Current Reading: Boom, Revival, or Crisis?', 1947.

7 G. Healy 'British Labour and the Tasks of the Fourth International', 1945.

8 G. Healy, 'The Marxist Method versus Eclecticism and Empiricism', 1946.

9 Jock Haston Papers, Hull University, JDH 15B/110, May 1950.

10 Labour Party Faction Report, August/September 1956.

11 Kenneth O. Morgan *Labour in Power* (Oxford: University Press, 1985) pp. 283–4 and ch. 6 *passim*.

12 Ibid., p. 239.

13 Mark Jenkins, *Bevanism, Labour's High Tide* (Nottingham: Spokesman, 1979) ch. 3 *passim*.

14 Ibid., p. 95.

15 M. Pablo *Where are we going?* reprinted in *Education for Socialists* (New York: Pathfinder, 1974) part 4, vol. 2, pp. 5–6.

16 *Trotskyism versus Revisionism: A Documentary History* (6 vols London: New Park, 1974) vol. 1, pp. 50 and 78.

17 Ibid., pp. 93–4.
18 M. Pablo, 'On the Duration and Nature of the Transition from Capitalism to Socialism' and E. Mandel, 'What Should be Modified and What Should be Maintained in the Theses of the Second World Congress of the Fourth International on the Questions of Stalinism?' Both reprinted *Fourth International* 1, winter 1958.
19 Ibid.
20 G. Healy, *The Way to Socialism in Britain*, (pamphlet, n.d.,) pp. 40–1.
21 M. Pablo, 'The Rise and Decline of Stalinism' reprinted in *Fourth International* 1, winter 1958.
22 'The 20th Congress of the CPSU' in *The Struggle to Re-Unify the Fourth International (1954–63) Education For Socialists* (New York, Pathfinder, 1974) vol. 3; 'De-Stalinisation, the Hungarian Revolution and World Trotskyism, documents 1955–7', *Education for Socialists* (New York: Pathfinder) pp. 53–4.
23 *De-Stalinisation*', p. 60. This report was given to the seventh plenum of the IEC in May 1956.
24 'The Hungarian revolution and the crisis of Stalinism' (resolution adopted by the SWP National Committee, January 1957) in *The Struggle to Re-Unify* vol. 3, pp. 33–9: G. Healy, *Revolution and Counter-Revolution in Hungary* (pamphlet), 1957).
25 R. Palme Dutt, Notes for the Month, *Labour Monthly*, December 1956.
26 G. Healy *Revolution and Counter Revolution*, p. 59.
27 D. Widgery (ed.) *The Left in Britain* (London: Peregrine, 1976) p. 59.
28 Richard Johnson, 'Thompson, Genovese and Socialist Humanist History', *History Workshop Journal*, 6, autumn 1978; B. A. D. Bryant 'The New Left in britain 1956–68' (Ph.D. thesis, London University, 1981).
29 Peggy Duff, *Left, Left, Left* (London: Allison and Busby, 1971) pp. 118–19.
30 Alan Jones, 'Battle of Ideas No. 1', *Red Weekly*, October 1976.
31 Nigel Young, *An Infantile Disorder? The Crisis and Decline of the New Left* (London: Routledge and Kegan Paul, 1977) p. 154.
32 *The Newsletter*, 10 May 1957.
33 'The Newletter Conference: National Industrial Rank and File Conference 16 November 1958' (internal bulletin).
34 'A Charter of Workers' Demands', p. 8.
35 G. Healy, *Our Answer to the Witch Hunt and Our Policy for Labour* (pamphlet, January 1959). First published in *The Newsletter*, 6 December 1958.

36 This is mentioned in 'Entrism' the Militant's *opus magnum* reprinted in November 1973. See also Tom Forrester, 'The Labour Party's Militant Moles,' *New Society*, 10 January 1980.

37 Editorial, *Labour Review*, April-May 1959.

38 Draft Constitution of the Socialist Labour League, 1959.

39 Internal Bulletin, no. 3, April 1960.

40 Internal Bulletin, no. 4, May 1960, p. 14.

41 J. Castle, 'Cuba: Marxism and the Revolution' in *Fourth International* 2, 2. This journal replaced Labour Review in 1964 as theoretical organ of the SLL.

42 'Draft Resolution on International Perspectives', January 1961 (Purdie Papers Warwick University, Modern Records Centre) p. 25.

43 See T. Ali, The Coming British Revolution (London: Cape, 1972).

44 Tony Whelan, *The Credibility Gap: the Politics of the Socialist Labour League* IMG pamphlet): E. Mandel *Marxism vs Ultra-leftism* (New York: Pathfinder, 1978).

45 From a letter to Bob Purdie (Purdie Papers, Warwick University, Modern Records Centre) 8 July 1968.

46 Robin Blick and David Caldwell, 'The Life and Times of Comrade H, *New Statesman*, 6 December 1985.

47 G. Healy, Internal Bulletin, No. 9, p. 9 (Tarbuck Papers Warwick University Modern Records Centre).

48 Quoted in G. Thayer, *The British Political Fringe* (London: Anthony Blond, 1965) p. 134. See also Robin Blick and David Caldwell, 'Life and Times'.

49 A. Thornett The Battle for Trotskyism (Oxford: Frampton, 1976) p. 2.

50 Ibid., see p. 94 for detail of the violence used.

51 Michael Banda, *Workers' Press*, February 7 1986.

52 *Intercontinental Press*, March 24 1986, p. 191.

53 *Spartacist*, 38–9, summer 1986; *Fourth International* 42 June-July 1986.

54 Peter Fryer describes the method of bullying dissenters which involved a visit from Healy and 'his thugs' in the early hours of the morning. See *Spartacist* 38–9.

55 *Workers Hammer*, February 1986.

56 This allegedly includes WRP photographers supplying the Iraqi embassy with pictures of Iraqi dissidents demonstrating in London. See *Workers' Vanguard*, 26 September 1986.

57 Michael Banda, *Whither Thornett?* (London WRP, 1975).

58 See the following instances: C. Slaughter, *The Class Nature of the*

International Socialists (Workers' Press pamphlet, 1970); C. Slaughter *Who are the International Socialists? (Workers' Press* pamphlet, 1971); P. Jeffries, *Falsifiers of Lenin* (Workers' Revolutionary Party Pocket Library No. 9, 1974); *A Marxist Analysis of the Crisis* (SLL pamphlet, n.d.); C. Slaughter, *A Balance Sheet of Revisionism* (Newsletter pamphlet, 1969); C. Slaughter, *Reform or Revolution?* (Workers' Press pamphlet, 1970).

Chapter 4   The Socialist Workers' Party and Leninist Industrial Politics

1 L. Trotsky, *The Revolution Betrayed* (London: New Park, 1969) p. 94.
2 'The World Situation and the Tasks of the Fourth International', November 1947.
3 'The New Imperialist Peace and the Building of the Parties of the Fourth International', April 1946.
4 'On the Coming European Revolution', April 1945.
5 A. W. Atkinson, 'On the Russian Question', July 1947.
6 D. Hallas (ed.) *Origins of the Innternational Socialists* (London: Pluto 1971) p. 3.
7 Trotsky, *The Revolution Betrayed*, p. 245.
8 T. Cliff, 'On the Class Nature of the People's Democracies', in D. Hallas (ed.) *Origins of the International Socialists*, p. 36.
9 Ibid., p. 36.
10 T. Cliff, interview in *The Leveller* 30 September 1979, pp. 20–1.
11 D. Hallas, *Trotsky's Marxism* (London: Pluto, 1979) p. 38.
12 T. Cliff *Russia: A Marxist Analysis* (London: Pluto, 1974) p. 153.
13 Hallas, *Trotsky's Marxism*, p. 40.
14 See ch. 1.
15 Cliff, *Russia*, pp. 169–70.
16 Hallas, *Trotsky's Marxism*, p. 107.
17 Cliff, *Russia*, p. 210, Cliff's argument is in places strikingly similar to N. Bukharin, *Economics of the Transformation Period* (London: Pluto, 1971).
18 Chris Harman, 'The Inconsistencies of Ernest Mandel', *International Socialism Journal* 41, December 1969/January 1970. p. 38.
19 Michael Kidron, *Western Capitalism Since the War* (Harmondsworth: Penguin 1968) p. 49.
20 Ibid., p. 56.
21 M. Kidron, *Capitalism and Theory* (London: Pluto, 1974) p. 160.
22 Ibid., p. 163.

23   V. Karalasingham, 'The War in Korea', in D. Hallas (ed.) *The Origins of the International Socialists*, p. 78.

24   Ian H. Birchall, *Workers Against the Monolith* (London: Pluto, 1974) pp. 59–60.

25   Editorial, *Socialist Review*, March 1955.

26   T. Cliff, 'Welfare State Capitalism', *New Politics*, winter 1962, pp. 51–65.

27   T. Cliff, *State Capitalism in Russia* (London: Pluto, 1974) p. 162.

28   T. Cliff, *The Crisis* (London: Pluto, 1975) p. 162.

29   M. Kidron, 'Two Valid Insights Don't Make a Theory', *International Socialism Journal* 100, July 1977.

30   D. Purdy in *The Bulletin of Socialist Economists*, spring 1973; G. Hodgson in *International*, January, 1973; B. Warren in *New Left Review* 72, March-April 1972; E. Mandel *Late Capitalism* (London: New Left Books, 1975)

31   Kidron, *Capitalism and Theory*, p. 84; Cliff, *The Crisis*, p. 16.

32   Ian Birchall, 'History of the International Socialists, Part 1' *International Socialism* 76, March 1985, p. 17.

33   T. Cliff, *Rosa Luxemburg* (London, 1959) p. 43.

34   Ibid., p. 54.

35   Ibid., p. 54.

36   Ian Birchall, 'History of the International Socialists' p. 20.

37   T. Cliff, C. Harman, D. Hallas and L. Trotsky, *Party and Class* (London: Pluto, n.d.) p. 15.

38   M. Shaw 'The Making of a Party', *Socialist Register*, 1978, p. 109.

39   Quoted by Peter Allen in *Socialist Worker* – paper with a purpose', *Media, Culture and Society* 7, 2, April 1985, p. 218.

40   Cliff, *The Crisis*, p. 182.

41   Shaw, 'The Making of a Party', p. 136.

42   J. Hinton and R. Hyman, *Trade Unions and Revolution* ((London: Pluto, 1957) p. 71.

43   R. Hyman, 'Industrial Conflict and the Political Economy', *Socialist Register*, 1973, pp. 107–9.

44   T. Cliff, *The Leveller*.

45   *Socialist Worker*, 14 November 1981.

46   Ibid.

47   See as an instance of this argument Roger Kline (n.d.) *Can Socialism Come Through Parliament?* (IS pamphlet, n.d.).

48   Cliff, *The Crisis*, p. 172.

49   R. Hyman, 'Industrial Conflict', p. 107.

50   Cliff, *The Crisis*, pp. 154–5.

51   Cliff, *The Employers Offensive* (London: Pluto, 1970) p. 201.

52   Hyman, 'Industrial Conflict'.

53 Hyman, *Marxism and the Sociology of Trade Unionism*, (pamphlet, London: Pluto Press, 1971) p. 37.

54 Cliff, *The Crisis*, p. 11.

55 S. Jeffreys, 'The Challenge of the Rank and File', *International Socialism*, March 1975, p. 7.

56 'In Defence of Marxism: Platform of the Left Opposition of IS', internal document, September 1974.

57 See Roger Rosewall, *The Struggle for Workers' Power*, (IS pamphlet, n.d.) p. 13.

58 Cliff, *The Crisis*, p. 121.

59 Cliff, *The Employers Offensive*, p. 231.

60 Alex Callinicos and Mike Simons, *The Great Strike: The Miners Strike of 1984–5 and its Lessons* (London: Socialist Worker, 1985) p. 234.

61 Ibid., p. 118.

62 Ibid., p. 219.

63 Ibid., p. 238.

64 Ibid., p. 211.

65 Michael Crick, *Scargill and the Miners*, (Harmondsworth, London: Penguin, 1985). p. 96.

66 Callincos and Simons, *The Great Strike*, p. 130.

67 Crick, *Scargill and the Miners*, p. 104.

68 SWP Internal Bulletin, June 1982.

69 Tony Cliff, *Lenin*, vol. 1 (4 vols. London: Pluto, 1975) pp. 263, 258, 254.

70 Ibid., pp. 66–7.

71 Duncan Hallas, *The Comintern* (London: Pluto, 1985) *passim*.

72 Donny Gluckstein, *The Western Soviets* (London: Bookmarks, 1985) p. 14.

Chapter 5   The New Left and the Politics of the International Marxist Group

1 See 'The 20th Congress of the CPSU' 1978 in *The Struggle to Re-unify the Fourth International (1954–63) vol. 3; De-Stalinisation, the Hungarian Revolution and World Trotskyism*, documents 1955–7; *Education For Socialists* (New York: Pathfinder) pp. 53–4.

2 This report was given to the seventh plenum of the IEC in May 1956.

3 See E. Mandel, 'Prospects and dynamics of the political revolution Against the Bureaucracy' in *The Development and Disintegration of World Stalinism* (New York: Pathfinder, 1970)

4   See 'The Hungarian revolution and the crisis of Stalinism' (resolution adopted by the SWP National Committee in January 1957) in *The Struggle to Re-Unify the Fourth International* (1954–63) vol. 3, pp. 33–9 and G. Healy *Revolution and Counter-Revolution in Hungary* (pamphlet, 1957).

5   *Trotskyism versus Revisionism* (London: New Park, vol. 3) 1974 pp. 37–8.

6   Quoted by Frank Richards, 'The Question of the International', *Revolutionary Communist* 2, May, 1975, p. 32.

7   The new 'colonialist' emphasis was pursued with especial zeal in the case of Michel Pablo, the ISFI's secretary, who became involved in the Algerian revolution in a personal capacity after having set up an Algerian Bureau under the auspices of the ISFI. Pablo and his supporters eventually broke with the ISFI on this issue in 1964. In Britain a tiny 'Revolutionary Marxist Tendency' of Pabolites existed until 1968: their removal from the ISFI did not lessen Healy's attacks on that organization for 'Pabloite liquidationism' – indeed such attacks increased!

8   See 'Draft resolution on international perspectives' adopted by SLL National Executive Committee 28/29 January 1961, p. 27.

9   The Re-unification Congress of June 1963 said of Castroism that it 'will more and more play a genuinely international role . . . It is at this stage . . . the most advanced political leadership by far of all the workers' states'. See 'The Sino-Soviet conflict' in *The Development and Disintegration of World Stalinism* (New York: Education for Socialists, 1970) p. 67.

10 *Trotskyism versus Revisionism*, vol. 3, p. 259.

11 For the SLL argument see *Trotskyism versus Revisionism* vol. 4, p. XIII.

12 In the absence of documents produced by this group the rest of this account of the origins of the IMG relies heavily on the accounts of Pat Jordan and Tariq Ali. Jordan was founder member of the IMG and Ali was its best-known spokesman. See 'Aspects of the history of the IMG' by Peter Peterson (alias Pat Jordan), IMG Pre-Conference document no. 6, January 1975, and T. Ali, *The Coming British Revolution*, pp. 137–40. (London: Cape, 1972).

13 The programme of *Young Guard* – which united several left-wing groups outside *Keep Left* – included unilateral nuclear disarmament, withdrawal from NATO, a programme of nationalization under workers' control and comprehensive education. In 1962 its supporters won four seats on the Young Socialists national committee while *Keep Left* obtained three amid accusations of

violence and intimidation. See Zig Layton-Henry 'Labour's lost youth' in the *Journal of Contemporary History* 11, July 1976, pp. 275–308.

14 Since 1960, and CND's Committee of 100, Russell had become organizationally dependent on Ralph Schoenman and politically influenced by him. See Bertrand Russell, *The Autobiography of Bertrand Russell* (London: Unwin, 1975) p. 603. According to Tariq Ali it was Schoenman who conceived the Vietnamese Solidarity Campaign, See *Red Mole* 1, 9. When the International War Crimes Tribunal was set up in the summer of 1966 IMG members such as Ali became involved in its international fact-finding missions. Indeed the IMG began to build a London branch in 1966 because Jordan had to move there to work full time for the VSC.

15 In 1961 the sixth congress of the ISFI had claimed that 'special attention must be paid to the situation in Great Britain where . . . the strongest left-wing tendency in Western Europe is developing under extremely favourable conditions for a decisive intervention of revolutionary Marxists' inside the Labour Party. See *Fourth International* 12, winter (1960). There is no doubt that the FI was as unrealistic as the Labour left in its hopes for the socialism of Harold Wilson and that the 'intense secrecy' under which the IMG laboured in the early sixties (see Ali, *The Coming British Revolution*, pp. 139–40) was justified in terms of an expected strengthening of the Labour left. Even when this hope was shown to be illusory the IMG persisted with entrism until 1969.

16 See Lewis Minkin, *The Labour Party Conference* (London: Allen Lane, 1978) p. 44.

17 Ken Coates has a rather different version of the events which caused the split between him and Jordan. According to his account the breach in relations between them was caused by Jordan 'unilaterally changing the basis of our working relationship. Our association had always been based upon an agreement that we were *not* establishing a classic Leninist type of organisation, but on the contrary, a novel kind of catalyst. Indeed Pat had declared himself to be quite as rigorously "revisionist" as any of us. All of a sudden, he was converted to an extreme form of organisational piety, not to say dogmatism' (from a letter to the author).

18 Recorded by Nigel Young *An Infantile Disorder? The Crisis and Decline of the New Left*, (London: Routledge, 1977). See also his typology of old and new lefts on p. 310.

19 This estimate is made by Martin Thomas in 'The Logic of

Scenario Politics: the IMG 1972–6' in 'The ICL and the Fourth International', *International Communist Special*, no. 1, 1976, p. 33. (theoretical journal of the International Communist League).

20   Young, *An Infantile Disorder?*, pp. 144 and 147.

21   *International*, July 1968, p. 13.

22   Adrian Mitchell resigned from the *Black Dwarf* editorial board over IMG's criticism of the African National Council.

23   E. Mandel, *A Socialist Strategy For Western Europe* (Nottingham: Institute for Workers' Control, Spokesman pamphlet, 1965 p. 1. This analysis appeared also in *International*, September 1968.

24   See E. Mandel, *The Lessons of May 1968* (IMG pamphlet). Yet, paradoxically, the May events rekindled faith in perspectives of insurrectionary roads to socialism, 'explosions' of consciousness, and economic collapses.

25   Mandel cites the following theses of the FI in particular:
(a) Lenin's conception of the epoch as one of wars, civil wars, and revolutions
(b) the crisis of proletarian leadership
(c) the necessity of a vanguard organization
(d) the revolutionary role of the proletariat
(e) the centrality of the demand for workers' control of industry in the transistion from capitalism to socialism. See E. Mandel, *A Socialist Strategy* pp. 16–22.

26   E. Mandel, *The Revolutionary Student Movement: Theory and Practice* (New York: Pathfinder 1971) p. 36. A similar analysis is presented by Gareth Steadman-Jones, *Student Power* (Harmondsworth: Penguin, 1969); by IS in Susan Buddle et al., *Students and the Struggle For Socialism* (Interational Socialist Pamphlet, 1972) and the Communist Party of Great Britain in D. Cook, *Students*, (CP Pamphlet, n.d.) and D. Cook, 'Students, Left Unity and the Communist Party, *Marxism Today*, October 1974.

27   *International*, December 1968, p. 7.

28   *Internatonal*, January 1969.

29   *Red Mole* 1 March 1970, p. 2.

30   *Red Mole 1*, 3, April 1970,. The title of Blackburn's essay is itself of interest since it was taken from a Rolling Stones LP and symbolizes the youth-oriented nature of the IMG. The notoriety achieved by Blackburn (through his expulsion from the LSE) accounts for *Red Mole's* public announcement of his subsequent recruitment to IMG: such 'news' was presumably of interest to the student left – though perhaps a little mystifying to anyone else who happened to read it.

31   See 'Proletarian and Bourgeois Democracy: a Reply to Geoff

Roberts'. Tariq Ali and Robin Blackburn, 'Battle of Ideas', monthly supplement to *Red Weekly*, no. 3, December 1976.

32 See, for example, 'Documents of the 1965 world congress of the Fourth International' in *International Socialist Review*, spring 1966.

33 For more detail on this see R.J. Alexander *Trotskyism in Latin America* (Stanford: University Press, 1973).

34 *Intercontinental Press*, July, 1969, p. 720.

35 Ibid., X, 1., p. 49.

36 *International*, 2, 1, 1973, p. 40. See also Geoff Roberts 'The Politics of the IMG', in *Marxism Today*, February, 1976, and the self-criticism of Tariq Ali and Robin Blackburn, 'Proletarian revolution and bourgeois democracy' 'Battle of Ideas' *Red Weekly*, no. 3, December, 1976.

37 *International*, May 1969, p. 4.

38 Much of this emphasized Connolloy's Marxism and the significance of the Easter Rising of 1916. *See International*, nos. 1, 3, 5 and 8 for examples.

39 *International*, July, 1970, p. 39.

40 *International*, 1, 3. January/February 1971; *Red Mole* 1, 12.

41 *International*, 1, 6, September/October 1971.

42 *Red Mole* 1, 3, 15 April 1970.

43 In 1971 the IMG briefly canvassed for Saor Eire – an ephemeral grouping based in the Republic which somewhat tentatively avowed that it 'could be called an urban guerilla group'. See *Red Mole*, 2, 1, January 1971.

44 This was stressed in 'Ireland: the Acid Test for British Socialists' in *Red Mole*, September 1971.

45 *Red Mole*, 2, 6, April 1971. As if to underline the IMG's ignorance of the republican movement in 1971 an article in which it declared its support for the latter's military campaign consisted of an interview with three Officials who condemned the 'catholic nationalist' project of the Provisionals. At this time the IMG supported both wings of the IRA. See *International* 6, September/October 1971.

46 *Workers Press*, 4 September 1971, objected that 'no socialist can tolerate or defend the indiscriminate bombings of the IRA'. Bob Purdie, for IMG, denounced this statement as 'slanderous'. See *Red Mole* 28, September 1971.

47 *Red Mole*, 15 November 1971.

48 *Red Mole*, 16 October 1972.

49 *Red Mole*, 27 November 1972.

50 *Notes to Organisers*, 1, 13, New Series, 28 August, 1973. In this the following resolution was put before the IMG Political Committee

meeting of 26 August 1973. 'The FI is opposed to individual terrorism. The IMG hold that the present bombings – for which both the Official and the Provision IRA deny responsibility – obstruct the struggle against capitalism.' This was unanimously defeated (7 votes against, none for). the members who put forward this resolution constituted themselves 'the Tendency' and declared unequivocal opposition to terrorism, noting that 'not one of Trotsky's statements on this question has ever appeared in the pages of *Red Weekly* (successor to *Red Mole*) or its predecssor – *not one*. See 'Internal Discussion Bulletin. 2, 8, November 1973. In fact, despite the emphasis to the contrary, *Red Mole* did, as we have noted, print Trotsky's article on Grynszpan (but the substance of the Tendency's objections is sound).

51 *International Socialism Journal* 70, mid-June 1974. p. 13.
52 This point was made by the Militant Tendency. See P. Taaffe *Marxism Opposes Individual Terrorism* (Militant Pamphlet n.d.) p. 10. Militant also recognized that the partition of Ireland no longer had any economic significance for British capitalism and have always regarded the defeat of the IRA as 'inevitable'. See, for example, Ted Grant 'British Perspectives and Prospects', in *Militant International Review* (MIR) 6, January 1973, p. 8.
53 The majority of the IMG National Committee decided in May 1973 that 'the issue of the repressive role of the army in Ireland is the key issue'. See Liam Sykes 'Ireland: a Review and Some perspectives', IMG Pre-Conference Discussion Bulletin 2, 22, 1973 p. 8.
54 *Red Weekly*, 15, 24 August 1973.
55 *Red Weekly*, 52, 16 May 1974.
56 See *Red Weekly*, 79, 5 December 1974, for both IS and IMG statements on the Birmingham pub bombing.
57 The Militant Tendency's position on Northern Ireland amounts to a restatement of its arguments concerning the advance of socialism in Britain (see chapter 7). This involved support for the still-born Northern Ireland Labour Party and the election of an 'independent' Labour Party in the South together with a call for the adoption of Militant's economic demands. Today Miltiant also calls for the establishment of a non-sectarian Trade Union Defence Force to act as a militia in defence of workers against terrorism after the army has been withdrawn. Militant now calls for the creation of trade union-backed Labour Party in the North to implement its economic programme. See P. Hadden, *Divide and Rule: Labour and the Partition of Ireland* (Militant pamphlet, 1980)

and his *Northern Ireland: Tory Cuts, Common Misery, Common Struggle* (Militant Pamphlet, 1980, reprinted 1981).

58 See the International Socialist – Socialist Workers Party pamphlet *Troops Out of Ireland* September 1980, and Geoff Bell *British Labour and Ireland: 1969–1979* (IMG Pamphlet, 1979) other statements of the two organizations.

59 See the publication *Hands Off Ireland*, quarterly bulletin of the Revolutionary Communist Group, no. 4, May 1978, pp.11–14.

60 S. Rowbotham et al., *Beyond The Fragments: Feminism and the Making of Socialism* (London: Merlin Press 1979 p. 95).

61 On several occasions in the early 1970s the intervention of the ISFI was a moderating and calming influence on tendencies within IMG engaged in prolonged dispute. There is no doubt that only the authority and prestige of the International leadership prevented splits in the IMG. See United Secretariat thesis, 'The Situation in Britain and the tasks of the IMG' in *International, 2, 2, Summer 1973, pp. 7–14* and United Secretariat theses 'The British Crisis' in *International*, 3, 1, Spring 1976, pp. 9–23.

62 J. Mitchell, *Women's Estate* (Harmondsworth, London: Penguin, 1971) p. 54.

63 Kathy Ennis 'Women's consciousness' in *International Socialism Journal* 68, April 1974, pp. 27–8.

64 J. Ross, 'Capitalism, Politics and Personal Life' in *Socialist Woman: A Journal of the IMG* 6, 2, summer 1977.

65 S. Rowbotham, 'Leninism in the Lurch' in *Red Rag* 12, spring 1977.

66 Rowbotham et al., *Beyond the Fragments*, pp. 21–50.

67 *Fourth International, Women's Liberation and the Socialist Revolution* (Sydney: Pathfinder 1979) p. 15.

68 Ibid., p. 69.

69 Ibid., pp. 75–7.

70 V. Beechey, 'Female Wage Labour in Capitalist Production, in *Capital and Class* 3, 1977 p. 61.

71 *Fourth International, Women's Liberation*, p. 210.

72 Ibid., p. 21.

73 See as an instance of this Marxist functionalism the Revolutionary Communist Group's argument in O. Adamson et al., 'Women's Oppression under Capitalism', *Revolutionary Communist* 5, 1976.

74 M. Barrett, *Women's Oppression Today* (London: Verso, 1980,) p. 85.

75 M. Coulson et al., 'The Housewife and Her Labour Under Capitalism – a Critique', *New Left Review* 89, January/February 1975, p. 61.

76 H. Hartmann, 'The Unhappy Marriage of Marxism and Feminism', in L. Sargent (ed.) *Women and Revolution* (London: Pluto Press, 1981) p. 7.

77 The most influential of these is J. Mitchell, *Psychonalysis and Feminism* (Harmondsworth: Penguin, 1975). See also R. Coward, 'Sexual Politics and Psychonalysis' in R. Brunt and C. Rowan (eds) *Feminism, Culture and Politics* (London: Lawrence and Wishart, 1982).

78 Mitchell, *Psychonalysis*, p. 415.

79 See W. Seccombe, 'Marxism and Demography', *New Left Review* 137, January/February 1983. p. 28–9.

80 *Big Flame* started as a local socialist newspaper in Liverpool in 1970 and developed into a Merseyside-based revolutionary group. By 1981 the group had established branches in most of the large towns in England. See J. Howell 'Big Flame: Resituating Socialist Strategy and Organisation', *Socialist Register*, 1981.

81 The Marxist Workers Group consisted of a dozen splitters from Workers Fight (itself a breakaway from the International Socialists-SWP) based on the Bolton and Leigh districts of Lancashire.

82 The so-called Communist faction consisted of only a handful of IMG members who were (unwittingly) led by members of the Spartacist Tendency intent on disrupting the IMG organization. The Spartacist Tendency is a tiny group of fundamentalists whose *raison d'être* is the disruption of political meetings and organizations of the Marxist left. The point appears to be a caricatured version of the splitting tactics endorsed by the Bolshevik Comintern and, later, by Trotskyist entrists, in the mass working-class organizations.

83 The attitude of IS to student politics switched dramatically from one which envisaged 'the mass of students against the system' to a position which relegated their role to a politically equivocal force that is useful in so far as it is linked to working-class struggles off campus. The change in position had its casualities as can be seen by comparing M. Shaw 'Which Way for Student Revolutionaries?' in *International Socialism Journal*, March 1973, and the pamphlet by Buddle et al., *Students and the Struggle For Socialism*.

84 A. Jones and R. Thompson, *After the Miners' Strike – What Next?* (pamphlet, 1972).

85 R. Miliband, *Capitalist Democracy in Britain* (Oxford: Oxford, University Press, 1982) p. 152.

86 IMG Pre-Conference Bulletin 5, January 1975, p. 8.
87 E. Mandell, *Late Capitalism*, (London: New Left Books, 1975).
88 See note 36.
89 See 'International Internal Discussion Bulletin', 10, nos 1, 7, 20, 21; 1983, for the terms of the dispute.
90 See 'Tactics for Building a Unified Revolutionary Organisation', Pre-Conference Bulletin 13, 1978.

Chapter 6   From Stalinism to Eurocommunism

1 *The Communist Unity Convention* (pamphlet, London: Communist Party, 1920) p. 10.
2 *Manual of Party Training* (London: Communist Party, 1924) p. 9.
3 Ibid., p. 21.
4 Hary Pollitt, *Looking Ahead* (London: CPGB, 1947) p. 87.
5 Ibid., p. 90.
6 See R. Black *Stalinism in Britain* London: New Park, 1970) pp. 285 and 286.
7 Noreen Branson, *History of the Communist Party of Great Britain 1927–41* (London: Lawrence and Wishart 1985) p. 191.
8 Milovan Djilas, *Conversations with Stalin* (London: Pelican, 1969) p. 90.
9. Black, *Stalinism in Britain*, p. 286.
10. *The British Road to Socialism* (London: CPGB, 1951) p. 14.
11 Ibid. pp. 14–15.
12 John Gollan, *Peoples Democracy for Britain* (London: CPGB, 1952) pp. 3–4.
13 Pollitt, *Looking Ahead*, p. 42.
14 Margaret Hudson, 'The Marshall Standard of Life' in *Labour Monthly* 3, 12, December 1948, pp. 383.
15 Pollitt, *Looking Ahead*, p. 10.
16 Ibid., p. 43.
17 Keith Jeffrey and Peter Hennessy, *States of Emergency: British Governments and Strikebreaking Since 1919* (London, Routledge and Kegan Paul, 1983) p. 196.
18 Ibid., pp. 220–1.
19 Phillip M. Williams, *Hugh Gaitskell* (Oxford: University Press, 1982). p. 207.
20 S. Parsons, '1956 and the Communist Party of Great Britain', Bulletin of the *Society for the Study of Labour History*, no. 47, Autumn 1983.
21 *Labour Monthly* 35, 4, 1953, pp. 163–4, p. 145, p. 159.

22 Sam Aaronovitch, *The Ruling Class* (London: Lawrence and Wishart, 1961) p. 162. This is the fullest statement of the argument by a British communist.

23 See Michael McCreery, *The Way Forward: A Marxist-Leninist Analysis of the British State, the CPGB and the Tasks for Revolutionaries* pamphlet, (London: Working People's Party of England, n.d.).

24 Lewis Minkin, *The Labour Party Conference: A Study in the Politics of Intra-Party Democracy*, (London, Allen Lane, 1978) pp. 86–7.

25 See for example T. Cliff, *The Crisis* (Pluto Press: London, 1975) p. 11.

26 E. J. Hobsbawm, 'Syndicalism and the Working Class' *New Society*, 48, 861, 5 April 1979, pp. 8–10.

27 John Foster and Charles Woolfson, *The Politics of the UCS Work-In*, (London: Lawrence and Wishart, 1986).

28 See *Comment*, 8, 51, 19 December 1970, p. 802.

29 See Jim Arnison, *The Shrewsbury Three: Strikes, Pickets and 'Conspiracy'* (London: 1974 Lawrence and Wishart).

30 B. Ramelson, *Social Contract: Cure-all or Con-trick?* (pamphlet, London: CPGB, n.d.).

31 Bill Warren and Mike Prior, *Advanced Capitalism and Backward Socialism* (Nottingham: Spokesman pamphlet No 46, n.d.) pp. 8–9.

32 David Purdy, 'British Capitalism Since the War: Part 2', *Marxism Today*, October 1976, p. 316. Part 1 of this article is in the same journal, September 1976.

33 Mike Prior and Dave Purdy, *Out of the Ghetto* (Nottingham: Spokesman, 1979) p. 13.

34 Ibid., pp. 90–91.

35 John Gollan, 'Socialist Democracy – Some Problems: The 10th Congress of the CPSU in Retrospect', *Marxism Today*, January 1976.

36 Ibid, p. 5.

37 Ibid., pp. 5 and 6.

38 See *Discussion of Socialist Democracy*, (pamphlet, London: CPGB, 1976)

39 *The British Road to Socialism*, 5th edition (London: CPGB, 1978) p. 3.

40 Ibid., p. 25.

41 *Report of Commission on Inner-Party Democracy* (CPGB, 1979) See pp. 5–46.

42 Ibid., p. 47.

43 Editorial, *Marxism Today*, September 1978.

44 See M. Jacques and F. Mulhearn (eds) *The Forward March of Labour*

Halted? (London: Verso, 1981). See Ken Gill's essay for a typical assertion that all is well, especially p. 21.

45 S. Hall, 'The Great Moving Right Show', *Marxism Today*, January 1979.
46 S. Hall and M. Jacques (eds) *The Politics of Thatcherism*, (London: Lawrence and Wishart, 1983) p. 16.
47 John Callaghan, 'The CPGB in Local Government' in B. Szajkowski (ed.) *Marxist Local Governmennt in West Europe and Japan* (London: Pinter, 1986).

Chapter 7   Militant and Entrism

1 G. Zinoviev, *History of the Bolshevik Party* (London: New Park, 1973) p. 143.
2 V. I. Lenin quoted in B. Lazitch and M. Drachkovitch *Lenin and Comintern* California: Stanford, 1972) pp. 329–30.
3. Stuart McIntyre, *A Proletarian Science: Marxism in Britain* (Cambridge: University Press, 1980) p. 231.
4 See John Callaghan, 'Leninism, Entrism and the British Labour Party' *Journal of Communist Studies*, December 1986.
5 Deane Archive, Manchester Polytechnic, closed section (henceforward DA) A55(1).
6 Ibid., Heffer to Deane correspondence 21 October 1956, 31 March 1957.
7 Ibid., 'The Present Situation and Our Tasks', C57(1).
8 Ibid., 'Organisational Persepctives', June 1957, G57–67.
9 For more on this see A. Z. Ehrlich, 'The Leninist Organisations in Britain and the Student Movement 1966–72' (Ph.D. thesis, London University, 1981).
10 DA, 'Committee for the Circulation of Documents for Internal Discussion', 8 August 1962, F62 (1).
11 DA, 'The Building of the Revolutionary Party and the Question of Entry', 6 October 1962, F62 (2).
12 DA, Draft Constitution 1962 (revised 1964), J62 (2).
13 DA, 'Notes on Council Work', February 1961, Q61(1).
14 Ibid.
15 Ibid.
16 DA, 'Joint Agreements Reached Between RSL – IG' Leadership Meeting, Seven Oaks, 13 September 1964, E64(5).
17 DA, Sub EC Minutes, 13 June 1964, B64(20).
18 DA, Taaffe to Deane, 27 June 1964, A64(49).
19 DA, 'Finance 1964', March 1964, P64.

20   'Entrism', internal document, November 1973, p. 8.
21   'History of the Labour Party' articles reprinted from *Militant*, West London Militant Supporters, n.d., pp. 10 and 18.
22   Reg Underhill, 'Entryist Activities of the Militant Tendency', report to the Constituency Labour Parties, March 1980, p. 21.
23   *Programme of the International*, (London: International Bureau for the Fourth International, 1970) p. 20.
24   *Committee for the Workers' International Bulletin* 2, January 1975.
25   Michael Crick *The March of Militant* (London: Faber and Faber, 1986) pp. 161–6.
26   'British Perspectives 1977', internal document, September 1977, p. 29.
27   Ibid., p. 15.
28   Quoted in Underhill, 'Entryist Activities', p. 21.
29   'British Perspectives and Tasks', internal document, 1975, p. 25.
30   Tom Forester, 'The Labour Party's Militant Moles', *New Society*, 10 January 1980.
31   Ted Grant, *Falklands Crisis: A Socialist Answer*, Militant pamphlet, 1982.
32   Pete Duncan, 'The Politics of Militant', (pamphlet, London: clause 4, 1980) p. 25.
33   Peter Taaffe, 'British Communist Party in Crisis', *Militant International Review* 15, Autumn 1978, p. 28.
34   *Programme of the International*, pp. 16–16.
35   *Programme of the International*, p. 19.
36   Peter Hadden, *Northern Ireland: Tory Cuts, Common Misery, Common Struggle* (London: Militant, 1980, reprinted January 1981) p. 9.
37   Alan Woods, 'The Crisis of Thatcherism', *Militant International Review* 19, spring 1980, p. 6.
38   Hadden, *Northern Ireland*, p. 15.
39   'British Perspectives 1977', pp. 10 and 12.
40   Ibid., p. 29.
41   Ibid., p. 11.
42   Woodrow Wyatt, *What's Left of the Labour Party?* (London: Sidgwick and Jackson, 1977) p. 177; Stephen Haseler, *The Death of British Democracy* (London: Elek, 1976), p. 219.
43   Blake Baker, *The Far Left* (London: Weidenfield, 1981) p. 5.
44   David Webster, *The Labour Party and the New Left* (Fabian Tract 477, 1981) p. 4.
45   John Gyford, *The Politics of Local Socialism* (London: Allen and Unwin, 1985) pp. 25–6.
46   Michael Crick, *The March of Militant*, p. 247.
47   The *Observer*, 23 November 1986: The *Guardian*, 24 November 1986.

48   See *Chartist* 7, 1, 'News and Views' January/February 1986 and *Chartist* April/May 1986.
49   See *Chartist* 7, 1, 'News and Views'.

Conclusion

1   K. Marx and F. Engels, *Manifesto of the Communist Party*, Selected Works (Moscow: Progress Publishers, 1968) p.46.

Index

Cliff, Tony 61, 86, 87, 88, 89, 90, 92, 93, 95, 96, 97, 99, 100, 101, 102, 104, 105, 106, 111, 112
Club 70, 71, 73, 74, 118
Coates, Ken 72, 73, 120, 121
Colquhoun, Maureen 137
Commission on Inner Party Democracy 181–2
Committee to Defeat Revisionism for Communist Unity 172
Committee for the Regroupment of the Fourth International 118, 191
Communist Campaign Group ix, 188
Communist Information Bureau (Cominform) 50, 171, 172
Communist International (Comintern) *see* Third International
Communist Party of Great Britain (CPGB) ix, 26, chs 2 and 6 *passim*, 49, 56, 69, 71, 101, 106, 125, 137
Communist Party of the Soviet Union (CPSU) 68, 168
Communist Solar System 44
Communist University of London 174
Congress Truth 186
Cooley, Mike 137
Cooper, David 139
Corrie Amendment 201
Cortonwood 108
Cowley 80, *see also* British Leyland
CPSA x, 151
Craven, Pat 196
Crawshaw, Richard 208
Crick, Michael 199, 209
Cripps, Stafford 43
Cuba 116, 117, 118, 130
Czechoslovakia 173

Daily Worker 41, 70, 164, 168
Daly, Lawrence 74, 120, 169
De Leon, Daniel 27
Deakin, Arthur 167
Deane, Brian 192, 195
Deane, Jimmy 61, 118, 191, 196, 208
Deutscher, Isaac x, 68, 73, 116
Dickinson, Keith 208, 210
Dimitrov, G. 43
Doctor's Plot 168
Dowling, Harry 196
Doyle, Clare 196, 199, 210
Duncan, Pete 201

Dunn, Jimmy 208
Dutschke, Rudi 179
Dutt, R. Palme 35, 36, 37, 46, 48, 52, 168

Edwards, Bob 196
ELAS 63
Engels, F. 146
entrism 25, 118–19; and Communist Party 32–3, 34, 45–7; and Gerry Healy 61, 62, 73–4; and Militant 189–215; *sui generis* 65–8, 69
ETU 167
Eurocommunism x, 109, 177, 184, 185, 188

Fabian society 11, 32, 45
Faction for Revolutionary Democracy ix
Falklands War 200–1
Feather, Vic 167
feminism 138–51
Fields, Terry 208
Focus 187
Foot, Michael vii, 210
Foot, Paul 99
For Soviet Britain 163
Foundry Workers 167
Fourth International (FI) 24–5, 55, 86, 87, 120, 130, 138, 142–8, 154, 155, 199, *see also* International Secretariat; International Committee
Fourth International (FI) 118
Fox, Ralph 53
Fryer, Peter 69, 70, 73, 169

Gallacher William 28, 50
Gaster, Jack 42
General Strike 35, 36
German Democratic Republic 170
GMBATU 211, 212, 214
Goldman, Albert 60
Gollan, John 165, 180
Goonewardene, Leslie 116
Gramsci, A. 3, 28, 71, 73, 172, 174, 177, 179
Grant, Ted 61, 118, 119, 192, 196, 197, 199, 202, 203, 208
Guild Socialists 30

Hall, Stuart 184
Hallas, Duncan 96, 97, 99, 102
Halliday, Fred 136